THE BIBLE AS LITERATURE

'The Elohim creating Adam'   WILLIAM BLAKE

THE BIBLE
AS LITERATURE

by

T. R. HENN

*President of St. Catharine's College,
the University of Cambridge*

1970

OXFORD UNIVERSITY PRESS

NEW YORK

First published 1970

Second Impression 1971

COPYRIGHT © 1970 T. R. HENN

ISBN 0 7188 1653 6

PRINTED IN GREAT BRITAIN BY
R. & R. CLARK, LTD., EDINBURGH

Contents

Acknowledgements

I AM INDEBTED in these essays to many sources and to many authorities. One major debt is to Messrs. Nelson, the publishers of *Peake's Commentary on the Bible* (1962) and to its Editors, Professors Matthew Black and H. H. Rowley; they have given me permission to develop in certain directions an article which I wrote for the Commentary, an article which was itself begotten out of a paper to The Society for Old Testament Studies. A second debt is to Dr. Cecil Northcott who invited me to undertake this book: and to his friends who have, at various stages, criticized the successive drafts. So also to Professor Winton Thomas, Regius Professor of Hebrew at Cambridge (and one of the Archbishops' Commission to Revise the Psalter); to whom I am also indebted for permission to quote from *Documents from Old Testament Times*, and for enlightening my ignorance over many aspects of translation from the Hebrew. I owe much to the late Professor C. S. Lewis, and to colleagues in my own College and in the English Faculty at Cambridge: notably Alan Wilkinson, G. T. Cavaliero and, above all, Edward Armstrong.

Among the many distinguished critical works which I have tried to record in the Bibliography, one book seemed (for this particular purpose) to be outstanding. It is George Adam Smith's *The Historical Geography of the Holy Land*; first published in 1894 and revised, after twenty-four previous editions, in 1931. It became clear that, for me at least, this book was supreme in the enlightenment it gave on certain of those literary qualities with which I was concerned: the whole varied 'inscape' of 'Syria', the climatic variations and abnormalities which give rise to (and, known, enable us to appreciate to the full) the immense range of imagery drawn from place and environment; the geographical factors which determine its boundaries; its bulwarks for the military operations on which Israel depended for survival. But more than any book the writer seems to me to have caught up from the Bible the subtlety of tone and response, the sense of high yet human poetry, into his own style; and that without a touch of pretentiousness, or, far worse, the vacuity of certain enthusiastic writers on this topic. For this and other reasons I have given in full his passage on the Shepherd.

I have attempted, in the Bibliography and in footnotes, to record my many debts, borrowings, sources. But the field of this literature is now so vast and complex that my reading must have been, in Dr. Johnson's words, 'desultory and unsystematick'; nor is it always possible to distinguish, over a period of years, between what one has read, what has been gleaned in conversation and in argument; or set out in lectures; or heard in discourse. For my inadvertent borrowings I ask pardon. For what might be thought original, by way of comparison and illustration from other literatures, I take full responsibility. Yet even in this area in which one might, perhaps, claim some knowledge, the sheer richness of the material in the category of 'imitatio' is immense and even daunting; to record and analyse more than a fraction of it was clearly beyond the scope of this book.

I am fully aware of the difficulties and dangers of such a designed treatment. In the first and last chapters I have set out my own views: which may, I hope, be taken as an apologia.

For permission to quote from material still in copyright, I am grateful to:—

Messrs. Faber & Faber, Ltd. (London) and Messrs. Harcourt, Brace and World, Inc. (New York) for 'Ash Wednesday' from *Collected Poems* by T. S. Eliot.

The Society of Authors, Messrs. Jonathan Cape Ltd. (London) and Messrs. Holt, Rinehart & Winston, Inc. (New York) for extracts from A. E. Housman's *Collected Poems*.

Mrs. George Bambridge, Messrs Macmillan & Co. Ltd., (London) and Messrs. Doubleday & Co., Inc. (New York) for extracts from Rudyard Kipling's *Verse*.

Mr. Michael Yeats, Messrs. Macmillan & Co. Ltd. (London) and the Macmillan Co. of New York for extracts from the *Collected Poems* of W. B. Yeats.

Professor G. H. Driver and *The Times* of London for his letter dated April 19, 1963.

CHAPTER ONE

Introduction

i

THE TITLE of this book is clearly open to many and grave objections, yet it is difficult, for this particular purpose, to find any alternative. The first task, therefore, is to attempt to strip it of pejorative or superficial associations, and suggest some kind of redefinition and method of control. For one objection is that the Bible is not, in any normal sense, a work of literature. It is a vast miscellany, by many authors, of many themes and kinds. Its unity has been imposed on it, as it were, from without; by the growth and establishment of the canon, by the historical perspectives that bind it together, by the interlocking prophecies, quotations and allusions that draw together the Old Testament and the New. It has, strictly speaking, no common style, for behind it lie three main languages; and each group, or individual, who undertakes to translate it, has little opportunity of impressing a style other than that of the age in which the translation is made, and the characteristics of the language out of which it comes. The texts from which the translations must be made have shown a steady and enlightened improvement; but the tools of the workers in that field must now include comparative philology in several languages, semasiology, palaeography, archaeology. They constitute the province of what is probably the most highly specialized form of textual criticism that we know. It is also true to say that there is now no *Textus Receptus* such as that on which the Forty-Seven Translators of the Authorized Version worked, and which, in 1604, they would have considered final.

Within the terms of this essay it is not possible to consider the overriding condition of the unity of the Bible: which is, and must remain, spiritual.

How far, then, can the Bible be considered as literature, in any coherent sense?

It is clear that it has been burned deeply into the fabric of the life

9

and literature of the English-speaking peoples. 'Burned' is, perhaps, a metaphor not without significance; its imprint has not been made without pain, and, as I have suggested later, a measure of potential evil. Its proverbs and its parables, its episodes sacred or profane, have been expounded in drama and poetry from the earliest written English. It has supplied the themes or framework for epic, satire, tragedy, comedy, farce, ballet; above all, its dramatic and choric potential make it specially suitable for oratorio. It has furnished allusions or depth-images to an incalculably great mass of writing. Its rhythms have been engrafted historically into much of our prose. But it seems impossible to discuss this immense variety as 'literature' except by breaking it down into arbitrarily-chosen examples of the 'kinds', such as epic, narrative, lyric, dramatic; and by offering some consideration of them by means of the normal critical methods.

Here the initial difficulty is formidable. Such a discussion requires a text—but which? There is a great variety of choice; with the further complication that the more recent the text the more likely we are to approach, not merely to verbal accuracy, but to certain complex shades of meaning of the originals. The two hundred and fifty years between the Authorized Version and the Revised Version show great changes; the R.S.V., still more accurate, will be super-seded in due course by the New English Bible in its complete form. One could choose among many of the admirable 'personal' versions. Moffatt, Knox, the Jerusalem Bible, the lucent inspiration of Phillips . . . the list is endless. But a glance at any of the 'parallel' Bibles shows at once the impossibility of the task of assessing the variants, even for the limited selection of subjects which I have suggested above. It was necessary to choose one text, and keep to it; though all versions that added to, or modified, meaning were clearly relevant to literary criticism, and the forging and reforging of style a subject of profound critical interest.

For this purpose there seemed no choice but the Authorized Version of 1611. This was not merely because of its familiarity. It alone of all the versions is the product of one of the great ages, and the first stable age, of English literature. It is one which is likely to sustain its historical interests, perhaps pre-eminence, because of Shakespeare and his contemporaries. The Revised Version and the Revised Standard Version seemed open to the objection of bearing too obviously (always for the purposes we have mentioned) 'literary' marks of ages whose literature was not always beyond criticism for sensitivity and taste. And of the modern or 'personal' versions it was clear that they were written in an idiom that might itself be 'dated' within a fairly short time; each succeeding age is likely to produce versions to suit what it considers to be its own special needs. This is wholly legitimate. The Authorized Version is at least stable. Wherever its 'antique style' is misleading it is not difficult to produce modern and better equivalents. And if (this is not impossible) the common reading of the Bible falls into disuse, the 1611 Version will remain, with Bacon, the Voyages, the Sermons of Donne and of Jeremy Taylor, the prose poems of Traherne, among the literary monuments of the time. Further, there are readily to hand comparative instances for the discussion of the structure of prose, and particularly of rhythm and of the cadence.

It seemed clear, too, that the significant failings in translations of the Authorized Version were such as to involve, on occasion, points of doctrine: and into these I do not propose to enter. The archaic features of the vocabulary, on the other hand, offer some interesting considerations on the nature of meaning as well as *exempla* of the growth of language.

A somewhat similar position arose over the Psalms. Here I have taken into consideration the recent revision,[1] based on Coverdale's version, and limited in that revision by the condition that they must have an essentially singable quality. Within such a condition the revisers have cleared up a number of the 'dark places' in the Prayer Book text, while preserving a consistency of language, idiom, and lyric qualities.

ii

But the phrase 'the Bible as literature' suggests, perhaps, a method of approach—and, necessarily, of assessment—which is in some way spurious; something that is less than relevant, even harmful, to its intrinsic character. Of this view the most forceful exponent is C. S. Lewis, who must be quoted at some length:

"It may be asked whether now, when only a minority of Englishmen regard the Bible as a sacred book, we may anticipate an increase of its literary influence. I think we might if it continued to be widely read.

[1] S.P.C.K., London, 1966. It keeps, in the main, Coverdale's characteristic rhythms.

But this is not very likely. Our age has indeed coined the expression 'the Bible as literature'. It is very generally implied that those who have rejected its theological pretensions nevertheless continue to enjoy it as a treasure-house of English prose. It may be so. There may be people who, having been forced upon familiarity with it by believing parents, have yet been drawn to it by its literary charms and remained as constant readers. But I never happen to meet them."[1]

That is one point of view; though the 'rejection of its theological pretensions' is a loaded phrase that requires closer examination. We have also to account for the impressive and rising circulation of the Bible in many languages, and it is too easy to dismiss these figures as irrelevant. More serious is Lewis' second major point:

"The Bible is so remorselessly and continuously sacred that it does not invite, it excludes or repels, the merely aesthetic approach."

While I should myself question the adjectives *remorselessly* and *continuously* in such a context, there remains the problem of giving offence to those who hold these or similar views. Nor is it sufficient to explore the connotations, pejorative and otherwise, of the term *aesthetic* in this context. It is probable that some damage has indeed been caused by attempts to isolate passages, by limited and therefore arbitrary selection, that appear to invite such an approach. Not least damaging to any serious assessment is the suggestion that an approach can profitably be made on some less intense level than the Bible demands; even to a hint of dilettantism.

But these are only the beginnings of the difficulties. Criticism will demand that there can be no separation between the thing said and the manner of saying it; the essential fusion of 'form' and 'content' must be respected. In considering this, the critic cannot but take a point of view which will inevitably be personal. He must, on occasion, tread a knife-edge: on one side, there is the dogmatic, the theological importance of the statements; on the other, values which may on many occasions be qualitatively different. Either way there may be causes of offence.

The same causes of offence are not unlikely to arise from the necessary discussion, in terms of language, of different versions. They are latent even in the act of translation. A new rendering may result in the abandonment of a reading which is not merely hallowed by

[1] *They Asked for a Paper*: 'The Literary Influence of the Authorized Version', London, 1962.

association, but which has acquired, by growth and usage, profound emotional significance. A cogent example is the rejection of the reading in *Psalm* 23:

Yea, though I walk through the valley of the shadow of death . . .

in favour of

Yea, though I walk through the darkest valley . . .

In poetry, prose, and painting[1] the 'Valley of the Shadow' has attained a formidable freight of associations of all kinds, as subsequent protest in some quarters made plain. The Revisers of the Psalter, who foresaw this, provided a special explanatory note. In this context it is relevant to quote a succinct statement of this and other problems by Professor G. R. Driver:[2]

"Your correspondent's objection[3] raises the whole question of this and indeed of any other revision of a translation, or fresh translation of the Bible. Are those charged with this task to accept an ancient mistranslation because it is hallowed by long association or is attuned to this or that reader's emotional reactions, or are they honestly to eliminate all that is wrong or misleading to the best of their ability in the light of modern knowledge? If they adopt the former method, whose emotions shall dictate what they say? For countless readers will react in as many different ways to every proposed correction. . . . At the same time, if they adopt this course they will be unfaithful to themselves and will ultimately be involved in much difficulty, e.g. in matters of doctrinal importance: here they will run the risk of raising a suspicion that as they have been unfaithful in small things, so they are also in great things. . . .

The translators or revisers have also to remember all those to whom their work is addressed. The older generation are set in their ways, any change will irk them or convey no sense of improvement to them; the younger, puzzled by much that they find in current versions, will be likely to prefer one that speaks to them more or less in their own language, which is immediately intelligible and less liable to be misunderstood. No good purpose can be served by offering them ancient mistranslations in the hope that some future generalization will put things right; the longer the error persists, the harder it is to eliminate it, as history shows only too well.

The Bible was originally written in languages which in time ceased to be, or which in time came to be but imperfectly understood, and each successive translation was only too apt to reflect contemporary misinterpretations; and its language became in due course obsolete and was

[1] e.g. Watts' *Love and Death.*   [2] In a letter to *The Times*, April 19, 1963.
[3] That is, to the change in *Ps.* 23.

13

then in its turn all too easily misunderstood. Language changes and knowledge increases; the Bible therefore needs to be reinterpreted every now and then as the generations go by, to offset the ever-accumulating misinterpretation and to bring new light to illuminate what it says. . . .''

Professor Driver's letter raised a very large number of questions, both directly and by implication. How far is it true that present-day versions of, say, the Epistles, when translated into 'contemporary language', can be considered to be 'immediately intelligible' and 'cannot be misunderstood'? It would seem that, as a fact of experience, large tracts of the Lectionaries evoke little response, either because of their complexity of reference (such as those to the Jewish Law or to some shading of a Hellenistic background[1]), from the ordinary congregation; and that some preparatory explanation, perhaps even taking the place of the formal sermon, is essential if they are not to be misunderstood, or, still worse, neglected.

And granted that Biblical Hebrew, Aramaic, and Biblical Greek are languages that are dead, the argument that translations into English 'age' in quite the same way may not provide a wholly accurate parallel. Much ink was spilt in the last half of the nineteenth century over the proper language into which to translate Homer; the argument ran that, since Homeric Greek was in itself archaic, some form of archaic English—often pseudo-Chaucerian— was appropriate.[2] How obsolete, in fact, is Elizabethan/Jacobean English compared with that of Moffatt or Knox or R.S.V.? How are we to weigh the relative importance of the actual mistranslations which no one would wish to perpetuate, and of which Professor Driver so rightly complains? How are they to be assessed—if and when they conflict unmistakably with other qualities—if their character is minor? Is it possible that language through usage acquires a kind of *patina* of its own, that whether 'hallowed' or not, we must look at carefully? We know, for example, that words manipulated in rhythmic settings of various kinds grow, as it were, into each other through usage and repetition, and draw from each other peculiar kinds of strength and significance.[3]

---

[1] As in the Pauline Epistles, or the Septuagint.

[2] The results are apparent in those varieties of prose and verse known as 'Wardour Street English'.

[3] We may think of certain poems of Gerard Manley Hopkins, where seemingly disjunctive words become fused by assonance and alliteration.

And in the last resort, how sure can we be? In note after note we read 'Meaning of the Hebrew uncertain'. This is inevitable in a consonantal script where the vowels have to be inserted by the reader. But if the translation has no certain support from the text, may it not be possible that some poetic insight may have brought us near to what Shakespeare calls

"—that unbodied figure of the thought
That gave't surmised shape."[1]

If, as so often, it is poetry that is being translated, and if there *are* obscurities in the text, may it not happen that the translator's lips may sometimes have been touched by fire from the altar? Is there, perhaps, some truth in Kipling's fancy, that made the group of Revisers working at Oxford send for Shakespeare to put the final polish for them on a passage of *Isaiah* at which they had been labouring? His fellow-workers have testified to the 'happy valiancy' of C. S. Lewis' contributions to the revision of the *Psalter*. If indeed the conditions of scribal transmission,[2] the considerable possibilities of misunderstanding, and the inevitable limitations of vocalizing the Hebrew script—as for example, when it was rendered into Greek by the Septuagint translators—the 'intelligent guess' might well be thought to be something more.

But even when we have arrived at the best texts that the palaeographers, philologists, textual critics and semasiologists can give us, and translated as faithfully as we can, there remains the central problem: what does this *mean*? The exegetical problem is immense. To it must be brought a knowledge of social habits, thought, illustrative usages, archaeology, history, geography. We must remember that Hebrew is a language with a comparatively small body of literature on which we can draw for comparisons of usage. Our knowledge is minute compared with that of the Classics. Again and again we have to speculate: what does this mean?

iii

At this point there may enter the subjective interpretations of which I have spoken. However we try to eliminate personality in the area of exegesis we can never completely succeed.

[1] *Troilus and Cressida*, I. 3. 16.
[2] See, e.g., H. J. Chaytor's *From Script to Print*, Cambridge, 1945.

We are aware historically of the many sects, not only of Christians, who draw their beliefs from a phrase or two, perhaps a few verses, of the Bible. We can accuse them, with some justice, of the lack of a balanced view of the whole; it is a risk to which any major work or body of work is subject.[1] But there is a further complication. We know that historical exegesis, from the twelfth century onwards, grouped itself under definite headings, and we may quote from *The Four Senses of the Scripture*:

> "They divide scripture into four senses, the literal, tropological, allegorical and anagogical. The literal sense is become nothing at all for the pope hath taken it clean away, and hath made it his possession. He hath partly locked it up with the false and counterfeit keys of his traditions, ceremonies and feigned lies; and driveth men from it with violence of sword, for no man dare abide by the literal sense of the text, but under a protestation, 'if it shall please the pope'. The tropological sense pertaineth to good manners (say they) and teacheth what we ought to do. The allegory is appropriate to faith; and the anagogical to hope and things above."[2]

Of allegorical exegesis we may give some examples:
For *Isaiah* 40 : 4 (Every valley shall be exalted . . .)

> "be the vallei is to make men understand that (which) shall be made high in everlasting joy: and by mountains be understand proud men and high men that shall be bowyd in everlasting damnacion."

The Miracle in Cana has been specially attractive to the commentators. 'The six stone-jars which were filled with water and were found full of wine are the six ages of the world. This water, in which unknown to men invisible wine was hidden, is the ancient Law behind whose letter Christ may be found. The Scriptures according to the letter are but tasteless water; but according to the spirit they are a generous wine. Christ was hidden from the world, like the wine in the water, during the six ages marked by Adam, Noah, Jechonias and John the Baptist. . . .'[3] Alternatively, the transformation signified the union of God and Man in the Incarnation. The six water pots were six attributes of Christ Incarnate, but also the six Heavinesses

---

[1] Compare the infinitely varied deductions as to outlook, religion, 'philosophy' that have been drawn from Shakespeare or Goethe; as well as the Messianic interpretations of Virgil and other 'sacred books'.

[2] *Doctrinal Treatises*, ed. H. Walter, Cambridge, 1878, p. 303.

[3] And much more in this kind: from Émile Mâle, *The Gothic Image*, Fontana Press, 1961, p. 195.

which the Apostles experienced at the Crucifixion. The Wise Virgins of the parable 'typify the five forms of mystical contemplation. ... The oil which burns in the lamps is charity ... The Five Foolish Virgins are symbols of the five forms of the lusts of the flesh, the pleasures of the senses which cause the soul to forget all holy thoughts and extinguish the flame of heavenly love ... The terrible cry in the night is the voice of the archangel, the trump of God which shall sound in the silence when none shall expect it, for "the Lord will come like a thief in the night".'[1] As a further example of ingenuity we may instance the interpretations that enjoined the persecution of heretics and schismatics on the grounds that they were 'the little foxes that spoil our vines'; or interpreted a passage from *Canticles* that the breasts of the Bride prefigured the Old and New Testaments, with Christ as the bundle of myrrh between them.[2]

In our own time explications of certain books in terms of current or future politics and world events are frequent, and often far more fantastic. We need not consider them here. But it is clear that in the later seventeenth century a kind of decadent metaphysical imagery led the preachers to strange imaginings. We may quote from John Eachard's *The Grounds and Occasions of the Contempt of the Clergy and Religion*, 1670,[3] on this kind of interpretative preaching:

"It seems pretty hard, at first sight, to bring into a sermon all the Circles of the Globe and all the frightful terms of Astronomy: but I will assure you, Sir, it is to be done! because it has been. But not by every bungler and ordinary text-divider; but by a man of great cunning and experience.

There is a place in the prophet *Malachi*, where it will do very nicely, and that is Chapter IV, Verse 2, 'But unto you that fear my name will the Sun of Righteousness arise with healing in his wings.' From which words, in the first place, it plainly appears that our Saviour passed through all the twelve signs of the Zodiac; and more than that, too, all proved by very apt and familiar places of scripture.

First, then, our Saviour was in *Aries*. Or else what means that of the Psalmist, 'The mountains skipped like rams, and the little hills like lambs!'? And again, that in Second of the *Kings*, Chapter III, Verse 4. 'And Mesha, King of Moab, was a sheep master, and rendered unto the

---

[1] *Ibid.*, p. 198.

[2] *cit.* H. H. Rowley, *The Unity of the Bible*, London, 1953, p. 17.

[3] Eachard was Master of St. Catharine's College, Cambridge, and subsequently Vice-Chancellor. We may think that the second paragraph suggests a change of tone as the writer satirizes the pulpit-voice of the preacher.

King of Israel an hundred thousand lambs' and what follows 'and a hundred thousand rams, with the wool.' Mind it! it was the King of Israel!

In like manner was he in *Taurus. Psalm* XXII. 12.

'Many bulls have compassed me! Strong bulls of Bashan have beset me round!' They were not ordinary bulls. They were *compassing* bulls! They were *besetting* bulls! They were *strong Bashan* bulls!"[1]

And so through other 'signs'.

iv

Eachard is of course satirizing a contemporary fashion; he is also, by implication, reproving those who search for hidden significance in texts which can by no stretch of imagination be forced into that category. But we must tread carefully. The line that divides symbol from allegory, from designed parabolic statement to wild interpretative imaginings, may be a thin and wavering one. *Revelation* is, in addition to much else, a covert attack on the Roman occupation. The Whore of Babylon became in certain circles synonymous with the Church of Rome; but a study of the contemporary fertility cults against which the prophets inveighed so assiduously suggests that their revulsions were well founded in taste as well as in morals. In modern exegesis of the Parables of the New Testament there are still dark places, faintly lit by a recourse to symbolic, even oblique explanations.

There is another consideration. We know that the great cathedrals and churches of Christendom were, from the twelfth century onwards, a kind of *Biblia Pauperum*. Such scholars as Émile Mâle and Panovsky[2] have shown the common patterns which they adopted for what we might call exegesis in stone. That the north side of a cathedral should represent the Old Testament, and the south the New, is perhaps obvious: it is at first sight less clear why the western door should represent the Place or Day of Judgment. A favourite subject is that of the Three Wise Men of the East, later to be transformed into the Three Kings: the gifts that they bore have traditional meanings that enrich and illuminate the episode. We do not, I believe, do wrongly if we consider that meanings may on occasion be reflected, as it were, from without the letter of the

[1] For a similar outburst by a Puritan preacher, see Walter Scott, *Woodstock*, h. i.   [2] *Studies in Iconology*, New York, 1939.

texts, and may be themselves the product of ancient wisdom and meditation. It is for this reason that I have included some reference to symbolism and—more hesitantly—to numerology.

v

For in the last resort a study such as this, undertaken in all humility in response to a specific request, must attempt to draw into itself a range of literary comparisons and *exempla* that is wider than many might think proper. In justification I would suggest that this aspect of the importance of the Bible can best be shown by some alignment with aspects of secular literature, and with art and iconography. Such a course contains peculiar difficulties and pitfalls. It would have been easy to have allowed one's critical judgment to be submerged in the loose superlatives and generalizations that so often attend the writings, and still more the lectures, of those who have taken as their title, 'The Bible as Literature'. It would also be easy to draw on the immense amount of material for destructive criticism that is manifest, in many kinds, in the writings of the past hundred and seventy years. It would, I think, have been impossible to retain any critical integrity if one were to accept the position of complete verbal inspiration. On the other hand,

> "The dangers of falling into a sickly semi-humanism by excess of the experiential approach are too obvious to need stressing."[1]

I have not found it possible, or desirable, to take up a neutral position. In the final chapter, 'Towards the Values', I have tried to draw together some of the conclusions which seem to emerge from this study. But perhaps it is fairer to make plain my own position at the outset. I cannot accept that every portion of the Bible is of equal sanctity and importance, for some study of the history of the texts and their editing leads me to believe otherwise. Equally, I do not accept the modern trend of the 'demythologizing' theologians, now so prominent. 'Myth' does not seem to me to be assessable in terms of historical truth or falsehood, both because of its nature and because of the complex conditions under which it passes into literature. I have preferred (following Jung and Kerényi[2]) the term 'mythologem' in order to avoid the pejorative associations of 'myth'. At the same

---

[1] T. R. Young, *A Basis for Religious Education*, Colin Smythe, 1967, pp. 27–28.
[2] G. C. Jung and C. Kerényi, *Introduction to a Science of Mythology*, Transl. R.F.C. Hull, London, 1951.

time I am clear as to the immense spiritual importance of what the Bible sets out in the central and perennial aspects of myth, and of the function of the archetypes as one road to religious experience. Of this, indebted as I am to Maud Bodkin, Jung, Rahner, Austin Farrer, and others, I have written below.

Through the dim and broken history of the Bible there passes a strange procession of events and images which alone can shadow forth, and in part satisfy, man's groping recognition of many kinds of hidden yet vital life; that the roots which the images send deep into our minds draw from the depths something that satisfies, we do not know how, the deepest need of the psyche. Many are, as Yeats said of Shaw, 'atheists who tremble in the haunted corridor'. Without the richness which the archetypes give us, and without the links with the past which the mythologems provide through the creative imagination, we may well be doomed to that starvation, that atrophy of the traditional life of the spirit, which many moralists have diagnosed as a malaise of our time.

I do not see the mythologems and the archetypes merely as a meeting-point of subjective human need and objective traditional image. I believe, with Jung, that the human mind brings to the encounter a creative activity; and that this creative activity is to be discerned in much of the greatest literature. 'But also I have come to believe that in this encounter there is the co-operation of an influence, termed by the philosopher Whitehead the Divine Persuasion, and, by theologians, the Grace of God.'[1]

[1] Maud Bodkin, *Studies of Type Images* . . . , Oxford, 1951, p. 175.

CHAPTER TWO

Themes and Kinds

i

WE MAY FIRST consider some of the basic qualities and limitations
of the Bible in such a context.

As 'literature' it is, in many ways, remote from our present consciousness. There is no single work of comparable quality and
intention (still less of current availability) with which we may
compare it. We may read the Koran, or the Granth Sahib, the
Upanishads, the Bhagavad Gita, the Egyptian *Book of the Dead*, the
Epic of Gilgamesh,[1] the Babylonian Epic of Creation,[2] the Law Code
of Hammurabi;[3] and these, together with various anthologies,
provide some material for comparisons, throw some oblique and
broken light; but little more. In its range, its unity, its diversity,
its two major symphonic movements of promise and fulfilment, in
its avoidance (in general) of arid and now pointless narrative or
gnomic reflections that are of little relevance to the West, the Bible
is unique. It regards history as a straightforward linear progression,
unlike the gyres and whorls of Greek thought. Yet we must realize
that the great unifying force is teleological. It is a record of man's
tentative and intermittent progression, through increasing awareness,
through spiritual warfare and the grasping of 'wisdom through
suffering', towards a comprehensive and comprehensible moral
situation: 'the city that hath foundations, whose builder and maker
is God . . .'.

But it would be wrong to minimize the difficulties: and the gap
between this mass of literature and that of our own time which
demands some imaginative historical leap. This is a literature of
simplicity, and of simplification. It communicates thoughts and
feelings arising out of limited situations. It is characterized by

[1] *c.* 2000–1800 B.C.   [2] *c.* 1750–1400 B.C.
[3] King of Babylon. *c.* 1792–1750 B.C.

profundity without complexity; at least until we are in the world of certain of the Epistles, with their Hellenistic background. The problem of evil that the Bible presents has not (with the possible exception of *Job*) the depth and complexity of the Greek dramatists, or of Shakespeare, or of such moralists as Matthew Arnold and Eliot. It makes little attempt to explore the workings of interior consciousness. Above all, it must speak largely through its own special kind of myths and images, and we must adjust ourselves to these.

From another angle it is the fragmentary history of a small tribe of the Eastern Mediterranean, which had settled by conquest a portion of what is sometimes called the 'fertile crescent'. The record of that conquest, the successive reduction of key-towns such as Jericho, the slaughter of the inhabitants, the raids, counter-invasions, oppressions and defeats, occupies much of the military narrative. This way of life is an essential part of the total pattern, as certifying the past and sustaining the promise of the future under the covenant of God. The nomadic habits of *Genesis* and *Exodus* yield to the more settled life of the cities and villages as the gains of warfare are consolidated.

Such warfare is constant: in narration, in prophecy, in the fabric of the poetry. The strategical situations of the Jews had made their country a buffer state, lying across the immemorial routes from Syria to Egypt, from Persia to the coast. They were always liable to local raids, or more massive invasions; living uneasily with their neighbours, the Bedouin of the desert, the Syrians, the Amalekites, the Philistines of the coastal plain. They were capable of undertaking, under David and Solomon, significant counter-actions of their own in order to extend the Empire. They suffered pillage, subjection, or captivity as the great empires about them rose and fell. So it comes about that much of their poetry is that of elegy, or of something verging on despair; the 'compleynt' so frequent in medieval literature. With the captivities or the occupations it was often necessary to compromise, to accept the restraints on liberty and to build their own lives in such a context.[1]

In such a situation, under constant pressures of every kind—military, religious, cultural, economic—from a host of neighbours—their

[1] e.g. their assumption of the roles of banker, accountants, middlemen, civil servants, in Babylon; even, on occasion, as political and religious advisers.

concern is to maintain their racial integrity, already complicated by the tribal structure of their nation, and the stern monotheism of the Mosaic Law. Within this broad intention, the Law itself expands and elaborates itself into extremity of detail, ritual, and hygiene, punishments and judgments, which are essential aspects of this maintenance of identity. Like all such codifications it could and did become arid with the weight of the centuries, with custom and priestly gloss; the letter tending to rise, as always with law, above the intention or spirit. But of its essential relevance, sanity, and cogency for a people in such a situation and setting, there can be no doubt.

Their history—itself an historical record of value, without parallel in the ancient world—is written, in general, long after the events which it commemorates. For this reason it is perceived in terms of action; the acid of time eating away all irrelevancies concerned with the emergence of human personality revealed in action, in some form of spiritual or military or judicial leadership. Of detail we have little; the imaginations of artists and sculptors have been free for centuries to depict Moses or Isaac or David, Peter or Paul or Luke, according to their personal visions and the type-figures or models of their time.

Such a narrative of action must be by its nature highly selective. It moves simply and strongly through time, its gaps omitted or compressed to throw into relief the more significant events; those that in any saga-literature find a permanent place because they are celebrated in memorable ballad or song. And here, as always in such literature, an essential part is the rehearsing of the names and places that such ballads or miniature epics have connected with events; monuments that make past warfare live again.

We must not underestimate the immense importance, to the Jewish community struggling against the Romans, or to the Puritans of Cromwell's New Model Army, of the deeds of the God of Battles; as certifying His past and present protection, and anticipating His justice for the future. Nor should we underestimate its effect to stimulate the heroic and patriotic virtues. Ulfilas, Bishop of the Goths about A.D. 350, is remembered for his version of the Scriptures, but perhaps more for Gibbon's comment:

"He prudently suppressed the four books of Kings, as they might tend to irritate the fierce spirit of the Barbarians."

So the total narrative moves, a little spasmodically, toward its objective, the Messianic prophecy that will one day be fulfilled. Its track through history is maintained by a constant retrospective correction of the course, through back-references to its history, the national epic and its related traditions, to the immensely important perception of prophecies fulfilled. So events seem to slide like weights down taut wires, from past to present: to build up in solid masses the miniature epics in which a single purpose, or the frustration of that purpose by human stupidity or evil, is made known.

Within this overall pattern of the Old Testament we have a literature of the utmost variety. In this lies a major difficulty. Those parts of it which we might select as of significant 'magnitude' for sustained examination as literature are, too often, brief and even fragmentary. If we set aside the books of the campaigns, there are great tracts of the Bible of which the interest today seems to belong, not to literature, but to a somewhat specialized kind of ancient history. Among the 'kinds' which seem to invite a wider examination it is possible to suggest a brief and perhaps arbitrary catalogue.

There would be the whole of *Genesis,* and part of *Exodus*; not much of *Leviticus*; all *Ruth, Job*; most of *Isaiah*; parts of *Daniel, Ezekiel* (after some study), *The Song of Solomon, Ecclesiastes*; all, or nearly all, of the *Psalms.* Dramatic episodes, some of them handled for their human interest as well as for their didactic potentialities by the dramatists of the Mystery and Miracle plays,[1] Noah's Flood, Cain and Abel, Baalam's Ass, the Sacrifice of Isaac, the Wanderings in the Desert, the Temptation in the Garden. One of the most popular—it is not difficult to see why—is the apocryphal Harrowing of Hell, first found in the 'Gospel of Nicodemus' and developed by various commentators.[2] The reasons for its popularity are clear; for it not only gave hope to the vast body of souls inhabiting Limbo, but might be thought to settle a problem that had vexed the early Christian world. For this was an anxiety to the men of the Renaissance, who had founded their education and scholarship on the Classics, and who had seen Aristotle incorporated into the *Summa Theologica* of Aquinas, Plato assimilated to St. Paul's teaching, Virgil acquiring

---

[1] It is perhaps surprising that we find no dramatization of one of the most dramatic of all stories, that of Jezebel. Was the 'moral' too obscure?

[2] *v.* Mâle, *op. cit.,* p. 224.

the character of a pagan prophet.[1] What was to happen in the Day of Judgment to all those who, by the accident of their birth in time, were deprived of the hope of salvation? 'Meanwhile Epicurus lies deep in Dante's Hell, wherein we meet with tombs enclosing souls which denied their immortalities. But whether the virtuous heathen, who lived better than he spake at least so low as not to rise against Christians . . . lie so deep as he is placed . . . were a quaery too sad to insist on.'[2]

Among other 'great' episodes which have been singled out are the Breaking of the Tables of the Law, the story of Jonathan and David, the end of Esther, Daniel; Joseph and his brethren; the satiric passage on the priests of Baal and their ecstatic attempts at the invocation of fire. Perhaps we may turn for a kind of summary to the Epistle to the Hebrews:

> And what shall I more say? for the time would fail me to tell of Gideon, and of Barak, and of Samson, and of Jephthaeh; of David also, and Samuel, and of the prophets: who through faith subdued kingdoms, wrought righteousness, obtained promises, stopped the mouths of lions, quenched the violence of fire, escaped the edge of the sword, out of weakness were made strong, waxed valiant in fight, turned to flight the armies of the aliens. . . . And others had trial of cruel mockings and scourgings; yea, moreover, of bonds and imprisonment: They were stoned, they were sawn asunder, were tempted, were slain with the sword: they wandered about in sheepskins and goatskins, being destitute, afflicted, tormented; (of whom the world was not worthy:) they wandered in deserts, and in mountains, and in dens and caves of the earth.[3]

ii

When we move to the New Testament we are in some measure in another world. The tradition is still emphasized by genealogy, reference, quotation, the triumphant or embittered recognitions of prophecies fulfilled. Often the atmosphere seems to carry a kind of gentle luminosity, as of the 'Italian Light' of the Campagna. The battle clouds, the thunder of Jahweh,[4] the denunciations of the prophets, have yielded to a quieter and sweeter air. The soldiery and the images of warfare are in the background. We are in a country

[1] On the strength of a famous passage in the Fourth Eclogue.
[2] Sir Thomas Browne, *Urn-Burial*, IV, 21. [3] *Heb.* 11: 32–38.
[4] Whom some consider to have been originally a Storm-god.

occupied by a stern but civilized nation; we are conscious always of
the Roman pressures on the perimeter, but we are aware of them
only in the complexities of civil administration, racial riots, judgment
of the Courts. We are aware of the jarring sects, split both by beliefs
and by differing interpretations of the Law, but animated always by
their nationalist aspiration to rid themselves, under some leader or
Messiah, from the hated Roman sway. A projection of that hope,
and its chronicle, is in Josephus; forming, perhaps, a link between
the Old and the New Testaments. The imagery is kinder; there is
more of the 'household language'; there is, even inland, a smell of
ships and nets, and we remember that prolonged ministry by the Sea
of Galilee. The logic and restraint of the Greek ethos has penetrated
to this world; so that in the Septuagint the Old Testament is
translated for the benefit of the Alexandrian Jews who have no
Hebrew, and Hebrew, Greek, and Aramaic interpenetrate each
other to provide subtle shadings of significance.

iii

Yet there is one profound change of theme that arises out of the New
Testament. An empty grave encourages men to look into other
graves, full or empty; either seeking to assure a congregation, as
Donne seems to have done,[1] that there was no bodily salvation in it,
or to build enormities of the romantic imagination by those on whom

> "Pale lies the distant shadow of the tomb,
> And all that draweth on the tomb for text."[2]

The Old Testament is objective, even laconic in its view of death. Its
heroes sleep with their fathers; man returns again to be dust, or
withers like grass, or descends into that Sheol of which no one speaks
with certainty. There is cruelty, there are even fragments of what
our civilization would call the macabre; as when the dogs lap the
blood from the chariots as they are washed out after the battle, or
reject the hands and feet of the dismembered Jezebel. But there is
nowhere, either in the Old or the New, the inflaming of a morbid
imagination by the thought of the grave,[3] speculation on the
physical circumstances of the resurrection, the central paradox of
overt corruption out of which is to come eternal life.

[1] As, for example, in the great and terrible sermon on *Vermiculation* (*Death's
Duell*, pp. 20–22).   [2] Meredith, *Modern Love*.
[3] The ghosts raised by the Witch of Endor are described in a matter-of-fact way.

It is this terrible morbidity that grows in later ages out of the grave; and out of the uncertainty as to the future of the soul. Few passages express more strongly the horror of the adolescent imagination than this from *Measure for Measure*:

> "Ay, but to die, and go we know not where;
> To lie in cold obstruction and to rot;
> This sensible warm motion to become
> A kneaded clod; and the delighted spirit
> To bathe in fiery floods, or to reside
> In thrilling region of thick-ribbéd ice;
> To be imprison'd in the viewless winds
> And blown with restless violence round about
> The pendant world; or to be worse than worst
> Of those that lawless and incertain thoughts
> Imagine howling: 'tis too horrible!
> The weariest and most loathed worldly life
> That age, ache, penury and imprisonment
> Can lay on nature is a paradise
> To what we fear of death."[1]

We have therefore the central paradox that the assurance of immortality, as in the triumphant assertion of *1 Corinthians* 15, leads men to every kind of speculation on the nature and consequences of that resurrection. Across the literatures are etched the 'horrible imaginings' of the tomb; the medieval Dance of Death, the all-pervading imagery of the skeleton, and the injunctions of St. Augustine to meditate on the terrible torments of hell-fire. Nathaniel Wanley stumbles by accident upon a skull, and takes it home with him:

> "For if wee
> Rightly define the true Philosophy
> To be a Meditation of the Grave,
> Then while I hugge thee I am sure I have
> The best Philosopher. . . ."[2]

In the Old Testament the dead go down into the underworld. Except for that allegorical vision of Ezekiel, the Valley of Dry Bones, there is no ague of the skeleton, any more than there is in the classics, and in the literature based upon the deaths they handle. In this matter it is profitable to compare Shakespeare's refractions; the world of death

[1] III. 1. 116
[2] From *The Philosopher, Poems, ed.* L. C. Martin, Oxford, 1928.

in *Antony and Cleopatra,* and that of the Christian *Measure for Measure,* or *Hamlet.* It is true that we may gather out of the New Testament the texts on which the minds of so many writers, from Dante to Beddoes, were to build:

> . . . depart from me, ye cursed, into everlasting fire, prepared for the devil and his angels.
>
> *(Mt.* 25:41)

> But the heavens and the earth, which are now, by the same word are kept in store, reserved unto fire against the day of judgement and perdition of ungodly men.
>
> *(2 Pet.* 3:7)

> But the fearful, and unbelieving, and the abominable, and murderers, and whoremongers, and sorcerers, and idolaters, and all liars, shall have their part in the lake which burneth with fire and brimstone: which is the second death.
>
> *(Rev.* 21:8)

It would be wrong to underestimate the imaginative fabrics of human torment, physical and mental, that have been built upon these and similar texts. For in the mind we have always to reckon with an element of morbidity, the impulse towards death, the pleasant shudder of horror at its trappings, the ceaseless attempts to obtain glimpses, however thick the veil, of the after-life. We may perhaps notice the calm assurance with which the Egyptian *Book of the Dead* presumed to chart, and to navigate with complex rituals, that undiscovered sea.

iv

This, the half-fearful promise of the opening tomb and its mysteries, is a consequence of the New Testament that we cannot escape. The whole superstructure of the Romantic macabre is built upon it. Psychologists tell us that man is, always,

> "Half in love with easeful death."[1]

and we may quote from Henry Vaughan:

> "Dear, beauteous Death! the jewel of the just,
>   Shining nowhere, but in the dark;
> What mysteries do lie beyond thy dust,
>   Could man outlook that mark!"[2]

[1] Keats, *Ode to a Nightingale.*   [2] *They are all gone into the world of light.*

Hagiography, miracles, reliques of saints and their uncorrupted bodies, have been added. At best—

"The body of Saint Theresa lies undecayed in tomb,
   Bathed in miraculous oil, sweet odours from it come,
   Healing from its lettered slab . . ."[1]

at worst—

"Send them home
To talk it with their wives: sow them with books
Of midnight marvels, witcheries and vision:
Let the unshaven Nazarite of stars
Unbind her wondrous locks, and grandame's earthquake
Drop its wide jaw; and let the church-yard's sleep
Whisper out goblins."[2]

The imagination has seemed reluctant to rest on the perennial, perhaps the ultimate, image of the mystery of the buried seed:

But some man will say, How are the dead raised up? and with what body do they come?

Thou fool, that which thou sowest is not quickened, except it die.[3]

It is probable that humanity might have been spared much torment if the imagination could have rested upon that saying, or upon the more sophisticated but no less noble confession of Sir Thomas Browne:

"I believe that our estranged and divided ashes shall unite again; that our separated dust, after so many Pilgrimages and transformations into the parts of Minerals, Plants, Animals, Elements, shall at the Voice of God return into their primitive shapes, and join again to make up their primary and predestinate forms. . . . As at the Creation, all the distinct species that we behold lay involved in one mass, till the fruitful Voice of God separated this united multitude into its several species; so at the last day when those corrupted reliques shall be scattered in the Wilderness of Forms, and seem to have forgot their proper habits, God by a powerful Voice shall command them back into their proper shapes, and call them out by their single individuals."[4]

v

One great difficulty in reading the Bible is that it is normally available only in texts divided into verses. It is of no use to lament

---

[1] Yeats, *Vacillation: To Von Hügel.*   [2] Beddoes, *The Second Brother*, III. 1.
   [3] *1 Cor.* 15: 35, 36.   [4] *Religio Medici*, I. xlviii.

this, or to point out that these divisions were not imposed till the early sixteenth century. For purposes of doctrine, quotation, reference, and exegesis the advantages are clearly very great, and it is unlikely that we shall see any permanent change.[1] It is helpful that those passages which are clearly lyric in structure, such as those discussed in Chapter 6, should be on occasion printed continuously, sometimes in a pattern that has at least some similarity to the original; or that passages of sustained argument, as in parts of *Romans*, should be printed consecutively.

At the same time we must realize clearly the limitations as well as the qualities of this verse-structure. In large tracts it can become intensely monotonous. So can the Spenserian stanza or the eighteenth-century couplet. Monotony may be reinforced by those structures, antithetic, parallel or incremental, which are considered in the next chapter. In general, it seems fair to suggest that this verse-pattern is most successful when it deals with comparatively limited areas of experience, selected and compressed; with lyric passages where the strength is derived mainly from the rapid impact of varied images; or with narrative which moves rapidly from one point to point with the minimum of detailed description. It is supremely efficient for the exposition of law or ritual, where the units of thought are often, perhaps usually, self-contained or for genealogical or dynastic memorials in which 'checks' in the pattern are of no great consequence. Above all, it is supremely fitted to any writing embodying proverbial or gnomic utterance. The *Psalms* of course are a special case. Custom and their position in the services of the Church, as well as the interjections, musical or moral, which we find in them, make it unlikely that any rearrangement into stanzaic form will ever be popular.

vi

Within the 'kinds'—we may use the Elizabethan term—we have a literature concerned with an immense *range* of events, but the units which compose each kind are relatively small. If we look for the books of the Old Testament which exhibit a complete unity of action

[1] Modifications such as printing consecutively and signifying the verses by small numerals in the text are not perhaps wholly satisfactory, though there is clearly a gain in printing lyric poetry in lines which follow the thought-units; even though they cannot reproduce the rhythms, and still less the occasional ambiguities, word-play, and puns, of the Hebrew.

and, in consequence of tone, there are not many which fulfil the condition. There is *Genesis*, though this splits into smaller movements; *Exodus* almost in its entirety; the military histories of *Kings*, *Judges*, and *Chronicles*. *Jonah*, the liveliest of all, is a consistent unity, though not without its difficulties. *Ruth* and *The Song of Songs* offer, perhaps, the best examples of unity of tone and intention. *Job*, though the geological strata of its text obscure its sweep and progress, is also notable.

One condition of this brevity is that, as we have previously suggested, we rarely find any development of character, or indeed any solid delineation of it. The great figures move in somewhat remote fashion, their characters illuminated as it were from the side by flashes of magnanimity, pity, anger; heroism, deceit, covetousness; suffering and the frequent cry of despair. *Proverbs* and *Ecclesiastes* are largely self-consistent; but to estimate them demands some comparative knowledge of similar forms. There are many of these in the literatures of the Middle East.

Perhaps we should indeed see the Book as this series of variegated patterns, lights and colours, shifting in time like a modern mobile, coalescing to break apart into new forms. In succession we have the archetypal patterns of myth; the dangerous journey, the ordeal, conquest and defence, subjection and captivity. There are miniature vignettes, dramas of individuals. There is song, prophecy, lamentation; struggles against man's recurrent disillusionment or despair; exaltation and courage, meanness and generosity.

Always we must perceive with whatever effort of the imagination, statements that are simple and profound, arising out of situations that are, in the main, statements of a simplified dichotomy; rain and drought, evil against good, the idols against the One God, the little cities and their heroes against the enemy. There is little concern with interior psychology. Men 'do evil in the sight of the Lord'; that mystery is perpetually before us, but its irrationality and attractiveness is never solved. We do not advance, except by Grace, beyond St. Paul's confession:

> For the good that I would, I do not: but the evil which
> I would not, that I do.[1]

[1] *Rom.* 7 : 19.

31

CHAPTER THREE

The Languages and their Energies

". . . Poetic rhythms, as a rule, are incorrigibly untranslatable;
the luckless fate of innumerable 'translations in the metres of the
original' bears eloquent witness to that mournful truth. But here
was a rhythm dependent upon an inner impulse rather than
upon external rule—ebbing and flowing, rising and falling with
the fluctuations of thought or mood, and carrying, through its
powerful beat, the impelling emotion into the reader's mind, to
stir in turn the springs of rhythm there."

(John Livingston Lowes, *Of Reading Books*)

i

IT IS OFTEN said, with considerable truth, that the English translators of both the Elizabethan and Jacobean versions were supremely
fortunate in having to their hands a language well suited to the
character of both the Hebrew and the Greek originals. Hebrew was a
simple, concrete and direct language, basing its imagery on the simple
events of daily life; not demanding any great complexity or subtlety
in its thinking. Above all, it used what we may call a psycho-
physiology which found its counterpart in the Elizabethan theories
of the humours, and the location of the emotions, with the description
of their effects, in the human body and its functions. The 'bowels' of
compassion, the 'telling' of individual bones in fever or despair, the
strength that was dried up like a potsherd: all were familiar. Later
developments of Elizabethan psychology were consonant with these:
the liver for the seat of love, the gall and spleen for the emotions of
bitterness and hatred, the triple divided functions in the anatomy of
the brain, the 'spirits' ascending in the blood, sorted out in the heart
and cooled by the lungs on their progress to the brain: all these were
ideas familiar to the Shakespearian world. Neuro-physiology was
equally developed in terms of

the sinewy thread my brain lets fall[1]

and Job's

> Thou hast clothed me with skin and flesh, and hast fenced me with bones and sinews.[2]

is echoed by Hamlet, Marvell, A. E. Housman and G. K. Chesterton.

Yet the initial problem of the matrix-languages demands some consideration. Biblical Hebrew is characterized by its small number of consonants—22 as against 28 in Arabic—and by a relatively sparse vocabulary, some 5,000 words. Its syntactical structure is simple. There is a poverty of connecting particles. The result is a simple disjunctive style, working in short units. Dramatic force is obtained by repetition, especially of significant words; by different kinds of variations, 'ringing changes' in the word order of a similar sentence repeated in parallel. We tend to a prose that can move with relative ease over simple narrative connecting a series, as it were, of peaks of action. It can carry admirably its own special type of lyric by repetition, contrasts, incremental statements. Something of its simple unpatterned accumulation can be seen if we set a passage from *Exodus* against one from Malory's *Morte d'Arthur*:

> And it came to pass, that at even the quails came up, and covered the camp: and in the morning the dew lay round about the host. And when the dew that lay was gone up, behold, there lay a small round thing, as small as the hoar frost on the ground. And when the children of Israel saw it, they said one to another, It is manna: for they wist not what it was.[3]

> "Then the king made the barget to be holden fast, and then the king and the queen entered with certain knights with them; and there he saw the fairest woman like in a rich bed, covered unto her middle with many rich clothes, and all was of cloth of gold, and she lay as though she had smiled. Then the queen espied a letter in her right hand, and told it to the king. Then the king took it, and said: Now am I sure this letter will tell what she was, and why she is come hither."

The simple disjunctive style can achieve, besides narrative, a considerable variety of the 'kinds'. It can compass sermons, letters, law; civic documents (provided that these are in the form of simple Eastern 'decrees' like those of Nebuchadnezzar); it rejoices in a certain quasi-consecutiveness, often dramatically unexpected, proper

---

[1] Donne, *The Funerall*.   [2] 10:11.   [3] 16:13–15.

C   33

to the fairy-tale, or the outrageously supernatural event (such as that of Balaam's Ass). Its gnomic quality is well suited to oracles, spells, or proverbial wisdom.

It is in the lyrical kinds that the language and its conventional poetic form find, perhaps, their most characteristic achievement.

The rhythm of Biblical Hebrew is based on significant elements, which are normally, but not invariably, single words. The major bases are 3:3 and 3:2: the latter is called 'balancing' or 'echoing' rhythm. Variants are 4:4 and 2:2. As an example:

> mayim / šā ál // chālábh / nāthánā
> water / he asked // milk / she gave
> beséphel / ʾaddīrīm // hiqríbhā / chem'á
> in a bowl of / nobleness // she proffered / curds

i.e.

> He asked water, // and she gave him milk
> She brought forth butter // in a lordly dish.[1]

—where the *A.V.* version seems to echo the caesuras and stresses of the Hebrew. The normal rhythm of the *Psalms* is that of two balancing clauses, each carrying a 4- or 3-stress movement on either side of the caesura, so that we are conscious of many variations upon the norm:

> I was glad when they said unto me,//Let us 'go into the house of the Lord.
>
> Our feet shall stand within thy gates, // O Jerusalem[2].

or they can carry (assisted by the chant) far longer units:

> My soul waiteth for the Lord more than they that watch for the morning: // I say, more than they that watch for the morning.[3]

The vitality is of the kind common to much primitive poetry: based again like the Scottish Ballads, on repetition, both parallel and incremental, and on antithesis, sometimes in a refrain. In its simplicity and in the activity of its verbs, it is also supremely fitted for curses, blessings, laments, songs of pilgrimage or battles, for parable, fable, allegory. We may note, and lament, the lack (for purposes of comparison) of any great body of significant literature in those forms to-day. From time to time the poverty of the adjectival resources

---

[1] *Jg.* 5:25 (see also pp. 81, 84). I am again indebted to Prof. Winton Thomas.
[2] *Ps.* 122:1.   [3] *Ps.* 130:6.

(for they are often, like the Scottish Ballads, restricted to a few clichés, a stylized diction) is relieved by an imaginative exuberance of imagery which Addison noted:

"There is a certain coldness and indifference in the phrases of our European languages, when they are compared with the oriental forms of speech; and it happens very luckily, that the Hebrew idioms run into the English tongue with a particular grace and beauty. Our language has received innumerable elegancies and improvements, from that infusion of Hebraism, which are derived to it out of the poetical passages in Holy Writ. They give a force and energy to our expression, warm and animate our language, and convey our thoughts in more ardent and intense phrases, than any that are to be met with in our own tongue."[1]

ii

The situation is a little different with the New Testament. Its Greek is a secular language of the three centuries before the Birth of Christ. It is widely divergent from classical Greek; its syntax and its verb-system are simplified. It has characteristics which suggest that it stands, in fact, half-way between a literary and a popular or 'household' language. This is important, for we are only now acquiring a thorough understanding of the peculiarities of this 'popular' language through recent discoveries of contemporary inscriptions and documents. This knowledge was not accessible to the scholars of the King James Bible, and has resulted in many important modifications in meaning in the New English Bible.

Like Elizabethan English, New Testament Greek was constantly borrowing and coining words. Furthermore, as the early Church developed, words began to acquire Christian overtones; which, as always, only become clear by a study of contextual usage. There is a vast increase, compared with the Old Testament, in what we might call, loosely, 'the philosophical concern'. But there is, also, through the Septuagint, a flavouring of Hebrew idiom in the ways of thought, partly perhaps through Aramaic, more by the constant reference to, and quotation from, the Old Testament. These need not concern us here; but again the Tudor structure of prose, of the 'Low' or 'Mean' Style, was eminently fitted to carry the weight of narrative, teaching, parables, and simple poems. Only when it has to face the complexities of neo-Platonic argument do we find that the skeins of the

[1] *Spectator*, No. 405 (see also Chapter 5).

Authorized Version tend to become a little tangled in the hand. Then we must often turn to the versions of the last half-century.

iii

We may illustrate some characteristics of the Hebrew and Greek, in the narrative kind, by comparing two 'maritime' passages with a piece of Tudor prose.

> But the Lord sent out a great wind into the sea, and there was a mighty tempest in the sea, so that the ship was like to be broken.
>
> Then the mariners were afraid, and cried every man unto his god, and cast forth the wares that were in the ship into the sea, to lighten it of them. But Jonah was gone down into the sides of the ship; and he lay, and was fast asleep.
>
> So the shipmaster came to him, and said unto him, What meanest thou, O sleeper? arise, call upon thy God, if so be that God will think upon us, that we perish not.[1]

> But not long after there arose against it a tempestuous wind, called Euroclydon.
>
> And when the ship was caught, and could not bear up into the wind, we let her drive.
>
> And running under a certain island which is called Clauda,[2] we had much work to come by the boat:
>
> Which when they had taken up, they used helps, undergirding the ship; and fearing lest they should fall into the quicksands,[3] strake sail, and so were driven.
>
> And we being exceedingly tossed with a tempest, the next day they lightened the ship;
>
> And the third day we cast out with our own hands the tackling of the ship.[4]

The writer of *Jonah* has no interest in ships or in the sea; his only concern is the bearing of the event on Jonah, his fate and that of the seamen. The narrative from *Acts* has all the circumstantial precision of men who use the sea. The vessel is trapped near a dangerous coast by a north-east gale, and cannot turn to windward; the seamen 'wear' her, take all possible canvas off her, and run for shelter. In

---

[1] *Jon.* 1:4–6.   [2] Now Gozzo, near Malta.
[3] The Gulf of Syrte, W. of Libya.   [4] *Acts* 27:14–19.

such a following sea the ship's boat, towed behind, has been swamped; to recover and bale her out is a highly dangerous task.[1] Then the pounding that the ship has taken causes some of the strakes to start; the seamen adopt the emergency procedure of passing hawsers under the keel at intervals, and securing them with Spanish windlasses, in the hope of holding the hull together.[2] But in this state the pressure of the sails on the hull is excessive, and they strip to bare poles, lowering the single great yard. The sea gets worse. They jettison, first, part of the cargo—wheat—and then the heavier, vital gear, such as spare anchors and spars: perhaps they even cut a mast away.

It will be noticed that the extract has one adjective, *tempestuous*. Against these two we may set a passage, comparable in scope and intention, of the mid-sixteenth century:

"We, with the other seven ships, cast about into the sea, the storm enduring ten days with great might, boisterous winds, fogs, and rain. Our ship, being old and weak, was so tossed that she opened at the stern a fathom under water, and the best remedy we had was to stop it with beds and pilobiers (pillows): and for fear of sinking we threw and lightened into the sea all the goods we had, or could come by; but that would not serve.

Then we cut our mainmast, and threw all our ordnance into the sea, saving one piece; which early in a morning, when we thought we should have sunk, we shot off: as it pleased GOD, there was one of the ships of our company near unto us, which we saw not by means of the great fog; which hearing the sound of the piece, and understanding some of the company to be in great extremity, began to make towards us, and when they came within hearing of us, we desired them 'for the love of GOD! to help to save us, for that we were all like to perish!' They willed us 'to hoist our foresail as much as we could, and make towards them; for they would do their best to save us;' and so we did."[3]

Here the prose, in its strong simplicity, its paucity of adjectives, its precisely accurate concern with professional seamanship, is wholly comparable with that of St. Paul. But it would be wrong not to recognize the limitations in vocabulary of all three passages, and it is

[1] We may note *R.V.* (better) 'We were able, with difficulty, to secure the boat.'
[2] For a more detailed account of this, see Kipling's story 'After the Manner of Men' (*Limits and Renewals*).
[3] Robert Tomson, of Andover, Merchant, *Voyage to the West Indies and Mexico 1556-1558 A.D.* From *Voyages and Travels*, ed. E. Raymond Beazley, Vol. I, 1903.

useful to set beside them a piece of modern prose to illustrate the depth and complexity achieved:

"The seas in the dark seemed to rush from all sides to keep her back where she might perish. There was hate in the way she was handled, and a ferocity in the blows that fell. She was like a living creature thrown to the rage of a mob: hustled terribly, struck at, borne up, flung down, leaped upon. Captain MacWhirr and Jukes kept hold of each other, deafened by the noise, gagged by the wind; and the great physical tumult beating about their bodies, brought like an unbridled display of passion, a profound trouble to their souls.[1] One of these wild and appalling shrieks that are heard at times passing mysteriously overhead in the steady roar of a hurricane, swooped, as if borne on wings, upon the ship, and Jukes tried to outscream it.

'Will she live through this?' "[2]

We may note two verbal debts to the Bible: *perished* and *trouble to their souls*. It will be noted that both Tomson and Conrad use the word 'perish', now in part obsolete: and in Conrad it suggests the utter irrevocable destruction of the ship, with, perhaps, an overtone of the familiar storm on the Sea of Galilee.

iv

Energy is communicated by rhythm. Rhythm is built on stress, tone and pitch. All are, to a greater or less extent, intrinsic in the structure of the Biblical 'kinds'. All may be, and are, modified within certain limits by the creative acts of reading aloud or chanting.

Rhythm is not an aspect of language that lends itself readily to critical analysis. Its physiological and mental effects are still far from clear. It is possible within limits to gesture towards an explanation of how certain effects are achieved; but the modulations of any scheme that can be usefully set down are so numerous and subtle that no medium exists for describing them.

Within these acknowledged limits we may suggest some of the qualities of prose and verse.

Prose (*prosus*, 'straight on') suggests a straightforward march, a progress without a repeating pattern; as it might be the Children of Israel moving from oasis to oasis through the Sinai Peninsula. Where this prose is, to eye and ear, divided or divisible into units, it appears

[1] cf. *Ps.* 107:26, 27 '. . . their soul is melted because of trouble. They reel to and fro, and stagger like a drunken man, and are at their wits' end. . . .'

[2] Joseph Conrad, *Typhoon*.

to embody a simple system of stresses, giving some degree of pattern;
as in these examples:

> Then Jacob went on his journey, and came into the
> land of the people of the east.
> And he looked, and behold a well in the field, and, lo,
> there were three flocks of sheep lying by it; for out
> of that well they watered the flocks: and a great
> stone was upon the well's mouth.[1]

This is 'disjunctive' prose, with a loose progressive organization.
When a rising pressure of emotion forces the structure into the repeating patterns of verse (*versus*, returning), we have the characteristic
4:4 or 4:2 base of the Hebrew which we have mentioned previously.
But we have in addition the aspect of prose known as the cadence.

The classical cadence is a metrical pattern marking the final
clauses of sentences in certain types of prose. It may be thought of as
analogous to the resolution of chords in music. It passes into English
through late Latin, and particularly through the rhythms of the
Cranmer prayer-book, deriving from the Mass. It appears strongly
in the Latin versions of the Psalms, and, widely dispersed, in the
Latin of St. Jerome's Vulgate which was so familiar to the early
Translators. We may consider it as a technical device that can give
to the endings of sentences or of paragraphs a peculiar energy,
weightiness and finality of rhythm: to conclude, round off, or lend
authority to the statement. There is no doubt that its effects, as with
all kinds of rhythm, are subtle, complex and profound; but there are
no satisfactory tools for analysis.

We may give first the bare facts. The classical cadence is a
rhythmical sequence denoted by counting the strong stresses *back-
wards* from the ending of the sentence. The result is shown in the
numerical sequences below.

The *cursus planus* is of the form / × × / ×, denoted by 5:2

> countless misfortunes, come to receive it

with an 'extension' to 6:2 or 7:2—

> tempore opportuno.

The *cursus tardus* is of the form / × × / × ×, denoted by 6:3 with
a possible extension to 7:3.

> Cana in Galilee

[1] *Gen.* 29:1, 2.

39

The *cursus velox* is of the form / × × / × /× ; 7:4:2.

It will be seen that the central condition is that the sentence should end with one, two or three unaccented syllables; so that their occurrence is more likely in a language which has unstressed case-endings, and which, through the aural conditioning of the translator, pass from the Latin into the English.

The 'native' English cadence is of less importance for our present purpose, but we may note that it invariably ends with a strong stress, which does not give the peculiar 'falling away' effect of the classical cadence. This strong-ending cadence is prominent in many of the Collects:

ármour of líght	(4:1)
(con)témpt of Thy Wórd	(4:1)

though if we continue the last sentence

(con)témpt ŏf Thy Wórd aňd commándmeňt

we have the whole forming a classical cadence of the structure 7:4:2.

An examination of the Communion Service of the Church of England will suggest, not only the steady building-up of rhythmic intensity towards the climax of the ritual, but also an alternation of the strong native cadences with variations on the classical types.

If we now apply the technique of cadence-analysis to the passage from *Genesis* quoted above, we can see the two types alternating to give the variety necessary to all good prose:

(be)hóld, ă wéll iň the fíeld	(6:4:1)
flócks of sheép lying bў iť	(6:(4):3)
(that) wéll they watered the flócks	(5:3:1)
a greát stóne wăs upoń the wéll's móuth	(7:6:4:1)

In general terms, it seems as if the cadences are most marked when the prose conveys a strong emotional pressure, as in ritual or lyric or prophecy; that the light or unstressed syllables before the final stress serve, in the 'English' cadence, to 'gather up' the stride of the prose before the emphatic stresses. But since any strongly-defined repeating pattern finally becomes monotonous (as in the 'poetic' prose of certain late Victorian writers) we shall find that the most distinguished and energetic lyrical passages of the Old Testament achieve their strength through a subtle alternation of pattern between these two main forms.

The cadence is seen perhaps at its clearest if we select a verse or two in the noble wrought-iron of the Latin; and to demonstrate at the same time its sheer density of meaning we may set beside it a rendering into French:

Ibi confregit potentias arcuum: scutum, gladium, et bellum.

C'est là qu'il a brisé toute la force des arcs: les boucliers, et les épées, et qu'il a éteint la guerre.

Illuminans tu mirabiliter a montibus aeternis: turbati sunt omnes insipientes corde.

Vous avez, ô Dieu, fait éclater votre secours d'une manière admirable du haut des montagnes éternelles: et tous ceux dont le cœur étoit rempli de folie ont été troublez.

Dormierunt somnum suum: et nihil invenerunt omnes viri divitiarum in manibus suis.

Ils se sont endormi du sommeil de la mort: et tous ces hommes qui se glorisoient de leurs richesses n'ont rien trouvé dans leurs mains lors qu'ils se sont éveillez.[1]

It is at first glance difficult to recognize the French translation as the familiar passage:

> There brake he the arrows of the bow, the shield, and the sword, and the battle. Selah.
> Thou art more glorious and excellent than the mountains of prey.
> The stouthearted are spoiled, they have slept their sleep; and none of the men of might have found their hands.

The Latin is massive, compressed and resonant, and flows like a mountain torrent over the boulders in its bed. The French, limpid and clear, has to use many more words in its attempt to give the sense of the Latin. It is not in the nature of French to carry strong speech-rhythms. But we are still perplexed by the way in which the A.V. seems to make so relatively little sense. What *are* 'the mountains of prey'? What is the meaning of 'none of the men of might have found their hands'? R.V. gives us no help, for it keeps the first and second phrases. We turn to the *Revised Psalter* of 1966:

> There brake he the flashing arrows of the bow: the shield, the sword, and the weapons of battle.
> Thou art of more honour and might: than the everlasting hills.

[1] *Ps.* 76:3–5. From *L'Office de la Semaine Sainte*, Brussels, 1738. (A.V. *Ps.* 76.)

> The mighty men were made a spoil, they sleep their sleep: and all the men of war have lost their strength.

This might be thought a cardinal example of the problem: what does it *mean*? Clearly, it celebrates the defeat of a raid or invasion. The *flashing* arrows seems to verge on poetic diction, perhaps inserted to 'fill up' the chant rhythm. The *everlasting hills* is nearer the *montibus aeternis* of the Latin, more meaningful by far than the *mountains of prey* in *A.V.* But we have lost completely, in all the versions except the Latin, the force of *omnes insipientes corde*, the foolishness or rashness of the defeated men: as well as the suggestion (which the French brings out) that part of this folly consists in glorying in riches.

v

In the New Testament we may note widely different kinds of prose. When the pressure of mind or emotion underlying a statement appears almost too great to produce any corresponding rhythmic intensity, we seem to fall (as often in verse drama) into a flat almost laconic statement,[1] as if the emotion were too overpowering to be reflected in complex rhythms; as in this:

> Then the soldiers, when they had crucified Jesus, took his garments, and made four parts, to every soldier a part; and also his coat: now the coat was without seam, woven from the top throughout.
> They said therefore among themselves, Let us not rend it, but cast lots for it, whose it shall be: that the scripture might be fulfilled, which saith, They parted my raiment among them, and for my vesture they did cast lots.[2]

The careful matter-of-fact phrasing moves deliberately, step by step, breaking free when it quotes *Psalm* 22:18 to complete the prophecy.

Against this we may set the strongly-marked rhythms of denunciation:

> Woe unto you also, ye lawyers! for ye lade men with burdens grievous to be borne, and ye yourselves touch not the burdens with one of your fingers.
> Woe unto you! for ye build the sepulchres of the prophets, and your fathers killed them.[3]

But the piece of New Testament prose which shows the most complex and subtle rhythmic variations, by reasons of its changes of

---

[1] The technical term for this understatement is *litotes*.
[2] *Jn.* 19:23–24.   [3] *Lk.* 11:46–47.

time and attitude, is *1 Corinthians* 15, the Lesson for the Burial of the Dead. This is discussed in Chapter 7.

vi

It is often said that the language of the Authorized Version (and, in places, of the English Prayer Book) is now so obsolete as to demand wholesale revision. We may attempt a somewhat closer examination of the problem.[1]

It seems to me that the 'obsolete' words and phrases fall into four classes:

(1) those which arise out of an actual mis-reading of the Hebrew or Greek, and which nobody would defend;
(2) those in which the changes in meaning between 1611 and today have been so considerable as to demand some modern equivalent;
(3) those words and constructions whose obsolesence I should call 'marginal', and which impose no great strain upon the common reader;[2]
(4) those in which modernization seems to involve a significant loss of meaning.

In the first category we cannot defend the astonishing misreading of the Hebrew words for *sixth* instead of *lead on* (*Ezekiel* 39:2): or *purchased possession* in *Ephesians* 1:14. *Allow* should be translated as *approve* (*Romans* 7:15) or *understand*, which is normal Shakespearian usage. Strangest of all is a passage of *Proverbs* 30:29–31:

> There be three things which go well, yea, four are comely in going:
> A lion which is strongest among beasts, and turneth not away for any;
> A greyhound; an he-goat also; and a king, against whom there is no rising up.

Now the Bible, like Shakespeare, usually mentions dogs only to abuse them; and this is understandable when we think of the curs about all eastern villages. Yet in the passage from *Proverbs* we might think well of the image of the greyhound that illustrates the 'going well', grace and vigour of movement: the slenderness of loin, depth of chest and so on. But here the Translators of *A.V.* were guessing,

---

[1] In this section I am indebted to the data (but not the opinions) in Luther A. Weigle, *Bible Words in Living Language*, London, 1957 edn.

[2] I am aware of the problems raised by the term. Perhaps we shall have to admit that his capacity to make out meanings, such as those which become apparent from a knowledge of classical languages, is steadily decreasing.

and the word seems to mean merely 'girt in the loins'; though the Septuagint has ' a cock walking proudly among the hens'.

'Taken with the manner'[1] (in the act) probably requires modernization, in spite of two Shakespearian usages, but 'manner' as used . . . 'of beasts', . . . 'of men', . . . 'of diseases', . . . 'of peoples' may have something to be said for it as suggesting both diversity and the habits of what the Middle Ages called 'the kinds'.

In the 'wholly changed' category we may think of *conversation*, not as 'speaking' but 'total bearing', 'manners', 'social intercourse', behaviour in general. Similarly with *communication*: not language or writing, but the totality of intercourse.

Prevent is used in the sense of 'anticipate', 'go before'; and is seriously misleading in *1 Thessalonians* 4:15:

> For this we say unto you by the word of the Lord, that we which are alive and remain unto the coming of the Lord shall not prevent them which are asleep.

We are reminded of Milton's sonnet 'On his Blindness':

> ". . . but patience, to prevent
> That murmur, soon replies . . ."

'lively' in the sense of 'living', 'vigorous', has been assumed to be misleading in the text of the Communion Service, and is now generally changed, though here, as elsewhere, we may pause to ask whether there is not some value in shocking the attention by an unfamiliar obsolescent word.

The Thessalonians are described as 'walking disorderly'[2] when they were 'playing truant', not going to work, because they expected the end of the world. The Prodigal Son did not 'gather together' all his share of his father's estate:[3] he realized it, turned it into ready money. The varying contextual uses, and hence the translation, of the Greek *ekklesia* ('church') and *aletheia* ('truth') raise questions of great complexity.[4]

There is a last source of energy: the images of the Bible. Something of their qualities and functions discussed in a later chapter. Their strength as an aspect of the energies falls perhaps into two categories. There is, first, their simplicity and the directness of the metaphors

---

[1] *Num.* 5:11–31.   [2] *2 Thess.* 3:11.   [3] *Lk.* 15:13.
[4] See, e.g., Hoskyns and Davey, *The Riddle of the New Testament*, ch. i, London, 1958.

used to adumbrate the always inadequate, ever-evolving concept of the godhead. The spirit moves upon the face of the waters;
after the defeat of the Egyptians, 'The Lord is a man of war'. He
comes on Sinai in thunder and lightning, in cloud or in thick smoke:
'and the sight of the glory of the Lord was like devouring fire on the
top of the mount'. He may answer Job out of the whirlwind, or
speak in a still small voice. He can judge, plead, threaten, denounce;
He can affright men with dreams, or enlighten them with visions. Of
His angels or ministers, we have some description in *Ezekiel*, as of
the 'terrible crystal' that is the likeness of the firmament;[1] but these
are settings only, 'the appearance of the likeness of the glory of the
Lord'. Only in *Revelation* do we get an attempt, tentatively, to depict
appearance of Alpha and Omega:

> . . . And in the midst of the seven candlesticks one like unto the Son of
> man . . .
> . . . his eyes were as a flame of fire . . .
> . . . his voice as the sound of many waters . . .[2]

His presence is by the sea of molten glass and fire; He is light; out of
His throne comes 'the pure river of water of life, clear as crystal'.

So the images move about the Image of God like flashing particles
in a vortex of men's thoughts, veering, occulting, dying into new life,
renewed as the creative imagination takes its many directions. They
crowd upon us, seeking to throw some light on God in His multiplex
aspects. Some measure of their relative success may be seen if we
consider the relative ineffectiveness of pictorial art. The Mosaic God
of the Sistine Chapel stretches a priestly finger across the abyss, to
wake Adam into life. The God of Tintoretto in *The Trinity adored by
the Heavenly Choir* is as characterless as, say, Fra Bartolommeo della
Porta's in *The Creation of Eve*. Only Blake's purity of vision saw, in
The Creation of Adam and in certain of the illustrations to *Job*, that
aspect of divinity that could be set down by the artist: the energy
that is eternal delight.

---

[1] 1:22.
[2] 1:13, 14, 15. Here are the archetypal symbols of light, fire, flood.

CHAPTER FOUR

The Forge of Style

"Neither did we disdaine to revise that which we had done, and to bring back to the anvil that which we had hammered."
(Address to the Reader by Dr. Smith, 1611)

"The Holy Ghost is an eloquent author, a vehement and abundant author, but not luxuriant."
(Donne, *Sermon* 79)

i

THERE ARE MANY images used to describe the processes of revision; Horace's *labor limae*, the labour of the file: Pope's 'polishing and refining', the critical 'stitching and unstitching' (for many reasons) revealed by a study of the changes made between the drafts by, say, Keats, Tennyson, Yeats. The committee under the chairmanship of Miles Smith and Thomas Wilson, charged with the forging of the 'King James' Bible, were ordered to use the previous versions, of which the chief, and the dominant influence is Tyndale's. We can do no more than gesture towards the many influences that determined and set out, among that large company of Translators, characteristic and coherent styles both for the Hebrew and for the Greek. It is not, I think, in question that the qualities we are considering, at this particular stage, grow out of an unfailing ear for the musical and rhythmical effects of which English was then capable; always fortified by the sonority, simplicity and *gravitas* of the familiar Vulgate. The Translators of the Old Testament had certain advantages in their basic versions which we can hardly overestimate. Let us take some arbitrary examples.

And he said, Go forth, and stand on the mount before the Lord.
And, behold, the Lord passed by, and a great and strong wind rent the mountains, and brake in pieces the rocks before the Lord; but the Lord was not in the wind: and after the wind an earthquake; but the Lord was not in the earthquake:

And after the earthquake a fire; but the Lord was not in the fire: and after the fire a still small voice.[1]

It is clear that this famous passage achieves its force from its balanced repetitions and negations, from the achievement of dramatic suspense in advance and retreat, and from a kind of resolution of musical chords in the last four words. In the Coverdale Bible they are rendered as a 'styll soft hyssinge'. The Matthew Bible has

> After the fyre / came a small still voice.

A.V. has omitted the 'came'—a slight anti-climax—and achieved a final harmony on the vowels *i—a—oi*, which drop in a descending scale, whereas the Matthew Bible has *a—i—oi*. It is this subtlety of cadence which appears to give the impression of the thing perfectly and finally said.

Let us take another instance, from Coverdale:

> But the deserte & wildernesse shall reioyse, ye waist grounds shall be glad, and shall florish as the lily. She shal florish pleasantly, and be joyful, and euer be geuing of thankes more and more.[2]

and set against it:

> The wilderness and the solitary place shall be glad for them; and the desert shall rejoice and blossom as the rose. It shall blossom abundantly, and rejoice even with joy and singing . . .[3]

R.V. alters this little, except to omit 'for them', but reminds us that the word for 'solitary place' (which is made singular) may also mean 'parched land', and 'the rose' may also mean—perhaps more accurately—'autumn crocus':

> The wilderness and the parched land shall be glad; and the desert shall rejoice and blossom as the autumn crocus . . .

Now both versions seem to have felt the need to ring the changes between 'desert'—'wilderness', but the 'solitary place' of *A.V.* give a stronger and more extended picture (involving the human aspect)—and is far more vivid than the semi-geographical 'parched lands'. But if we substitute the more accurate 'autumn crocus' for the rose we have lost a whole mass of western references and of submerged images; which include, not only the metaphor for woman's beauty in all its stages, but the imagery that attaches, for instance, to

---

[1] *1 Kgs.* 19:11, 12.   [2] *Isa.* 35:1.   [3] *A.V.*

47

Rosicrucianism. Similarly, the 'desert' has ampler meanings than the abstract 'waist places'. The old sense of 'pleasantly' (which includes the idea of sensuous delight) has yielded to 'abundantly': the rhythmically undistinguished 'geuing of thanks more and more' to the strong 'rejoice even with joy and singing', though we may regret some euphonic clash between 'joy' and 'rejoice'.

For another instance of the filing and fitting of language, we may consider the description of the war horse in *Job*,[1] and note the elimination of archaisms, and consequent compression, as between the Wycliffite version of 1395 and *A.V.*

> An arowe caas schal sowne on hym, a speare and scheeld schal florische. He is hoot, and gnastith, and swolewith the erthe; and he arettith not[2] that the crie of the trompe sowneth. Whenne he herith a clarioun, he saith, Joie! he smellith battle afar, the excityng of duykis, and the yellyng of the oost.

By contrast—

> The quiver rattleth against him, the glittering spear and the shield. He swalloweth the ground with fierceness and rage: neither believeth he that it is the sound of the trumpet. He saith among the trumpets, Ha, ha; and he smelleth the battle afar off, the thunder of the captains, and the shouting.

R.V. sets the passage out in verse:

> The quiver rattleth against him,
> The flashing spear and the javelin.
> He swalloweth the ground with fierceness and rage;
> Neither believeth he that it is the voice of the trumpet.[3]
> As oft as the trumpet soundeth he saith, Aha!
> And he smelleth the battle afar off,
> The thunder of the captains, and the shouting.

I have quoted these passages to suggest that the progress from Wycliffe may not be all gain. There is a peculiar vividness in

> Whenne he hereth the clarion, he saith, Joye!

'The excitying of duykis', as well as the 'yelling of the oost', have a Chaucerian freshness; we may recall the description of the Temple

---

[1] 39:23.   [2] does not consider, does not worry about.
[3] *R.S.V.* has a footnote: *or,* 'Neither standeth he still at the voice of the trumpet'; which I find more convincing as the picture of a cavalry charger.

of Mars in *The Knight's Tale*. And though we may approve (through long familiarity)

"The thunder of the captains and the shouting"

we may, on reflection, question the propriety of 'thunder' for an Israelitish battle, as well as the relative flatness of 'shouting'.

It is probable that the Twenty-Third Psalm has been paraphrased and versified more than any other; and I have alluded previously to the now notorious instance of the Valley of the Shadow. We may trace the growth of some of its characteristic phraseology, beginning with Coverdale (1535):

> The Lorde is my shepherde I can want nothing. He fedeth me in a greene pasture and ledeth me to a fresh water. He quickeneth my soul and bringeth me forth in the waye of righteousness for his name's sake. Though I shulde walke now in the valley of the shadowe of death yet I feare no evell for thou art with me, thy staffe and thy shepehoke comforte me.

The Great Bible of 1539 introduces 'waters of comfort', translating the Vulgate's 'super aquam refectionis', but 'still waters' returns to the Genevan Bible of 1560, to become 'calme waters' in the Bishops' Bible eight years later. We can see the successive versions feeling towards the familiar 'green pastures' through 'pastures full of grasse' and 'goodly lusty pasture', but the Forty-Seven return to Coverdale. *R.S.V.* gives the 'still waters', and the Hebrew 'the waters of rest'. The first line disregards the Latin title, *Dominus regit me*, in all but a very early version, a 'Book of Hours' of 1410, where it becomes 'Oure Lord governeth me'.

In the same way we can trace 'and fyllest my cuppe . . . full' through 'and my cuppe shall brymee full', the unfortunate 'my chalice inebriating how goodlie it is' to the final my 'cuppe runneth over'; we can see, too, how the Prayer Book Version returns to that of the Great Bible of 1539, '& my cuppe shalbi full', instead of *A.V.*'s 'my cup runneth over'.

ii

We may illustrate both the patterns of consecutive prose, and the rate of change of the language, by setting out the same passage in Wycliffe's version of 1378, Tyndale's in 1534, and the King James

Bible of 1611: over a period of two hundred and thirty-five years. This is *Luke* 2:1–7:

> Forsothe it was don in tho dayes, a maundement went out fro Caesar August that al the world shoulde be discruyed. This first discruyinge was maad of Cyrene iustice of Cirye, and alle men wenten that thei schulde make profescioun ech by himself to his cite. Sothly and Joseph stighede up fro Galilee of the cite of Nazareth in to Jude, in to a city of Dauith that is clepid Bedleem, for that he was of tho house and meyne of Daueth, that he schulde knowlache with Mary with child spousid wyf to hym.
>
> Sothly it was don whanne thei weren there the dayes weren fulfilled that she shulde bere child. And she shildede her first born sone and wlappede hym in clothis and putted hym in a craache, for ther was not place to hym in the comyn stable.

Wycliffe is translating from the Vulgate.

Here is Tyndale:

> Hit folowed in thoose dayes that there went out a commaundement from Auguste the Emperour that all the woorld shulde be valued. This taxynge was first executed when Syrenus was leftenaunt in Syria. And every man wente in to his awne shire toune there to be taxed. And Joseph also ascended from Galile oute of a cite called Nazareth, unto Jewry, into a city of David which is called Bethleem, because he was of the housse and linage of David, to be taxed with Mary his wedded wyfe, which was with childe. And it fortuned while they there were her tyme was come that she shulde be delyvered. And she brought forth her first begotten sonne and wrapped hym in swaddlynge clothes, and layed him in a manger be cause there was no roume for them within in the hostrey.

The corresponding passage in *A.V.* is familiar in many contexts, but we may quote it:

> And it came to pass in those days, that there went out a decree from Caesar Augustus, that all the world should be taxed.
>
> (And this taxing was first made when Cyrenius was governor of Syria.)
>
> And all went to be taxed, every one to his own city.
>
> And Joseph also went up from Galilee, out of the city of Nazareth, into Judaea, unto the city of David, which is called Bethlehem; (because he was of the house and lineage of David:)
>
> To be taxed with Mary his espoused wife, being great with child.
>
> And so it was, that, while they were there, the days were accomplished that she should be delivered.

And she brought forth her first-born son, and wrapped him in swaddling clothes, and laid him in a manger; because there was no room for them in the inn.

Setting aside the vagaries of spelling (and we should remember that there is no consistency in this art till well into the seventeenth century), Wycliffe has eight 'obsolete' words, Tyndale only one. All translators were worried by the need to find an equivalent for the Roman 'census'. Tyndale thinks in terms of his England when he writes 'own shire town' instead of the somewhat pretentious 'city'. *A.V.* has the graceful and weighty 'when the days were *accomplished*', giving something of the sense of the natural term of pregnancy, and perhaps a completed and difficult task, as well as the fulfilment of prophecy.

iii

We may make other points clearer by comparing two versions of *Mark* 11 from *R.S.V.* and *N.E.B.* It will be seen that the first retains much of the familiar Authorized Version:

> And when they drew near to Jerusalem, to Bethphage and Bethany, at the Mount of Olives, he sent two of his disciples, and said to them, 'Go into the village opposite you, and immediately as you enter it you will find a colt tied, on which no one has ever sat; untie it and bring it. If any one says to you, "Why are you doing this?" say, "The Lord has need of it and will send it back here immediately." ' And they went away, and found a colt tied at the door out in the open street; and they untied it. And those who stood there said to them, 'What are you doing, untying the colt?' And they told them what Jesus had said; and they let them go. And they brought the colt to Jesus, and threw their garments on it; and he sat upon it. And many spread their garments on the road, and others spread leafy branches which they had cut from the fields.

The characteristic 'flavour' of *A.V.* narrative is still retained in the number of conjunctive 'ands', as well as the 'garments'. By contrast, *N.E.B.* is at pains to transpose into the easiest and most natural of everyday speech; varying the 'ands' so as to smooth down the rhythm into a simple but dignified colloquial tone. We may remember one helpful note that *N.E.B.* provides 'Its owner' as a variant translation of 'Our Master', which may be thought to add another dimension to the narrative:

> They were now approaching Jerusalem, and when they reached Bethphage and Bethany, at the Mount of Olives, he sent two of his

51

disciples with these instructions: 'Go to the village opposite, and, just as you enter, you will find tethered there a colt which no one has yet ridden. Untie it and bring it here. If anyone asks, "Why are you doing that?" say, "Our Master needs it, and will send it back here without delay."' So they went off, and found the colt tethered to a door outside in the street. They were untying it when some of the bystanders asked, 'What are you doing, untying that colt?' They answered as Jesus had told them, and were then allowed to take it. So they brought the colt to Jesus, and spread their cloaks on it, and he mounted. And people carpeted their road with their cloaks, while others spread brushwood which they had cut in the fields . . .

N.E.B. has achieved a continuous pellucid style. Yet we may question several things: one 'mounts' a horse, but hardly a donkey; 'garments' cover a wider range of probability than 'cloaks'; and 'brushwood' implies something drier, more friable, than the 'leafy branches' of the other version. We remember with regret George Herbert's

> "I got me flowers to straw Thy way;
> I got me boughs off many a tree:
> But Thou wast up by breake of day
> And brought'st Thy sweets along with Thee."[1]

It would be possible to multiply examples indefinitely, but we must confine ourselves to one more instance in this kind, from the famous last chapter of *Ecclesiastes*. We may take first the passage as it appears in The Great Bible, 1539–40:

Remembre thy maker in thy youth, or ever the dayes of adversytie come, and or the yeares drawe nye, when thou shalt saye: I have not pleasure in them: before the sunne, the lyght, the moone and starres be darckened, and or the cloudes turne agayne after the rayne, when the kepers of the house shall tremble, and when the stronge men shal bowe them selves: when the myllers stande styll, because they be so few, and when the syght of the wyndowes shall waxe dymme: when the dores in the stretes shal be shutt, and when the voyce of the myller shalbe layed downe: when men shall ryse up at the voyce of the byrde, and when all the daughters of musike shalbe brought lowe: when men shall feare in hye places, and be afrayed in the stretes: when the Almonde tree shall florysh and be laden with the greshoper, and when all lust shall passe (because when man goeth to hys longe home, and the mourners go aboute the stretes.) Or ever the sylver lace be taken a waye, and or the golden bande be broken: Or the pot be broken at the well, and the

---

[1] *Easter.*

whele upon the cysterns: Then shall the dust be turned agayne unto earth from whence it came, and the sprete shal returne unto God, which gave it. All is but vanite (sayth the Preacher) all is but playne vanyte.

It is clear that there are dark places in the Hebrew.[1] One critic proposes 'your grave' instead of 'creator' or 'maker'; 'the voice of the bird' may mean 'and the sound of the bird is silent'; 'although as it stands it hints at the old man's sleep being early disturbed'.[2] There are many exegetical comments on the almond tree, the grasshopper, and the alternative reading to the next clause, 'when the caper-berry shall no longer stimulate desire'; or, in another sixteenth-century version, 'and concupiscence shall be driven away'. There are also many interpretations of the 'silver lace'—later 'silver cord', and of the 'golden bowl'. These all involve culminating death images: the golden lamp-bowl (light and oil imagery combined with the 'gold' of value) suspended by the tenuous thing, as in the perennial thread metaphors. Of this kind are Milton's

> "Comes the blind Fury with th'abhorrèd shears,
> And slits the thin spun life."[3]

and Sir Thomas Browne's:

> "But I, that have examined the parts of man, and know upon what tender filaments that fabrick hangs . . ."[4]

We can now consider the passage in the King James Version:

Remember now thy Creator in the days of thy youth, while the evil days come not, nor the years draw nigh, when thou shalt say, I have no pleasure in them;

While the sun, or the light, or the moon, or the stars, be not darkened, nor the clouds return after the rain:

In the day when the keepers of the house shall tremble, and the strong men shall bow themselves, and the grinders cease because they are few, and those that look out of the windows be darkened,

And the doors shall be shut in the streets, when the sound of the grinding is low, and he shall rise up at the voice of the bird, and all the daughters of musick shall be brought low;

Also when they shall be afraid of that which is high, and fears shall be in the way, and the almond tree shall flourish, and the grasshopper shall be

---

[1] c.f., e.g., E. T. Ryder's article on the Book in *Peake's Commentary*, p. 458 ff.
[2] Ryder, *op. cit.*, p. 466. [3] *Lycidas.* [4] *Religio Medici*, I, xliv.

a burden, and desire shall fail: because man goeth to his long home, and the mourners go about the streets:

Or ever the silver cord be loosed, or the golden bowl be broken, or the pitcher be broken at the fountain, or the wheel broken at the cistern.

Then shall the dust return to the earth as it was: and the spirit shall return unto God who gave it.

Vanity of vanities (saith the preacher); all is vanity.

Now the dominant mood conveyed is one of pessimism at the coming of 'evil days': including, but not confined to, the onset of old age; the lyric statement, the nobility of the language, redeeming (in part at least) that pessimism. We have a picture of the half-deserted village, its few and feeble inhabitants subjected to a nameless fear. The changing seasons are no more; the drought is permanent in the waste land,

> —nor the clouds return after the rain.

The village is poverty-stricken; the sounds of daily living are muted. Perhaps its crops are destroyed by beasts. We are puzzled, but hardly question, the cryptic almond tree. The 'long home' seems deliberately ambivalent; the eternity of the grave, Shakespeare's

> "But now two paces of the vilest earth
> Is room enough."[1]

There is a final impression of the streets empty except for those black figures, the mourners in this lyrical life-and-death. Blake might have drawn it.

We are conscious that the lyrical quality of *A.V.* has been achieved largely by a transition to trisyllabic rhythms, as from

> the light, the moon and starres be darkened

to

> while the sunne, ŏr thĕ líght, ŏr thĕ Moóne, oř thĕ
> starřes bĕ nŏt daŕkenĕd

from

> The sylver lace be taken away

to the 'feminine endings' of:

> Or ever / the silver / cord / bĕ loosĕd
> Or the golden / bowl / bĕ brokĕn.

[1] *I Henry IV*, V. 4.

54

The patterns, as in all good rhythmic prose, just avoid the monotony of purely 'poetical' patterning by their intricate variations.

But we turn to the Rabbinical interpretation. What the passage really means is, we are told, that the 'keepers of the house' are the hands, the 'strong man' the knees, the 'grinders' the teeth, 'those that look out of the windows' are the eyes; and that the last lines should read

> ". . . When one fears to climb a height,
> And terrors lurk in a walk.
>
> The hair grows white, like ripe almond-blossom,
> The frame, bent like a grasshopper, becomes a burden,
> And the caper-berry can no longer stimulate desire.
>
> So man goes to his eternal home
> While the hired mourners walk about in the street . . ."[1]

We may count, a little sadly, our gains and losses. We have lost the prophetic ambiguity of 'that which is high'—the 'terror of the skies', storms, divine vengeance. The 'fears in the wayside' suggested, perhaps, robbers or wild beasts, more cogent than in aversion to steps or rough ground. Our ear may disapprove the cacophony of 'lurk'—'walk'. We may think that a man bent by old age is by no means like a grasshopper, and prefer our earlier, less accurate, response to the desolate land eaten by a plague of locusts. 'Desire shall fail' is dignified, and seems to cover the facts. 'Eternal' is perhaps a cliché, and robs us of the ambiguity of 'long' to which I have referred. The 'hired mourners' may be an accurate translation, but we have been robbed of the wider 'the mourners' which might be thought to include the inhabitants themselves, mourning and uncomforted.

iv

I have already referred to J. B. Phillips' outstanding work in making certain of the *Epistles* far more comprehensible. But the following passage raises, in an acute form, two questions: How difficult is the *A.V.* in its familiar form, and how necessary is it to 'paraphrase down' into present-day idiom phrases which have grown wholly familiar? A short test passage may be found in *Romans* 13:11. In *A.V.*—

> And that, knowing the time, that now it is high time to awake out of sleep: for now is our salvation nearer than when we believed.

[1] Robert Graves, *Ecclesiastes*, New York, 1945; *cit.* Daiches, *Literary Essays*, Edinburgh, 1956.

The night is far spent, the day is at hand: let us therefore cast off the works of darkness, and let us put on the armour of light.

It is true that the phrases 'knowing the time', 'now is our salvation nearer', imply the Apostles' consciousness of Christ's Second Coming; and without some intelligent voice-stress in reading it is easy to make the passage sound confused. Yet 'high time', 'to awake out of sleep' have passed so completely into the language, together with the phrase 'the night is far spent', that there seems little possibility of confusion. We may note that *R.S.V.* and *N.E.B.* make little change, except for *R.S.V.*'s alternative 'salvation is nearer to us'. We may admire the consummate rhythmic skill in the varied patterns of the lyric movement in v. 12

and the way in which the second sentence gathers up, as it were, its rhythmic impetus, to dissolve it in the 'English' cadence of

If we set beside this the Phillips version—

> Why all this stress on behaviour? Because, as I think you have realized, the present time is of the highest importance—it is time to wake up to reality. Every day brings God's salvation nearer.
>
> The night is nearly over, the day has almost dawned. Let us therefore fling away the things that men do in the dark, let us arm ourselves for the fight of the day!

We are now reading a passage which seems a little uneven in its language and rhythm. Both 'the highest importance' and 'wake up to reality' are collapsed or cliché phrases; nor is 'wake up *to* reality' more impressive, in its meaning (for what is *reality?*) than the original 'awake out of sleep'. In the second verse we begin with an over-metrical sentence (the patterns suggest a poetic rather than a prose rhythm)

nor is there much, to all appearances, gained by the device used in the paperback edition of capitalizing Day to suggest or enhance its apocalyptic meaning. 'The works of darkness' has a far wider meaning than 'the things that men do in the dark' for the former covers the general blackness of all sin and crime, by suggesting the archetypal light–darkness dichotomy. 'Fling', in the attempt to give more of the 'household language', is perhaps weaker than 'cast'. 'Arm ourselves for the fight of the Day' seems to suggest that the day of Christ's coming will in fact be a battle, whereas the older version keeps before us the idea of a *total* moral achievement, the stress being on the general 'fight', and not as for some particular occasion. 'Put on the whole armour of God'—*induite vos armaturam dei*; we may compare two versions continuing this passage:

> Put you on the armour of God, that you may stand against the deceits of the Devil. For our wrestling is not against flesh and blood: but against Prince and Potestats, against the rectors of the world of this darkness, against the spirituals of wickedness in the celestials. Therefore take the armour of God, that you may resist in the evil day, and stand in all things perfect. Stand therefore having your loins girded in truth, and clothed with the breastplate of justice, and having your feet shod to the preparation of the Gospel of peace: in all things taking the shield of faith, wherewith you may extinguish all the fiery darts of the wicked one. And take unto you the helmet of salvation: and the sword of the spirit (which is the word of God) in all prayer and supplication praying at all time in spirit: and in the same watching in all instance and supplication for all the saints. (Douai, 1582)

The second is from *N.E.B.*:

> Put on all the armour which God provides, so that you may be able to stand firm against the devices of the devil. For our fight is not against human foes, but against cosmic powers, against the authorities and potentates of this dark world, against the superhuman forces of evil in the heavens. Therefore, take up God's armour; then you will be able to stand your ground when things are at their worst, to complete every task and still to stand. Stand firm, I say. Buckle on the belt of truth; for coat of mail put on integrity; let the shoes on your feet be the gospel of peace, to give you firm footing; and, with all these take up the great shield of faith, with which you will be able to quench all the flaming arrows of the evil one. Take salvation for helmet; for sword, take that which the Spirit gives you—the words that come from God. Give yourselves wholly to prayer and entreaty; pray on every occasion in the power of the Spirit. To this end keep watch and persevere, always interceding for all God's people. (1961)[1]

Certain things stand out. The second version has had to expand, but cannot avoid, the imagery of the armour. Beyond this, it relies on a

[1] *Eph.* 6:11–18.

series of abstractions. We have lost the expressive and proverbial 'wrestling . . . flesh and blood' with its overtones of Jacob and the Angel. 'Cosmic powers' is clearly more comprehensible than the vivid 'Prince and Potestats, against the rectors of the world of this darkness, against the spirituals of wickedness in the celestials'. This is taken literally from the Latin of the Vulgate:

> . . . Sed adversus principes, et potestates, adversus mundi rectores tenebrarum harum, contra spiritualia nequitiae, in coelestibus.

A.V. produces a notable ambiguity:

> against spiritual wickedness in high places

when the 'high places' may be the secular power, or the evil in heaven itself. 'Devices' of the Devil is hardly more obsolete, and far more concrete in suggestion, than his 'deceits'. 'The world of this darkness', again literal from the Latin, is richer than the cliché of 'this dark world'. 'The evil day' is more comprehensive in meaning than 'when things are at their worst'. The sword of the Spirit, which is the word of God' has also been weakened—the meaning seems no clearer—into 'for sword take that which the Spirit gives you—the words that come from God'.

v

It may be well to remind ourselves of what the forges cannot do. They cannot render for us the many acrostics, puns, the 'wit' of words that carry double meanings. Even the play on the word Peter as 'Rock' now requires a gloss. Nor can we ever recover the ambiguities, the subtle overtones, with which we are so familiar in English poetry; whether by memories of the origins of words, or of their rich and varied freightage of meaning which they derive from the contextual usages in our own literature. They cannot give us (even supposing that the available texts, in the best traditions, have reported them accurately) the speech-rhythms of the Hebrew or Aramaic. The words of Christ at the Last Supper, in their simplicity and beauty, reflect what *ought* to have been said on that occasion; that they are, in content and rhythm, wholly credible is due as much to the imaginative insight, or the inspiration, of the Translators as to the intrinsic qualities of the Greek. Again we may take an instance from *Luke* 10:21, in *A.V.*:

In that hour Jesus rejoiced in spirit, and said, I thank thee, O Father, Lord of heaven and earth, that thou hast hid these things from the wise and prudent, and hast revealed them unto babes: even so, Father; for so it seemed good in thy sight.

All things are delivered to me of my Father; and no man knoweth who the Son is, but the Father: and who the Father is, but the Son, and he to whom the Son will reveal him.

And he turned him unto his disciples, and said privately, Blessed are the eyes which see the things that ye see. . . .

Here is Phillips:

At that moment Jesus himself was inspired with joy, and exclaimed, 'O Father, Lord of Heaven and earth, I thank you for hiding these things from the clever and intelligent and for showing them to mere children! Yes, I thank you, Father, that this was your will.' Then he went on,—'Everything has been put into my hands by my Father; and nobody knows who the Son really is except the Father. Nobody knows who the Father really is except the Son—and the man to whom the Son chooses to reveal him!'

Then he turned to his disciples and said to them quietly, 'How fortunate you are to see what you are seeing!'. . .

Now whatever we may think of the detailed differences in meaning (such as the difference between *rejoiced in spirit* and *was inspired by joy*) it is clear that the tone of the Phillips version represents something completely different from the *A.V.* rendering. It may or may not have been nearer to the accents of the Aramaic. What we are concerned with is the power of the rendering to communicate what may have been said, in language that should be more intelligible, in this century, than the original *A.V.* We have then to consider whether 'clever and intelligent' does in fact represent any equivalent to 'wise and prudent' (clearly, it is something different), or whether 'babes' is well paraphrased by 'mere children'. In this last instance, we have to consider not only the force of the loaded adjective 'mere' but a contrast with the tone of

Suffer little children to come unto me

and reject overtones such as those of

Out of the mouths of babes and sucklings hast thou ordained strength[1]

[1] *Ps.* 8:2.

59

or even of

> And I, brethren, could not speak unto you as spiritual, but as unto
> carnal, even as unto babes in Christ.[1]

Probably the shade of meaning we require is the suggestion of
innocence, but not of childishness; something, perhaps, of the
praeternatural wisdom of the children in Blake's *Songs of Innocence*.
So *N.E.B.*:

> At that moment Jesus exulted in the Holy Spirit and said, 'I thank
> thee, Father, Lord of heaven and earth, for hiding these things from the
> learned and wise, and revealing them to the simple. Yes, Father, such
> was thy choice.' Then turning to his disciples he said, 'Everything is
> entrusted to me by my Father; and no one knows who the Son is but the
> Father, or who the Father is but the Son, and those to whom the Son
> may choose to reveal him.'
>
> Turning to his disciples in private he said, 'Happy are the eyes that
> see what you are seeing!'. . .

Much of the complexity of certain Epistles, which the *A.V.*
handles with extreme difficulty, arises out of what we may call the
co-ordinates of the argument in allusion to, or quotation from, the
O.T.; and these would be assumed as familiar and authoritative
to the recipients of the Letter. We may quote a passage from
Galatians:

> For as many as are of the works of the law are under the curse: for it is
> written, Cursed is every one that continueth not in all things which are
> written in the book of the law to do them.
>
> But that no man is justified by the law in the sight of God, it is evident:
> for, The just shall live by faith.
>
> And the law is not of faith: but, The man that doeth them shall live in
> them.
>
> Christ hath redeemed us from the curse of the law, being made a curse
> for us: for it is written, Cursed is every one that hangeth on a tree:
>
> That the blessing of Abraham might come on the Gentiles through
> Jesus Christ; that we might receive the promise of the Spirit through
> faith.
>
> Brethren, I speak after the manner of men: Though it is but a man's
> covenant, yet if it be confirmed, no man disannulleth or addeth
> thereto. . . .[2]

---

[1] *1 Cor.* 3:1.   [2] 3:10–15.

The passage when read aloud—even in its larger setting—is difficult to apprehend, and it contains a number of specific problems. Its authority depends in some degree on the number of texts embodied in it, and which, for us, must be isolated and studied separately; though we may suppose instant recognition by the original audience. There are also a number of technical terms belonging to the theological background, each demanding special consideration: *works, law, the curse, justified, faith, Spirit, covenant*. There are obsolete constructions—*the law is not of faith*; and the ponderous legal word *disannulleth*.[1] We may think too that the Greek has come over into Jacobean English in a somewhat crabbed and contorted fashion. Phillips, by isolating the embedded quotations, goes a considerable way towards clarifying the passage; there was clearly a need to expand on the close-knit text of *A.V.*, at the expense—wholly justified for this kind of argument—of stylistic elegance.

"Everyone, however, who is involved in trying to keep the Law's demands falls under a curse, for it is written:

Cursed is everyone which continueth not
In *all things* which are written in the book of the Law
To do them.

It is made plainer still that no one is justified in God's sight by obeying the Law, for

The righteous shall live by *faith*.

And the Law is not a matter of faith at all but of doing, as, for example, in the Scripture:

He that *doeth* them shall live in them.

Now Christ has redeemed us from the curse of the Law's condemnation, by Himself becoming a curse for us when He was crucified. For the Scripture is plain:

Cursed is every one that hangeth on a tree.

God's purpose is therefore plain: that the blessing promised to Abraham might reach the Gentiles through Jesus Christ, and the Spirit might become available to us all by faith.

[1] Though we may remember George Herbert's
"Wilt thou His laws of fasting *disannul*
Enact good cheer?
Lay out thy joy, yet hope to save it?
Would'st thou both eat thy cake and have it?"
where the Latin words crack, whip-like in their scorn, across the gentle 'household language'.

Let me give you an everyday illustration, my brothers.

Once a contract has been properly drawn up and signed, it is honoured by both parties, and can neither be disregarded nor modified by a third party."[1]

But the matter is (for the common reader) still more complex for there is no explicit text for

Cursed is every one that hangeth on a tree.

though the convergence of trees and cross is familiar enough in literature. Nor, in the descriptions which we know, does this matter of the tree and the curse seem appropriate: as in this:

And if a man have committed a sin worthy of death, and he be to be put to death, and thou hang him on a tree:

His body shall not remain all night upon the tree, but thou shalt in any wise bury him that day; (for he that is hanged is accursed of God;) that thy land be not defiled, which the Lord thy God giveth thee for an inheritance.

(Deut. 21:22–23)

For a final example I give, without analysis, the opening verses of the Gospel of St. John. Into it then enters everything that has been said previously: but behind it lies the profound and complicated meaning of the Word, the Logos. I would suggest only that the revision, its attempt at clarification, has darkened the mystery: by its series of compromises with language, and also by the destruction of the rhythms which are integral with the poetic statements:

In the beginning was the Word, and the Word was with God, and the Word was God. The same was in the beginning with God. All things were made by him; and without him was not anything made that was made. In him was life; and the life was the light of men. And the light shineth in darkness, and the darkness comprehended it not.

In the *N.E.B.*:

When all things began, the Word already was. The Word dwelt with God, and what God was, the Word was. The Word, then, was with God in the beginning, and through him all things came to be; no single thing was created without him. All that came to be was alive with his life, and that life was the light of men. The light shines in the dark, and the darkness has never quenched it.

[1] *Letters to Young Churches*, pp. 114–115.

CHAPTER FIVE

The Imagery

"A symbol is characterized by a translucence of the special in the Individual, or the General in the Especial or of the Universal in the General. Above all by the translucence of the Eternal through and in the Temporal. It always partakes of the Reality which it renders intelligible; and while it enunciates the whole, abides itself as a living part in the Unity of which it is representative."

(Coleridge, *Statesmans Manual*, 1816)

i

BY 'IMAGERY' I mean in this section both simile and metaphor; by 'parable', the method of communicating, by means of simple narrative, transferred applications of the narrative to the activities of body and soul. 'Allegory 'may on occasion overlap the attributes of parable, but will be more commonly used for the meanings, derived or superimposed, by subsequent commentators. The values of a symbol may attach themselves to, or grow into by context or repetition, any of the images; instances are the simple archetypes of tree, river, fire, clay, wine, thorns. These are often linked to basic, recurrent and apparently universal symbols, which suggest conscious or subliminal meanings in many literatures. I shall use these in terms of current psychology, of Jung, Freud, and particularly of the use made of them by Maud Bodkin,[1] Austin Farrer,[2] W. H. Auden,[3] Rosamund Tuve,[4] and others.

The imagery of the Bible is built, in the main, on simple and vivid sense-objects; derived, not from literary sources, but from the everyday life of a people whose problems of living are themselves simple yet profound. They reflect in the Two Testaments the common life of each. For a people at first nomadic and then agricultural, cave,

[1] *Archetypal Patterns in Poetry; Studies of Type-Images in Poetry, Philosophy and Religion.*   [2] *A Rebirth of Images.*
[3] *The Enchaféd Flood.*   [4] e.g. *A Study of George Herbert.*

desert, river, well and fountain, storm and rain and drought, tower and wall, have a special immediacy. Images of the plough, the seed and the sower, the vineyard and the shepherd, are more germane to the settled life of the New Testament than the Old. The manifestations of God may commonly be perceived in thunder, lightning, in the pillar of fire, or even in the mulberry-trees as He gives the signal for a flank attack upon the enemy.[1] Images from warfare are frequent: spear, shield, arrow. They tend now to become 'collapsed' or lifeless; either an imaginative effort must be made to assess their full significance, or they may be strained (as Blake's 'arrows of desire') to provide some Freudian significance. This, indeed, is a perpetual difficulty: the need to re-create the images in their context and against their background of living, if we are to be aware of their full force. Thus 'the arrow that flieth by day'[2] acquires a peculiar sinister force of its own, as if it had its own autonomous life, and were set in a kind of tension with 'the pestilence that walketh in darkness'.[3]

There are many fear-images drawn from the perpetual subjection to war and captivity. To the light-armed forces of the Israelites the chariots and horses of the peoples of the Plain, as of the Egyptians, were especially terrible; so that Israel must, in a double sense, lift up its eyes unto the hills. The destruction of the chariots trapped in the marsh by a sudden rising of the river is celebrated in the Song of Deborah; it was the first time, in this intermittent warfare, that infantry had triumphed over armour. Iron stands for captivity, cruelty, destruction; wood, by contrast, is valued, kind to the workman and the artificer, or, like cedar and fir, carries royal qualities. Value is, as always, in terms of the precious metals and stones. They stud the High Priest's breastplate; the price of the virtuous woman is above rubies;[4] the pearl of great price is worth all a merchant's resources. Gold and silver, metals that are purified by smelting, serve to set forth the immortal character of the soul. It is instructive to follow up some of the ramifications.

Fire-imagery, in all literatures, may connote destruction, inspiration, purification (as in the lips touched with fire), inspiration

---

[1] *1 Chron.* 14:15.

[2] *Ps.* 91:5. We may note the multiplex character of the arrow imagery: as for slander, pestilence, God's judgments.

[3] Is there, perhaps, an echo in 'the invisible worm' of Blake, *The Sick Rose?*

[4] An alternative rendering is *corals.*

(*Ezekiel,* and the Cloven Tongues of Pentecost); the intensities of love or lust. There is the whole complexity of the altar-imagery, the ascending smoke or scent, the meaning of incense in all ritual. By fire gold is purified, 'tried in the furnace', a parable of endurance in the fires of suffering. Fresh from the fire, it may suggest youth, its beauty and its energies:

> "Golden lads and girls all must
> Like chimney-sweepers, come to dust."

But we may watch the image being projected, as it were, into other great poetry. Donne's *The Ecstasy* concerns the relationship between soul and body in the act of love. One dominant Elizabethan image for the begetting of a child was the stamping of the father's image upon the softer metal of the woman:

> "Your mother was most true to wedlock, prince;
> For she did print your royal father off,
> Conceiving you."[1]

But in the striking of the coin the soft metals in their pure states were unserviceable. Hence Donne uses the gold as the symbol of the soul, but the alloy of the body—the base metal which must be mixed with the purer metal before it can take permanent shape and be used—is necessary to the minting. So:

> "We owe them thanks because they thus,
> Did us, to us, at first convey,
> Yielded their forces, sense, to us,
> Nor are dross to us, but allay."[2]

Another kind of projection is to be seen in Donne's *A Valediction: Forbidding Mourning,* which concerns the spirituality of love as tested by the fact of the lovers' separation. Here the souls are not broken in their unity:

> "Our two souls, therefore, which are one,
> Though I must go, endure not yet
> A breach, but an expansion,
> Like gold to ayery thinness beat."

---

[1] *The Winter's Tale,* V. i. 124.

[2] 'We are grateful to our bodies because it was through them that we first became aware of each other's presence and identity. They gave to us their special quality, which is the power of sensation. They are not like the worthless scum which rises to the top of the crucible and is thrown away; they are the baser metal which must be mixed with the nobler before it can be worked, become current.'

The sorrow of separation beats the precious metal, as gold is hammered between folds of gold-beater's skin to produce gold-leaf: still most precious, but also approaching in its substance to the lightness of air. But of this near-air, angels, in the system of the Schoolmen, might be formed by condensation[1] into the angelic forms. So the symbol is varied to suggest the changing of the immortal substance, through the agency of the suffering caused by separation into one yet more angelic in character.

Other value-images derive from ivory (carved as for the decorations of a palace, or a simile for the beauty of man's body), linked, with needlework, to royalty: the spices for their rarity, their household healing and scenting, the adornment of the bride: 'All thy garments smell of myrrh, and aloes, and cassia, out of the ivory palaces, whereby they have made thee glad.'[2] Gold, frankincense, and myrrh have their special symbolisms—the gifts of the Magi: royalty, adoration, the spices for burial. *The Song of Songs* is full of the scents of the early morning, the vineyards, the perfumes of the bride and bridegroom.

The images that decorate the beloved are from the natural world: there is no need to stress their recurrence in all literatures. But here again they may lose their vitality, through staleness of usage, unless we are forced, by some new circumstance, to consider them afresh. Thus the Woman-Flower imagery is archetypal and takes many forms; the rosebud-virginity aspect is familiar in Herrick's

"Gather ye rosebuds while ye may"

but we can trace its origin to the phrase in *Wisdom*:[3]

Let us crown ourselves with rosebuds, before they be withered.

This begets image upon image; the swift decay of beauty, the Shakespearian 'eating canker' in the heart, the festering lily, the alliance with thorns, the sensations of touch, texture, perfume: culminating perhaps in George Herbert's

"Sweet rose, whose hue angrie and brave
Bids the rash gazer wipe his eye:
Thy root is ever in thy grave
And thou must die."

[1] *v.* Donne's *Air and Angels*: following Porphyry.
[2] *Ps.* 45:8. [3] 2:8.

Several aspects are combined in Rossetti's *Barren Spring*:

> "Behold, this crocus is a withering flame;
>   This snowdrop, snow; this apple-blossom's part
>   To breed the fruit that breeds the serpent's art.
> Nay, for these Spring-flowers, turn thy face from them,
> Nor gaze till on the year's last lily-stem
>   The white cup shrivels round the golden heart."

The rose is a constant symbol: Burns'

> "My love is like a red red rose"

is trite compared with the complexity of Blake's *The Sick Rose*. But in medieval iconography we see the rose as a blossom on the Tree of Life, and then on the tree of the Cross, to become an emblem of Christ Himself, and to give rise to the esoteric philosophy known as Rosicrucianism. Other woman-images appear in the lily, to become too familiar in the pictures of the Annunciation, from the early Renaissance to the Pre-Raphaelites; a symbol of purity associated with the Madonna:

> I am the rose of Sharon, and the lily of the valleys.
> As the lily among thorns, so is my love among the daughters.[1]

In *The Song of Songs* the flowers and plants of the spring are invoked with their multiplicity of energies and joys and scents. One of the strangest is the simile of the apple:

> As the apple tree among the trees of the wood, so is my beloved among the sons. I sat down under his shadow with great delight, and his fruit was sweet to my taste.[2]

The Middle Ages considered that the fruit of the Tree was an apple, and the fruit appears in general to be linked to woman, as in the Judgment of Apollo. In a famous Celtic legend, that of Baile and Aillinn, two trees spring from the grave of dead leaves, the apple and the yew, and their timbers grow into one: here the apple seems to stand for woman, the yew (with its overtones of death and of violence[3]), for the man:

> ". . . All know their tale: all know what leaf and twig,
>   What juncture of the apple and the yew
>   Surmounts their bones . . ."[4]

---

[1] *Cant.* 2:1, 2.   [2] *Ibid.*, 2:3.
[3] cf. Shakespeare's 'double-fatal yew': as poisonous to animals, and as furnishing the wood of the bow.   [4] Yeats, *Ribh at the Tomb of Baile and Aillinn.*

All flowers suggest beauty, as well as the rapidity of its passing. Among the birds the dove, in its soft and delicate brilliance, its gentleness, purity, and helplessness; with perhaps some shadow of its original significance as a symbol of fertility, and the link with Venus' doves:

> Open to me, my sister, my dove, my undefiled.[1]

It was for the Middle Ages to discover further anagogical significance in the dove; as representing the Church, the two wings for the Old and New Testaments, the blue feathers for Heaven, the indeterminate iridescent grey feathers for man's voyage through life, the golden eye for wisdom, the feet red from the blood of the martyrs.[2]

The roe-deer stands for graceful strength in the male, but also for the qualities of the woman:

> Let her be as the loving hind and pleasant roe; let her breasts satisfy thee at all times; and be thou ravished always with her love.[3]

Honey and honeycomb are linked to the lover, and we remember the Elizabethan imagery, reverent or at times ribald, built round the breath taken in a kiss. Honey is the image of the sweetness of God's judgment as in the well-known passage from the Psalm[4] and from Samson's lion. Later, it appears as a symbol of longevity; there is a Renaissance picture of Samson presenting his parents with this symbolic gift. It is also to be linked with sex and the sexual act; Kranach's *Venus* shows Cupid at her feet pointing to a piece of honeycomb and a bee upon it; so that we are drawn into the strange orbit of the honey-bee-sting-death image cluster. Of these, two illustrations will serve:

> O death, where is thy sting? O grave, where is thy victory?[5]

—where the image is that of the Serpent.

So Romeo contemplates Juliet's body in the tomb:[6]

> "Death, that hath suck'd the honey of thy breath,
> Hath had no power[7] yet upon thy beauty:
> Thou art not conquer'd; beauty's ensign yet
> Is crimson in thy lips and in thy cheeks,
> And death's pale flag is not advancéd there."

[1] *Cant.* 5:2.   [2] Mâle, *op. cit.*, p. 30.   [3] *Prov.* 5:19.
[4] 19:10.   [5] *1 Cor.* 15:55.   [6] *Romeo and Juliet*, V. 3. 93.
[7] *sc.* 'And death shall have no more dominion over them'; as well as the sexual sense of *power*.

Among the birds, we are familiar with the multiple aspects of the eagle, its qualities, of godhead, mystery, strength. 'Swan and Dove' is in fact the title of a section of Yeats' *A Vision*, suggesting in his mythology the first annunciation, of Jove to Leda, and the second that of the Spirit. The eagle is the king, the sun-gazer, the hunter of the upper air, the protector of its young, standing for swiftness and strength, the symbolic bearer (as in church lecterns) of the Word. With it is the second of the 'noble' overtones, the lion; again strength, majesty, kingship, fear, and among the Desert Fathers, the friend of man. They are joined in David's lament:

They were swifter than eagles, they were stronger than lions.[1]

Eagle and lion appear with man and ox as the beasts of the Four Evangelists: Matthew the man, Mark the lion, John the eagle, Luke the ox. The labouring ox is naturally the symbol of patient fortitude, so that an ox's skull becames a Renaissance emblem of those qualities. The predatory animals are, as always, emblems of fear and destruction; like the 'wolf of the evenings', and the leopard that will watch over the desolate cities.[2]

By contrast there are the birds of the desert, or those imagined in it. They can be conveniently seen in a passage of *Isaiah*:[3]

But the cormorant and the bittern shall possess it; the owl also and the raven shall dwell in it . . .

And thorns shall come up in her palaces, nettles and brambles in the fortresses thereof: and it shall be an habitation of dragons, and a court for owls.

The wild beasts of the desert shall also meet with the wild beasts of the island, and the satyr shall cry to his fellow; the screech owl also shall rest, and find for herself a place of rest.

It is a common experience, in bombed cities or in buried and forgotten towns such as those of the Ganges Valley, to see how quickly the wilderness returns in its calm or fierce fertility. We have all seen how

"Nettles wave above a shapeless mound
And saplings root among the broken stone."[4]

---

[1] *2 Sam.* 1:23.　　　　[2] *Jer.* 5:6.
[3] 34:11, and 13–14. Note the 'prohibited birds' of *Leviticus*.
[4] Yeats, *Coole Park, 1929*.

Yet there is a specially ominous quality in the description from *Isaiah*; the incursion from the marshes, the predators, the sinister night-birds, the eaters of carrion, the scavengers of the battle-field:

> "The raven himself is hoarse
> That croaks the fatal entrance of Duncan
> Under my battlements."[1]

We may quote a similar passage from a modern play:

> I see the flames of Emain starting upward in the dark night; and because of me there will be weasels and wild cats crying on a lonely wall where there were queens and armies and red gold, the way there will be a story told of a ruined city and a raving king and a woman will be young for ever.[2]

ii

We should expect from the writings of a landlocked people that the sea and the great floods should provide emblems of fear; in the Old Testament at least, for in the New we are aware of an easy familiarity with ships and boats, nets and fishermen, and the Greek slides easily, in *Acts*, into the practised narrative of the Elizabethan voyages. We may quote from *Proverbs* 23:

> Yea, thou shalt be as he that lieth down in the midst of the sea, or as he that lieth upon the top of a mast . . .

and remember Shakespeare's adaptation of the image:

> "Wilt thou upon the high and giddy mast
> Seal up the ship-boy's eyes, and rock his brains
> In cradle of the rude imperious surge?"[3]

But to the Jews those waters provided images of awe mingled with fear: Leviathan, the Great Fishes, Dragons, Serpents, Behemoth, the Crocodile of the Nile. The dragon, which Otto describes as the 'numen of terror', is both an agent of destruction and a monster to be destroyed.

> And though they hide themselves in the top of Carmel, I will search and take them out thence; and though they be hid from my sight in the bottom of the sea, thence will I command the serpent, and it shall bite them.[4]

[1] *Macbeth*, I. 5. 38.   [2] Synge, *Deirdre of the Sorrows*, Act III.
[3] *II Henry IV*, III. 1. 18. This is quoted in the Elizabethan *Homilies*, as well as being one of Matthew Arnold's 'touchstones'.   [4] *Amos* 9:3.

For that most dramatic moment of the binding of the Dragon by Michael[1] we must go to Blake's drawing, the writhing protagonists set in a circular structure as Michael seeks to chain the open-jawed beast: dark and light forming strange patterns with the jagged outline of the dragon's tail. We are reminded of Milton's dragon that

> "Swinges the scaly horror of his folded tail."[2]

So the image of God's power is in the destruction of the dragon:

> . . . thou brakest the heads of the dragons in the waters. Thou brakest the heads of leviathan in pieces, and gavest him to be meat to the people inhabiting the wilderness.[3]

But it was the image of Leviathan that stirred most greatly the imagination of the medieval world; and perhaps—remembering *Moby Dick* and *The Old Man of the Sea*—our own.

> Canst thou draw out leviathan with an hook? or his tongue with a cord which thou lettest down?
> Canst thou put an hook into his nose? or bore his jaw through with a thorn? . . .
> Canst thou fill his skin with barbed irons? or his head with fish spears? . . .
> Out of his nostrils goeth smoke, as out of a seething pot or cauldron . . .
> Darts are counted as stubble: he laugheth at the shaking of a spear.[4]

The Middle Ages saw Leviathan as Satan, 'God threw the line into the sea: the cord of the line is the human descent of Christ, the bait is His divinity. Attracted by the smell of flesh Leviathan tries to seize it but the hook tears his jaws.'[5] In a miniature, the Kings of Judah are shown as the links in the line of the fisherman as Christ, who is using a frail but modern-looking rod.[6] But the description of the boiling pot suggested a type-illustration of Hell, so that artists showed a boiling pot in the jaws of the monster.[7] We are reminded of Hell-Fire, the painted gaping jaws with the cauldron of pitch below, a familiar stage property of medieval drama.

---

[1] *Rev.* 20:1, 2. [2] "Ode on the Morning of Christ's Nativity."
[3] *Ps.* 74:13, 14. This is presumably the hippopotamus.
[4] *Job* 41, *passim.*
[5] Mâle, *op. cit.*, p. 380: quoting Honorius of Autun.
[6] *Ibid.*, p. 380. [7] *Ibid.*, p. 381.

iii

The 'creeping things' of *Leviticus* 11:41 are clearly animals not only unclean but dangerous, as they so often are in the East. Some have passed into proverbs, such as 'the deaf adder that stoppeth her 'ʲare. So are all things 'that go in the dust', even the supposedly 'scaleless' fishes. (This is presumably because of the resemblance of eels to serpents, and this explanation is still given by peasant peoples who refuse to eat them.) But the adder provides many images of the familiar kind: slander, ingratitude, even the effects of wine. The poison of the asp is also used for slander, joined with the cockatrice in the famous passage of *Isaiah*:

> And the sucking child shall play on the hole of the asp, and the weaned child shall put his hand on the cockatrice' den.[2]

But the dominant images from the dust are, of course, provided by the serpent. The literature on the serpent, its cults and its archetypal symbolism, is a formidable subject. From the Garden onwards we are conscious of many attributes: subtlety, craft, wisdom; the capacity to renew his life, (the sloughing of its skin), as in Shelley's image of the spring:

> "The earth doth like a snake renew
> His winter weeds outworn."

It was a type of wisdom or subtlety in that it exposes its whole body to save its head from being bruised; that the horned viper (*Cerastes*, the burning fiery serpent of *Exodus*) hides in the sand in order to bite the heels of the horses that pass over it. It is worth noting that the Hebrew word for serpent is *sārāph* (the root sāroph means 'to burn'); either because of the pain of the wound—we remember Sophocles' *Philoctetes*—or its habitat in the desert sand. Yet while it is the cursed beast, and as such stands for Satan, its wisdom is not to be despised:

> . . . be ye therefore wise as serpents, and harmless as doves.[3]

and the erection of the Brazen Serpent in the Wilderness became an emblem on Christ on the Cross.[4]

Symbols involving the serpent shape themselves into patterns of the

[1] *Ps.* 58:4.   [2] 11:8.   [3] *Mt.* 10:16.

[4] *Jn.* 3:14. We may note 'the Talmudic tradition that the venom of the serpent, which had corrupted Eve and through her all mankind, lost its strength through the Revelation on Mount Sinai, but regained it when Israel began to worship the golden calf.' C. G. Scholem, *On the Kabbalah and its Symbolism* (1965) p. 69.

utmost complexity and subtlety of interactions. We may describe two of them.

On the inside lid of a bride's linen chest[1] there is a pen and ink drawing. In the background are the roofs and towers of two stylized Italian towns. In the centre is Eve, standing in a posture of crucifixion against the Tree of Life. She is being penetrated by the serpent. On the branches of the Tree are stylized roses, the emblem of Christ. On her left hand a figure like St. George is advancing with drawn scimitar as if to attack the serpent.

The second, more complex, is also of the Tree of Life: from a Salzburg Miniature of 1481. Adam lies, as if wearied or fainting, at the foot of the tree. Eve stands holding an apple in each hand. One she gives to the serpent twined round the trunk: the other, she hands to a kneeling figure in medieval dress, and to him she turns her eyes. The stylized Tree is covered with round fruits. In the midst there is a miniature representation of Christ crucified; and balancing this figure on the other side of the Tree a skull is suspended. On the medallions round the miniature are various Biblical scenes.[2]

iv

But perhaps the most powerful and multiplex emblems are those of the clay, the dust, the tree and the garden. The image of the making of man out of clay, the suggestion of the potter moulding the *materia prima*, is frequent in medieval iconography. A German alchemical picture of the fourteenth century shows the Creator drawing Adam upwards out of a mass of clay,[3] the *prima materia*: 'And the Lord God formed man out of the dust of the ground . . .' Beside the potter and the clay a river is depicted, flowing through Eden in which the newly-created beasts are grazing. 'Dust thou art, to dust thou shalt return . . .' 'Then shall the dust return again to the earth as it was, and the spirit shall return to God who gave it.'

There are ramifications. 'Thou shall break them in pieces like a potter's vessel.' 'My strength is dried up like a potsherd'; and in the famous passage of *Ecclesiastes* 12:

> Or ever the silver cord be loosed, or the golden bowl be broken, or the pitcher be broken at the fountain, or the wheel broken at the cistern.

[1] of *c.* 1630: in the writer's possession.
[2] Reproduced by Hugo Rahner, *Greek Myths and Christian Mystery*, p. 42.
[3] Jung, *Psychology and Alchemy*, Vol. XII, p. 139. This clay is by tradition red.

The pitcher may contain one of the three life-symbols, water, oil, or wine. It is often connected, as Sir Thomas Browne noted, with the Roman funerary urns, made in the form of the womb: adding yet another dimension of birth and death. And though it is the container of that which is most precious, it is most fragile, thus supplying the dying Hotspur with a thought:

> "I better brook the loss of *brittle* life
> Than those proud titles thou hast won of me."[1]

Imagery from the dust is everywhere: most cogent perhaps in seventeenth-century literature, where the custom of digging up old graves

> "Some second guest to entertain"

turned, literally, the dust of the church and the churchyard into human dust, and provided a series of images for Shakespeare, Herbert, Donne. We may quote one of great nobility:

> "The ashes of an oak in the chimney are no epitaph of that oak, to tell me how high or how large it was; it tells me not what flocks it sheltered while it stood, nor what men it hurt when it fell. The dust of great persons' graves is speechless too; it says nothing, it distinguishes nothing. As soon the dust of a wretch whom thou wouldest not, as of a Prince whom thou couldest not look upon, will trouble thine eyes, if the wind blow it thither; and when a whirlwind hath blown the dust of the churchyard into the Church, and the man sweeps out the dust of the Church into the churchyard, who will undertake to sift those dusts again, and to pronounce, this is the patrician, this the noble flour, and this the yeomanly, this the plebeian bran."[2]

The dust is the serpent's meat. It is an emblem of misery, degradation, earth's ultimate reduction of man. It has overtones of the desert and the waste places. Yet, mixed with spittle, it may heal the blind;[3] and in it Christ writes with his finger.[4]

V

A projection of the Images is the symbolism of numbers, structures, patterns. 'All things began in order, so shall they end and so shall they begin again; according to the ordainer of order and mystical mathematics of the city of Heaven.'

[1] *I Henry IV*, V. 4. 78.
[2] Donne, *Eighty Sermons*, p. 148. We may note the skill of the variations between the 'English' and 'classical' cadences.   [3] *Jn.* 9:6.   [4] *Ibid.*, 8:6.

Sir Thomas Browne, when he wrote these words at the end of *The Garden of Cyrus*, was thinking of the proportions of the celestial City as described in *Revelation*; but we may examine the subject in more general terms. No aspect of the Bible has had more nonsense written about it than what we might call 'inferred numerology', deductions based on prophetic and other texts. But it is well to examine the subject; standing back, as it were, from its more ludicrous manifestations.

The Hebrew cosmology was one of order in the heavens; the circling of the planets, the seasons that come in their settled order (itself an example of the divine providence) provide a mass of imagery. The stability of the universe, the outward sign of the power of the Godhead, underlie Jehovah's question to *Job*

> Canst thou bring forth Mazzaroth in his season? or canst thou guide Arcturus with his sons?[1]

The rhythm of the celestial bodies was a joyful one; its harmonies were to provide recurrent imagery everywhere. Sir John Davies' *Orchaestra*, Dryden's *Ode on St. Cecilia's Day*, are examples among many. Jehovah's hymn in *Job*

> When the morning stars sang together, and all the sons of God shouted for joy.[2]

is echoed in the garden at Belmont:[3]

> "There's not the smallest orb which thou beholdest
> But in his motion like an angel sings,
> Still choiring to the young-eyed cherubins."

and reinforce the divine harmonies of Plato's myth.

Pattern, order, constancy are attributes of the Creation. The world could be interpreted in terms of such a dynamic design: moving towards a Day of Judgment or to the coming of the Messiah. We may contrast Bishop Ussher's time scale for these events. The Creation took place in October, 4004 B.C. According to the Babylonian Talmud '6000. years the world stands 2000. years *Tohu* (or before the Law) 2000. in the Law. 2000. in the dayes of Messias which is by interpretation Christ.'[4] By the time of the Renaissance that world

---

[1] 38:32.   [2] *Ibid.*, 38:7.
[3] *The Merchant of Venice*, V. 1. 60.
[4] cf. Hugh Broughton, *A Treatise of Melchizadek. cit.* Désirée Hirst, *Hidden Riches*, p. 148.

was in its autumnal phase. Sir Thomas Browne wrote that

> "We who are ordained in this setting past of time, are providentially taken off from such imaginations: and being necessitated to eye the remaining particle of futurity, are naturally constituted unto thoughts of the next world. . . .

The fifteenth chapter of Corinthians had placed at the two poles of time, the first man and the last, Adam and Christ. The text

> I am Alpha and Omega, the beginning and the end

seemed to certify the same pattern. The desire to perceive a symmetrical order in history, prophecy and parable is a natural one, and gave rise to many myths of many kinds. The Gardens of Eden and of Calvary were the same in Donne's great *Hymn to God my God in my Sickness*:

> "We think that Paradise and Calvary,
>   Christ's Cross and Adam's Tree, stood in one place:
> Look, Lord, and see both Adams met in me:
>   As the first Adam's sweat surrounds my face
>   May the last Adam's blood my soul embrace."

The imagery of the garden is everywhere. 'God Almighty first planted a Garden.' It is, naturally, linked to water, and the fountain in the midst of the garden serves to express subtle and complex relationships. It is an emblem of fruitfulness and prosperity; as in *The Song of Songs*:

> Awake, O north wind; and come, thou south; blow upon my garden that the spices thereof may flow out. Let my beloved come into his garden, and eat his pleasant fruits.[1]

And in Ezekiel's vision.

> The cedars in the garden of God could not hide him . . . nor any tree in the garden of God was like unto him in his beauty.[2]

To Hamlet the world is an unweeded garden: Marvell is overwhelmed by its sensuous luxuriance. In *Richard II* it serves for a parable of order in the state.[3] A garden is a fitting place for a sepulchre.

From the beginning there was clearly a significant numerology. The seven days of Creation provided a basis; the seven candlesticks

---

[1] *Cant.* 4:16.   [2] 31:8.   [3] III, 4.

of *Revelation*, the Seven Spirits of God. The twelve tribes of Israel are represented by the four and twenty elders of *Revelation*, and the measurements of the Holy City are in terms of the square of twelve. The Four Books and the Four Riders of the Apocalypse are perhaps related to the Four Beasts of Ezekiel, two of which become symbols of the Four Evangelists. The thirty-three years of Christ's life on earth are a frequent object of comment by medieval theologians. The conception of Christ, and His death, both take place, according to their chronology, at the spring solstice. There are twenty-six kings in His ancestry from David.

Some glimpse of the fascination of the symbolism of numbers may by obtained from a single passage from *The Garden of Cyrus* of Sir Thomas Browne, and we may note that writer's perplexity:

> "More considerables there are in this mystical account, which we must not insist on. And therefore, why the radical letters in the pentateuch should equal the number of the soldiery of the tribes? Why our Saviour in the wilderness fed five thousand persons with five barley loaves, but four thousand with no less than seven of wheat? Why Joseph designed five changes of raiment unto Benjamin; and David took just five pebbles out of the brook against the Pagan champion;—we leave it unto arithmetical divinity, and theological explanation."[1]

The projection goes further. Three is the number proper to Spirit, and to the Trinity. It seems to have a basic relevance to form in nature, birds and insects.[2] Four is the province of matter, familiar in the tables of correspondences of the medieval and Elizabethan worlds: having their basis in the four elements of earth, air, fire, and water, and related to a highly developed physio-psychology. But if three is added to four—Spirit combining with matter—we have again the mystic seven. If we multiply, we have twelve, the number of the apostles, and of the tribes. Allow two Elders for each tribe, and we have the four and twenty Elders of *Revelation*. If the City is laid out on a *mandala*-pattern, it is natural that its basic dimensions should be the square of twelve.

The search for 'patterns' led to many strange places. There is a legend that Christ was exactly six feet tall. He, like Adam, was

---

[1] *Cyrus's Garden, or the Quincunx Mystically Considered*, ch. v, §8. I do not know the allusion in the second sentence.

[2] For this form in architecture, see, e.g., Trystan Edwards, *Good and Bad Manners in Architecture*, and his *Architectural Style*; where the form of a butterfly is used to exemplify what he calls 'resolved duality'.

presumed to be Man in his physical perfection, made in the image of God. If that were so, then the details of that perfection would be consonant with a mathematical structure, a secret but fixed ratio of part to part. If these proportions could be recovered, then it would be possible to reconstruct in statuary the very image of God. Hence the innumerable attempts to find a modulus, a root proportion, in the human form; especially by inscribing it in circles or ovoids which are sometimes related to the signs of the Zodiac. So in Austin Farrer's explanation of the plan of *Revelation*[1] he demonstrates an elaborate correspondence between the Festivals, the Seasons, The Twelve Tribes, the precious stones, and the signs of the Zodiac. Nor is it difficult, or inappropriate, to perceive different aspects of *mandala*-symbolism[2] in the complex structure, box within box, of the Temple, and in the circular structure of the *hortus clausus* so common in medieval representations of Eden.[3]

The Bible has been a forcing-ground for this imagery: so much is a platitude. It is expanded, modified, set out in countless ikons, carvings, church decorations, paintings. Artists have conventional-ized, modified, distorted, enlarged it in countless ways. The very sacredness of the text justified the typological inferences from it. The Five Wise Virgins typify the five forms of mystical contemplation. The oil that burns in the lamps is charity. The Foolish Virgins symbolize 'the five forms of the lusts of the flesh, the pleasures of the senses which cause the soul to forget all holy thoughts and extinguish the flame of heavenly love'.[4] In the alchemists pagan and Christian imagery converge, as in the Renaissance classical legend is constantly adapted to express correspondences with it. Ulysses tied to the mast as he is borne past the Sirens becomes an emblem of the Crucifixion, the sloping yard-arm forming the cross-piece.[5] An anchor with its cruciform structure becomes the emblem of hope, and salvation. On its flank may be impaled the Fishes, the anagram for Christ: so that, by extension, the heron, the killer of the fish, may become an anti-type of God. The frontispiece to Vico's *The New Science* contains one

[1] See Austin Farrer, *A Rebirth of Images*.

[2] See Jung and Kerényi, *op. cit.*; also ch. 9 of D. H. Lawrence's *The Symbolic Meaning*, London, 1962.

[3] There is a delightful representation of this in *The Duc du Berry's Book of Hours*, pl. xiii: with a Gothic fountain in the centre of the Garden.

[4] Mâle, *op. cit.*, p. 198.

[5] H. Rahner, *Greek Myths and Christian Mysteries*, London, 1963, p. 266.

of the most complex allegorical pictures ever devised: so packed with meaning, pagan and Christian, that we are fortunate to have Vico's own detailed explanation of its thirty involved symbols.[1]

It would be wrong to consider these developments from their sources as undeserving of attention. Every archetype is capable of infinite growth and differentiation. It is when the images become fantastic through the failure of the poets and mystics to realize their organic connection with each other, and to the roots of the spiritual life, that we dare to begin to mistrust them.

We may conclude this essay with a quotation from Austin Farrer:

"Who first saw life as a springing fountain, or guilt as dirt to be purged away? When did favourable deity begin to be an irradiating light, or divine sanctity a jewel wrapped by a veil within a veil, and guarded by jealous hands from the profane? When did the sky first marry the earth, to generate her fruits? . . . When did the traditions of the Elders or the justice of a king first seem to be the act of an authority controlling the stars?

In ages in which religion and poetry were a common possession, the basic images lived in the conserver's mind; men saw their place and destiny, their worth and guilt, and the process of their existence, in terms of them. Being externalized, the images taken for the reality of the divine became idolatry, and taken for the reality of nature became a false science. The rejection of idolatry meant not the destruction but the liberation of the images. Nowhere are the images in more vigour than in the Old Testament, where they speak of God, but are not he."[2]

[1] *Works*, ed. T. G. Goddard Bergin and Max Harold Fisch, Cornell, 1948.
[2] Austin Farrer, *op. cit.*, pp. 13–14.

CHAPTER SIX

Three Songs

i

The Growth of a Ballad

LET US RECALL the events of *Judges* 4 and 5. The children of Israel
have 'done evil' and the Lord 'sold' them into the hand of Jabin,
King of Canaan. Jabin's captain is Sisera. The prophetess Deborah
is the 'judge' of those Israelites who are not in bondage. A local
resistance movement begins under the guidance of Deborah, who
tells the leader of Naphtali and Zebulun (who had presumably been
outside the Canaanitish range of control) to concentrate on the high
ground near Mount Tabor. Barak refuses unless Deborah goes with
him. She agrees, but warns him that he will thereby lose credit in the
victory: 'for the Lord shall sell Sisera into the hands of a woman'.

Heber the Kenite, whose wife is the leading figure in the drama
that follows, is an 'outlander' who has cut himself off from the tribe,
and is living with his household on the plain of Kedesh.

Sisera is informed of the concentration of the Israelites, and moves
towards them with nine hundred chariots[1] and an unspecified force
of infantry. At Deborah's word 'Up, for this is the day in which the
Lord hath delivered Sisera into thine hands: is not the Lord gone
out before thee?' Barak comes down from the high ground. What
follows is not quite clear: either the Canaanitish cavalry and
armoured forces are bogged down in the marshes of the river
Kishon,[2] or the river itself rises rapidly, perhaps because of a sudden
rain-storm in the hills, so that the chariots cannot manœuvre and
are thrown into confusion. At any rate the Israelites cut Sisera's

---

[1] It is difficult to conceive of the power and terror of the iron chariots. We
might perhaps equate this force (if the figures are at all accurate) with the tanks of
three armoured divisions.

[2] Like the French knights in the marsh at Agincourt.

host to pieces; 'there was not a man left'. Sisera flies from the battle, and, weary and thirsty, chances on the tent of Heber, who, we should note, has concluded some sort of treaty of peace with Jabin. Then comes this most strange episode from *Judges* 4:18ff.:

And Jael went out to meet Sisera, and said unto him, Turn in, my Lord, turn in to me; fear not. And when he had turned in unto her into the tent, she covered him with a mantle.

Jael's invitation[1] emphasizes the double enormity of her subsequent crime; Heber is at peace with Sisera's master, and Jael is about to abuse the sacredness of Bedouin hospitality. *R.V.* reads 'rug' for 'mantle'. The latter has, perhaps, slight magical and courtly connotations. cf. *The Ballad of Tam Lin*.[2]

And he said unto her, Give me, I pray thee, a little water to drink; for I am thirsty. And she opened a bottle of milk, and gave him drink, and covered him.

Milk for water; the ritual of additional and re-vivifying hospitality. This will be 'intensified' as *butter* in the ballad.

Again he said unto her, Stand in the door of the tent, and it shall be, when any man doth come and inquire of thee, and say, Is there any man here? that thou shalt say, No.

The normal precautions of the escaping man: certain that he has found a friend, or that, at the least, hospitality will not be betrayed.

Then Jael Heber's wife took a nail of the tent, and took an hammer in her hand, and went softly unto him, and smote the nail into his temples, and fastened it into the ground: for he was fast asleep and weary. So he died.

R.V. has 'tent-pin', changing the rhythm from 'náil öf the tént' to the more prosaic and abrupt 'tént-pin' with its clashing n's: there is little clarification of meaning.

R.V. 'for he was in a deep sleep, so he swooned and died'. We have lost both the homeliness of 'fast asleep' and the dramatic suddenness of 'so he died'. 'And swooned and died' seems tautologous, even feeble. We

[1] Which is probably a sexual one as well.
[2]   "She shaped him in her arms at last,
           A mother-naked man:
       She cast her mantle over him,
           And so her love she won."
("The Ballad of Tam Lin.")

remember Tennyson's first version
of the "Sacrifice of Iphigenia":
"One drew a sharp knife through
my tender throat,
Slowly, and nothing more".[1]

And, behold, as Barak pursued
Sisera, Jael came out to meet him,
and said unto him, Come, and I
will shew thee the man whom thou
seekest. And when he came into her
tent, behold, Sisera lay dead, and
the nail was in his temples.

Here is a sordid story of treachery.[2] It may well have been written
after the ballad that celebrates this Women's Epic; for Deborah the
prophetess and Jael are the heroines. The song is celebration of the
traditional kind, a sort of ritual recapitulation of the whole battle
and its climax. We may select some of the verses:[3]

Gilead abode beyond Jordan:
and why did Dan remain in
ships?
Asher continued on the sea shore,
and abode in his breaches.

R.S.V. 'Why did he remain with
the ships?'
R.S.V. 'settling down by his land-
ings'. These are the tribes who did
not come to the help of others in
this popular revolt.

Zebulun and Naphthali were a
people that jeoparded their lives
unto the death in the high places
of the field.

R.S.V. has 'heights of the field',
which though accurate of the
Israelites concentrated on the high
grounds, seems to lose a little of the
numinous associations of *high places*.
'Jeopardied' is wholly archaic.[4]

The kings came and fought, then
fought the kings of Canaan in

Many battle-songs employ such
'namings';[5] to give the feeling of

---

[1] *A Dream of Fair Women*; one of the many passages excoriated by Lockhart in
The Quarterly Review.

[2] There is another side: Sisera should never have attempted to enter a woman's
tent.   [3] *Jg.* 5:17ff.

[4] But still widely understood: cf. *1 Cor.* 15; 30. (*A.V.*)
              "Why stand we in jeopardy every hour?"
and Kipling's *The Storm Cone*:
              "And worse than present jeopardy
              May our forlorn tomorrows be."

[5] cf. the passage from *Paradise Lost*, p. 222 *infra*, as well as much Celtic Saga.

Taanach by the waters of Megiddo; they took no gain of money.

actuality, and a certain memorable 'weight' of place. *R.S.V.* 'they got no spoils of silver'. Either seems irrelevant.

They fought from heaven; the stars in their courses fought against Sisera.

Here *R.S.V.*, by a poeticizing inversion, seems to have destroyed a classic simplicity. 'From heaven fought the stars,/from their courses they fought against Sisera.' The phrase 'the stars in their courses' is weighted by usage, and is expansive: suggesting God's intervention, the storm, destiny.

The river of Kishon swept them away, that ancient river, the river Kishon.
O my soul, thou hast trodden down strength.

R.S.V. has *torrent* for *river*, with little gain. This appears to be a battle cry in *R.S.V.*—
'March on, my soul, with might' —which may be thought to have unfortunate connotations to-day.

Then were the horsehoofs broken by the means of the pransings, the pransings of their mighty ones.

Better, 'Their horses hoofs hammered, from the galloping, galloping of the stallions.'
R.S.V. is again perhaps overpoetical: 'Then loud beat the horses' hoofs, with the galloping, galloping of the steeds.'

Few to-day can visualize the terror of a cavalry charge, or even that of a team of run-away horses. Yet we know that the nightmare, the treading under the hoofs, the biting teeth of the stallion; these are archetypal fear-images. We think of Fuseli's picture *The Nightmare*, or Macbeth's vision (refracted in Blake's picture)

And pity, like a naked new-born babe
Striding the blast, *or heaven's cherubin horsed*
Upon the sightless couriers of the air. . . .

or the Four Riders of the *Revelation* and of Dürer and his interpretation of *Revelation*; perhaps of Wagner also.

Curse ye Meroz, said the angel of the lord.

We do not know what this means, or what Meroz was. Perhaps it is a

Curse ye bitterly the inhabitants thereof; because they came not to the help of the Lord, to the help of the Lord against the mighty.

balancing curse against the blessing that follows; for we are now as it were in the aftermath of battle, having traced out the phases of the fight.

Blessed above women shall Jael the wife of Heber the Kenite be,
blessed shall she be above women in the tent.

R.S.V. 'tent-dwelling women' which seems clumsy.

He asked water, and she gave him milk;
she brought forth butter in a lordly dish.

But—though the last phrase has become proverbial, and though there is even to-day a ring of truth (one does ask for water among nomadic or peasant people and one *is* given milk) this is sheer hyperbole: reinforced by the strong rhythms.
R.S.V. 'curds in a lordly bowl'[1] gives a similar rhythm:

$$'|\quad \times\times\quad |'\times\quad |'$$
$$'\times|\quad \times\times\quad |'\times\quad |'$$

but with a wholly different cadence.

She put her hand to the nail, and her right hand to the workmen's hammer;
and with the hammer she smote Sisera,
she smote off his head, when she had pierced and stricken through his temples

R.S.V. 'She put her hand to the tent-peg and her right hand to the workmen's *mallet*;
she struck Sisera a blow,
she crushed his head,
she shattered and pierced his temple.'
The more accurate version seems to lose something of 'the woman's part', in the assassination with the nail.

The repetition, the tasting as it were of this ferocity of revenge, we find in the Norse Sagas and in the Scottish Ballads; as in this:

"I lighted down my sword to draw,
I hackèd him in pieces sma',
I hackèd him in pieces sma',
For her sake that died for me."[2]

---

[1] See p. 34 *ante*.   [2] *Helen of Kirconnel*.

This triumphant re-enactment seems to require this repetition; to certify as it were the nature of the deed.

> At her feet he bowed, he fell, he lay down:
> at her feet he bowed, he fell:
> Where he bowed, there he fell down dead.

Here *A.V.* might be thought clumsy, doubly so because the repetition does not quite succeed in conveying any suggestion of intensity; and we turn to *R.S.V.*:

> He sank, he fell,
> he lay still at her feet;
> at her feet he sank, he fell;
> Where he sank, there he fell dead.

There follows, as a sort of epilogue to Deborah's triumph-song, the intense and perennial drama of the soldier who does not return from the war, and of the women who wait for him.[1] It is possible that the irony, pity and depth-imagery which we may find in it are qualities which are wholly or in part subjective. Yet again we may remember a Scottish Ballad:

> "Hie upon Hielands
> And low upon Tay,
> Bonnie George Campbell
> Rade out on a day:
> Saddled and bridled
> And gallant rade he;
> Hame cam' his gude horse
> But never cam' he."[2]

Here is the song:

The mother of Sisera looked out at a window, and cried through the lattice,	*R.S.V.* seems to do violence both to the action and to the rhythm: 'Out of the window she *peered*', which makes the action mean and furtive.
Why is his chariot so long in coming? why tarry the wheels of his chariot?	

Her wise / ladies / answered her,
yea, she returned answer to herself.

> Have they not sped?
> have they not divided the prey;
> to every man a damsel or two;

[1] As Andromache waits for Hector.

[2] *Bonnie George Campbell.*

85

to Sisera a prey of divers colours,
a prey of divers colours of needlework,
a prey of divers colours of needlework on both sides,
meet for the necks of them that take the spoil.

In commenting on this portion of the poem we must remember our previous warnings against subjective or contemporary interpretation; yet the perception of other dimensions of irony and archetypal imagery seem too important to omit. Sisera's mother is in her house, surrounded by the women of her household. She *cried* through the lattice; impatience, anxiety, grief. *R.S.V.* has *gazed*: less strong and giving nothing of the tension, the lament, of *cried*. Another reading is *exclaimed*.

The return is delayed; intensified and picked up by the homely *tarry*. For *wheels R.S.V.* has *hoofbeats*, spoiling the cadence of *A.V.* and perhaps robbing us of such a remembered allusion as:

> "Wherefore rejoice? What conquest brings he home?
> What tributaries follow him to Rome
> To grace in captive bonds his chariot wheels?"[1]

'Her wise / ladies / answered her'—the three strides of the rhythm prepare for the woman's further outcry. As we speak it, there is a slight pause before *ladies* so that we linger on the possible irony of *wise*. (We are robbed of this by *R.S.V.* which reads *wisest*: but this version might be thought to gain by a dramatic transfer to the present tenses: *make answer, she gives answer*.) The pause suggests her anguished thought of disaster, rationalized in her mind to explain the delay.

'Have they not sped?' We need not object to the archaism, remembering 'God-speed'. But as it stands 'sped' has overtones, not merely of success in battle, but of the *speed* of the stallions and the chariots of the imagined returning: so that it picks up the chariots, the wheels, the hoof-beats. (*R.S.V.* omits this, and moves to the weaker

> Are they not finding and dividing the spoil?)

The spoils of women are divided up among the conquerors, as after the fall of Troy:

> To every man a damsel or two.

[1] *Julius Caesar*, I. i. 35.

R.S.V. has 'a maiden or two for every man', with a slight shift, perhaps, from the gay, 'devoted', perhaps musical 'damsel' to the 'maidens' or 'hand-maidens' who will be enslaved. This follows the seemingly irrelevant

> To Sisera a prey of divers colours

—strangely intensified by repetition, through which seems to come a tone of agony as she continues to attempt to reassure herself; lingering, almost in hysteria, on the household values—

> a prey of divers colours of needlework,
> a prey of divers colours of needlework on both sides.

We must consider *R.S.V.*:

> spoil of dyed stuffs for Sisera,
> spoil of dyed stuffs embroidered,
> two pieces of dyed work embroidered for my neck as spoil?

But *A.V.* has simply

> meet for the necks of them that take the spoil.

Is she imagining the spoil of needlework for herself? If so, we weaken two images. The first is that of the victorious army *wearing* the spoils. The second is the irony of Sisera: the head hewn off at the neck.

ii

"The loveliest song"[1]

That is the meaning of the title; Canticles, 'The Song of Solomon' seems less cogent. For it is clear that Solomon is not the author, who is unknown. It is a cycle of love songs which have been divided into as many as nineteen movements, or edited, with stage directions, to form a miniature drama. The book owes its inclusion in the sacred canon to its potential for allegorical interpretation; containing types of the Church as the Bride, the Word and the Soul, and other extensions of this kind.

For the purposes of this essay I propose to treat it as a series of love poems. There are not many great love-poems in English that are

---

[1] We may note this method of expressing the superlative in Hebrew: cf. 'god of gods', 'slave of slaves'.

direct and simple, built without shame on the delighted senses of bride and bridegroom. Much western poetry is concerned with the divided soul of the lover, with despair, frustration, rejection or loss. A whole convention is founded upon unsatisfied desire.[1] Often it is turned inward in some form of agonized self-analysis. Here the poetry is pure, uninhibited, sensuous without a trace of sensuality or lust. In these respects, as in the extreme and minute sensitivity to taste and scent, in the minutely-perceived freshness of nature, it has (as many commentators have noted) a delicate, almost feminine quality.

The ability to write love poetry of this kind we should expect in Elizabethan and Jacobean literature; but too often it is over-shadowed by memories of Theocritus, of baroque classicism, of the staled mechanisms of mythology. There are, in fact, few passages of genuine freshness after Chaucer. The following seems to approximate to the spirit of the Song of Songs, but even these are sometimes spoilt by the intrusion of 'impurities'. First, the third stanza of Ben Jonson's *The Triumph*:

> "Have you seen but a bright lily grow
>   Before rude hands have touch'd it?
> Have you mark'd but the fall of the snow
>   Before the soil hath smutch'd it?
> Have you felt the wool of beaver
>   Or swans' down ever?
> Or have smelt the bud o' the brier,
>   Or the nard in the fire?
> Or have tasted the bag of the bee?
> O so white, O so soft, O so sweet is she!"

This clearly owes something to *Canticles* (*lily, bud o' the brier, nard*) as does this of Spenser in the *Epithalamium*:

> "Her goodly eyes lyke Saphyres shining bright,
> Her forehed yvory white,
> Her cheeks lyke apples which the sun hath rudded,
> Her lips lyke cherryes charming men to byte,
> Her breast lyke lyllies budded,
> Her snowie necke lyke to a marble towre
> And all her body lyke a pallace fayre . . ."

[1] cf. C. S. Lewis, *The Allegory of Love.*

We could, we feel, have done without the fourth line. Herrick is a little clumsy in his woman-flower comparisons, and over-moralizes:

> "You are a full-spread fair-set vine
> And can with tendrils love entwine
> Yet dried ere you distil your wine.
>
> You are like balm enclosèd well
> In amber or some oystal shell
> Yet lost ere you transfuse your smell,
>
> You are a dainty violet,
> Yet wither'd ere you can be set
> Within the Virgin's coronet."

We may, indeed (though somewhat roughly) suggest some of the essentials of great single-minded love poetry. It arises out of the pressures of unsatisfied desire. Its hyperboles are the measure of that intensity. So Polonius:

> ". . .   I do know
> When the blood burns, how prodigal the soul
> Lends the tongue vows."[1]

But the balance is a delicate one. The imagery that the poet uses must carry a load of sensual meaning, yet that meaning must be controlled by taste and tact. The imagery must be capable of translation into sensual terms, though it may revolve constantly on the perimeter of the decorations proper to the physical qualities of the beloved. We remember Marvell's

> "A hundred years should go to praise
> Thine eyes, and on thy forehead gaze;
> Two hundred to adore each breast,
> But thirty thousand to the rest . . ."[2]

On that perimeter moves, as co-relatives of the imagery, what may be gleaned by the five senses; behind which lies the world of observed nature, and, in a purer time, the energy of the seasons:

> "The April's in her eyes: it is love's spring."[3]

or

> "O white violet of a woman, with the April in your face."[4]

---

[1] *Hamlet*, I. 3. 115.   [2] Marvell, *To his Coy Mistress.*
[3] *Antony and Cleopatra*, III. 2. 43.   [4] Masefield, *Enslaved.*

So the scents and sounds and sights of the springtime are drawn upon as in the *Love Song of Egypt*:[1]

> "The voice of the swallow[2] speaks, saying,
> 'The land is bright. What of thy way?'
> Prithee, do not, O bird, scold me.
> I have found my brother[3] in his bed,
> And my heart is pleased even more.
> We have said (to one another),
> 'I shall not go far away
> While my hand is in thy hand.
> I shall stroll about
> Being with thee in every beautiful place.'
> He has made me the chief of his lovely women
> Lest he should wound my heart."

We can now turn to parts of 'the loveliest song'. Its imagery is pastoral: wild animals, hunting, flocks, gardens, vineyard; and, sometimes, the decoration of craftsmanship in ivory, embroidery. The girl's belovéd is a roe or a young hart (perhaps best translated as an antelope or gazelle) suggesting grace, energy, the light sure-footedness of young men upon the hills, shepherds or warriors, in Eastern stories.[4] We may pause to think for a moment of the imagery-in-depth, setting aside some of the tedious Elizabethan puns on deer, horns and cuckoldry. Behind it is the terrible energy of the stag or buck in the rutting season; the gentleness and grace of the round-eyed does;[5] to us, perhaps, with the Artemis or St. Hubert associations; or such a contrast-value as in the exquisite music of Yeats' *Lullaby*:

> "Sleep, belovéd, such a sleep
> As did that wild Tristram know
> When, the potion's work being done,
> Roe could run or doe could leap
> Under oak and beechen bough,
> Roe could leap or doe could run . . ."

---

[1] From D. Winton Thomas (ed.) *Documents from Old Testament Times*. (Late Empire *c*. 1300–1100 B.C.)

[2] cf. the Itylus legend.   [3] i.e. husband or lover.

[4] cf. Kipling:

'With that he whistled his only son, who dropped from a mountain-crest;
He trod the ling like a buck in spring, and he looked like a lance in rest.'

(*The Ballad of East and West*)

[5] Familiar in Persian poetry: cf. also Homer, 'ox-eyed' Athena.

8. The voice of my beloved! behold, he cometh leaping upon the mountains, skipping upon the hills.

R.S.V. has 'bounding over the hills', which avoids the associations of 'skipping'. But 'upon the hills' seems to add another dimension: see (e.g.) *Lycidas:* 'For we were bred upon the self-same hill.'

9. My beloved is like a roe or a young hart: behold he standeth behind our wall, he looketh forth at the windows, shewing himself through the lattice.

R.S.V. 'gazelle or a young stag'. And 'gazing *in* at the windows, looking through the lattice', gives an important sense-change.

10. My beloved spake, and said unto me, Rise up, my love, my fair one, and come away.

R.S.V. changes to present tense, and has *Arise* for *Rise up*: which does not help, in spite, or because of, Yeats' 'I will arise and go now, and go to Innisfree'.

11. For lo, the winter is past, the rain is over and gone:

This is the supreme moment, celebrated again and again: the renewal of life in the spring. The juncture of *rain* with *winter*[1] suggests the clarity of the spring air, the bursting fertility of the rain-soaked land.

12. The flowers appear on the earth; the time of the singing of birds is come, and the voice of the turtle is heard in our land;

There is little need to add 'dove' to turtle. *Our* land conveys a sort of possessive pride in it.

13. The fig-tree putteth forth her green figs, and the vines with the tender grape give a good smell. Arise, my love, my fair one, and come away.

Figs, vines, grapes are capable of being used for sexual imagery, but there is no suggestion of it here: only the joy of the 'delighted senses'.

14. O my dove, that art in the clefts of the rock, in the secret places of the stairs, let me see thy

'Cleft of the rock', 'secret places of the stairs' have no oblique intention: they merely emphasize the

[1] cf. Swinburne, *Atlanta in Calydon*:
"For winter's rains and ruins are over,
    And all the season of snows and sins;
The days dividing lover and lover,
    The light that loses, the night that wins . . ."

countenance, let me hear thy voice for sweet is thy voice, and thy countenance is comely.
(*R.V.* Let me see thy countenance, let me hear they voice; for sweet is thy voice, and thy countenance is comely.)

15. Take us the foxes, the little foxes, that spoil the vines: for our vines have tender grapes.

16. My beloved is mine, and I am his: he feedeth among the lilies.

17. Until the day break, and the shadows flee away, turn, my beloved, and be thou like a roe or a young hart upon the mountains of Bether.

bride's shyness, carrying on the image of the dove.
R.V. reads 'in the covert of the steep place', which fits better with the idea of a rock-dove. The turtle-dove is a spring migrant.

Is this a fragment of the song of labourers in the vineyards? If we keep *A.V.* the image of the 'tender grapes' seems to return to the qualities of the girl. If we take *R.V.* something of this connection is lost: 'Take us the foxes, the little foxes, that spoil the vineyards; for our vineyards are in blossom.'

R.V. has 'he feedeth *his flock* among the lilies'. *A.V.* suggests the continuing attributes of the beloved as a roe or stag, as well as the purity of the lily-pond; is there perhaps, a hint, as in Shakespeare,[1] of her breasts?

R.V. Until the day be *cool*, but gives other words *break* or *breath*. If we keep *break* we have all the association of the *aubade*; the many poems of the dawn, in many languages, that celebrate or lament the passing of love's night.[2]

We may consider another section, this time the Bride's dream:

6: 1. Whither is thy beloved gone, O thou fairest among women? whither is thy beloved turned aside? that we may seek him with thee.

2. My beloved is gone down into his garden, to the beds of spices, to feed in the gardens, and to gather lilies.

She is looking for him frantically.

This is her reassurance to herself: she returns to her favourite image of the stag or antelope, among the sweet-smelling flowers.

[1] e.g. *Venus and Adonis*, 229 ff.

[2] *v.* A. T. Hatto, *Eos.*

3. I am my beloved's, and my beloved is mine: he feedeth among the lilies.

That is what he is doing: he is gathering his strength and sweetness for me. Now she is happy, and turns again to new imagery to glorify him.

4. Thou art beautiful, O my love, as Tirzah, comely as Jerusalem, terrible as an army with banners.

Tirzah is the 'city of delight'. Jerusalem and its beauty we may remember from Psalm 50:2 (*R.V.*) 'Out of Zion, the perfection of beauty, God has shined forth', which is very different from the familiar chant-version.

But the simile, 'terrible as an army with banners', is a strange one; the stranger in that it is repeated in the same chapter, this time of the Bride, after the Bridegroom has praised her as a 'dove' the undefiled one whom the queens and the concubines praise:

Who is she that looketh forth as the morning, fair as the moon, clear as the sun, and terrible as an army with banners? (6:10)

We feel that it is wholly appropriate that the Bridegroom's virility should be conveyed by the images of warfare:

Thy neck is like the tower of David builded for an armoury, whereon there hang a thousand bucklers, all shields of mighty men. (4:4)

and it is right that there should be 'three score valiant men about his bed' (3:7). But how can we say that the identical words—'terrible as an army with banners'—are appropriate to the Bride?

Very few people have seen an army, or even a battalion, on parade: fewer still have seen one with banners. Yet it is something that the Elizabethan world knew, and which would not have sounded wholly strange to the translators. They knew, of course, that a woman's proper qualities were to be mild and timorous:[1] but they also knew the extreme beauty of an army, freshly arranged and accoutred, in the morning light. In a famous simile Vernon reports the condition of the rebel army before Shrewsbury:

—"all furnished, all in arms,
All plum'd like estridges that wing the wind,
Baited like eagles having lately bath'd."[2]

[1] See, e.g., Sir Thomas Eliot, *The Governor*.
[2] *I Henry IV*, IV. 1. 98.

where the glittering sleek tension of the troops is noted in terms of the estridge, the short-winged hawk.

So, perhaps, we see two sets of qualities, complementary but not opposing, in the battle-image. He is fierce, strong, virile; *her* beauty has the freshness of the morning, the pure beauty of the moon. Then comes the *power* of the sun image; and from that we move to the image of the army. The poet wishes to convey ideas of tautness, splendour of her radiant personality, dignity and power. We may perhaps think of Yeats' *No Second Troy*:

> "What could have made her peacefull with a mind
> That nobleness made simple as a fire,
> With beauty *like a tightened bow*, a kind
> That is not natural in an age like this,
> Being high and solitary and most stern?"

But perhaps this Syrian Bride is remembering (for so are metaphors made) the flocks of goats on the hills by her home, the black tents of the herdsmen, the troops of fighting men that would have crossed the great highways to Joppa or Damascus.

iii

I have taken, for a third example, a New Testament Song. It may be thought that it is too familiar to bear, or require, scrutiny; but it has many features of profound interest. It is a lyric built on a complicated system of allusiveness. Let us consider, first of all, the *A.V.* version of *Luke* 1:46, setting beside it its somewhat similar *O.T.* passage (1 *Samuel* 2, also from *A.V.*) on which it appears to be partly built:

And Mary said, My soul doth magnify the Lord, and my spirit hath rejoiced in God my Saviour.	And Hannah prayed, and said, My heart rejoiceth in the Lord, mine horn is exalted in the Lord: my mouth is enlarged over mine enemies; because I rejoice in thy salvation.
For he hath regarded the low estate of his handmaiden: for, behold, from henceforth all generations shall call me blessed.	There is none holy as the Lord; for there is none beside thee: neither is there any rock like our God.
For he that is mighty hath done to me great things; and holy is his name.	

And his mercy is on them that fear him from generation to generation.

He hath shewed strength with his arm; he hath scattered the proud in the imagination of their hearts.

Talk no more so exceeding proudly; let not arrogancy come out of your mouth: for the Lord is a God of knowledge, and by him actions are weighed.

He hath put down the mighty from their seats, and exalted them of low degree.

The bows of the mighty men are broken,[1] and they that stumbled are girded with strength.

He hath filled the hungry with good things, and the rich he hath sent empty away.

They that were full have hired out themselves for bread; and they that were hungry ceased: so that the barren hath born seven; and she that hath many children is waxed feeble.

The Lord killeth, and maketh alive: he bringeth down to the grave, and bringeth up.

The Lord maketh poor, and maketh rich: he bringeth low, and lifteth up.

He raiseth up the poor out of the dust, and lifteth up the beggar from the dunghill, to set them among princes and to make them inherit the throne of glory: for the pillars of the world are the Lord's, and he hath set the world upon them.

He hath holpen his servant Israel, in remembrance of his mercy;

He will keep the feet of his saints, and the wicked shall be silent in darkness; for by strength shall no man prevail.

As he spake to our fathers, to Abraham and to his seed for ever.

The adversaries of the Lord shall be broken to pieces; out of heaven shall he thunder upon them: the Lord shall judge the ends of the

---

[1] v. p. 41 *supra*.

earth; and he shall give strength
unto his king, and exalt the horn of
his anointed.

But in addition the *Magnificat* contains a whole tissue of allusions to
the Old Testament: we may note briefly a few of them:

For he that is mighty hath done to me great things.

(cf. *Zeph.* 3:17)

. . . and those that walk in pride he is able to abase.

(*Dan.* 4:37)

He hath remembered his mercy and his truth toward the house of
Israel; all the ends of the earth have seen the salvation of our God.

(*Ps.* 98:3)

And God said moreover unto Moses, Thus shalt thou say unto the
children of Israel, The Lord God of your fathers, the God of Abraham,
the God of Isaac, and the God of Jacob, hath sent me unto you: this is
my name for ever, and this is my memorial unto all generations.

(*Ex.* 3:15)

I will sing of the mercies of the Lord for ever: with my mouth will I
make known thy faithfulness to all generations.

(*Ps.* 89:1)

We should also remember Zacharias's Song that follows immediately
in Luke 1:68: familiar as the Canticle, the Benedictus. It is worth
while noting that the Prayer Book Version differs little from the
A.V. substituting only

he hath raised up a mighty salvation for us

for the common but difficult image (as in Hannah's Song)—

and hath raised up a horn of salvation for us.

And in view of some recent versions, we may note there an alternative
translation of *handmaiden* as *bondmaiden*, and the previous verse in
Luke 1:38:

And Mary said, Behold the handmaiden of the Lord.

We remember Rossetti's famous picture, *Ecce ancilla Domini* and
reflect that in so describing herself Mary has joined a whole company
as it were of such 'handmaidens' of the Old Testament—Hagar,

Zilpah, Bilhah, Ruth, Hannah. Perhaps we may even recall Rossetti's poem.[1]

But what we have in the *Magnificat* is a wholly new poem; recalling by quotation or half-quotation so much of past history, yet gentle, reticent, working with a verbal economy which seems to achieve a peculiar feminine quality by its quiet rhythms. Its structure works outward from the fate of Mary herself to the doings of the Lord, to close with a liturgical phrase (for this is the common benediction) recalling the Covenant. It has none of the tautologies, the balanced repetitions, of Hannah's Song. What has been achieved is a gentle unified poem.

There are other things that we may note. The Prayer Book version substitutes

> and hath exalted the humble and meek

for

> and exalted them of low degree.

Apart from the superior 'singable' qualities of 'hŭmblĕ aņd ḿeek' we may reflect that of 'low degree' has tended to be drained of its former meaning by its use in spurious 'romantic writing': 'a squire of low degree', and so forth, whereas 'humble and meek' looks forward, rightly, to the Benedictions. But this verse, and the following one, deliberately achieve a generalized, even ambiguous statement:

> He hath filled the hungry with good things, and the rich he hath sent empty away . . .

does not merely recall Dives and Lazarus, or the several images from feasts, but also the more general qualities (beyond that of food) implied in such a reversal. So, too, the difficulty raised by

> he hath done to me great things

against the Prayer Book reading *magnified* me, picking up the first verse. In the light of subsequent versions *magnify* is clearly felt to be a

[1] " 'We two' she said, 'will seek the groves
Where the lady Mary is,
With her five handmaidens, whose names
Are five sweet symphonies:—
Cecily, Gertrude, Magdalen,
Margaret and Rosalys . . .' "
(*The Blesséd Damozel*)

difficult, perhaps ambiguous word, in a modern context. I can suggest no solution.

We may also note the cadences which, alternating between the Latin and the English, mark out as it were the lyrical qualities:

> . . . doth magnify the Lord
> . . . rejoiced in God my Saviour
> . . . hungry with good things
> . . . and the rich he hath sent empty away.
> . . . in remembrance of his mercy
> . . . Abraham and his seed for ever

—thus ending with the two 'classical' cadences.

The problems of the *Magnificat* as a Song can be considered in an acute form in the version of *The New Testament in Modern English*:

> Then Mary said, 'My heart is overflowing with praise of my God, my soul is full of joy in God my Saviour. For he has deigned to notice me, his humble servant and, after this, all the people who ever shall be will call me the happiest of women! The one who can do all things has done great things for me—oh, holy is his Name! Truly, his mercy rests on those who fear him in every generation. He has shown the strength of his arm, he has swept away the high and mighty. He has set kings down from their thrones and lifted up the humble. He has satisfied the hungry with good things and sent the rich away with empty hands. Yes, he has helped Israel, his child: he has remembered the mercy that he promised to our forefathers, to Abraham and his sons for evermore!'

I do not wish to appear captious, especially in view of the outstanding achievements of *Letters to Young Churches*; but we must make some assessment of the losses as well as gains. The *lyrical* qualities of the original have been dissipated; it is no longer a song. The loss of the original rhythms is more apparent because of the vestigial and perhaps irrational survivals of them, breaking the original unity of tone. We have replaced dignified archaisms by hardly less archaic clichés.

So

> He hath *deigned to notice me, his humble servant*

which is wholly different in meaning from

> He hath regarded the low estate of his handmaiden

as well as recalling the unfortunate cliché-ending of letter-endings. *All the people who shall ever be* is again different, and weakly abstract, compared with

All generations shall call me blessed

which recalls the freight of meanings from the genealogies in the Old Testament and in the New; and the emphatic *generations* is retained three lines later. In the attempt to get rid of *Behold, from henceforth* —surely not incomprehensible, and marking by its rhythm the triumphant moment of the Incarnation—we have the feeble *and, after this*. Mary, by foreseeing that she will be called *blessed*, is clearly not calling herself the *happiest* of women ('Yea, a sword shall pierce through thine own heart also'). Yet we have replaced

For He that is mighty hath done to me great things, and holy is His name.

(the Prayer Book version has *hath magnified*, though in a larger but wholly comprehensible phrase) by a sentence of a monosyllabic clumsiness that might have come from Basic English:

The one who can do all things has done great things for me.

and in place of the dignified and reticent statement

and holy is His name

we have the second of three exclamation marks, each unnecessary (for the rhythms should contain their own emphasis without external aid) coupled with the expletive Oh!¹

Oh, holy is his Name!

'He has swept away the high and mighty' again introduces an objectionable and dead cliché, with idiomatic connotations which seem unpleasant: and the original *put down* seems far more cogent (and works in wider dimensions) than the domestic *swept away*. We might also object that

He has set kings down from their thrones

is a good deal narrower, perhaps more provincial, than

He hath put down the mighty from their seat.

'Set kings down' is hardly English, and in *A.V.* it is not merely the kings that have been 'put down'. The phrase has wide connotations; it is surely all men of arrogance and power.

The Song of *Magnificat* remains as much beyond analysis as

¹ Perhaps *O* would have been preferable.

beyond praise; behind all the qualities towards which we can gesture there remains something enduring. This is so in all great poetry. It is not irrelevant to give some verses from St. Bernard of Cluny:

> "L'Ange du conseil
> Est né de la Vierge,
> Le soleil de l'étoile.
>
> Soleil sans déclin,
> Étoile toujours scintillante,
> Toujours lumineuse.
>
> Comme l'astre le rayon,
> La Vierge enfante le Fils,
> De la même manière.
>
> Ni l'astre par le rayon
> Ni par son fils la Vierge
> Ne sont altérés dans leur éclat."

CHAPTER SEVEN

Some Types of Persuasion

i

"FOR I am persuaded . . ." The famous opening sentence of *Romans* 8:38 is a convenient starting-point:

> For I am persuaded, that neither death, nor life, nor angels, nor principalities, nor powers, nor things present, nor things to come,
>
> Nor height, nor depth, nor any other creature, shall be able to separate us from the love of God, which is in Christ Jesus our Lord.

The phrase is now often rendered as 'I am certain . . .' 'I am sure', but I suggest that the implications are stronger, and with complex overtones. 'Persuasion' is the province of rhetoric; the employment of all the available means of convincing an individual or an audience of a particular point of view. As such it embodied, traditionally, a technique which could be taught; it could also be prostituted by many forms of artificial embellishment, as in Roman forensic oratory. When Agrippa said 'Almost thou persuadest me to be a Christian,'[1] he implied that both the logic and the emotional content of St. Paul's arguments were drawing him near to a state of conviction or conversion.

In the passage from *Romans* we must consider some of the aspects of an earlier part of this chapter:[2]

> For the earnest expectation of the *creature* waiteth for the manifestation of the sons of God.
>
> For the *creature* was made subject to vanity, not willingly, but by reason of him who hath subjected the same in hope,
>
> Because the *creature* itself also shall be delivered from the bondage of corruption into the glorious liberty of the children of God.
>
> For we know that the whole *creation* groaneth and travaileth in pain together till now.

[1] *Acts* 26:28.   [2] 8:19–22.

The theme is the hope to come; *creature* and *creation* are stressed repeatedly in order to emphasize the state of man before the redemption. The climax of the chapter follows. Death, and what has been previously called the 'bondage of corruption', is the most terrifying of the forces in opposition: unless there is hope. Angels are the most powerful of spirits; they may be good or evil.[1] In their evil aspects they are hinted at as 'principalities and powers', whether of the agents of the captivities or of the Roman occupation. 'Height' and 'depth' may imply astrological factors; or, to us, the powerlessness of man's mind when he contemplates infinity. Events are set in an inexorable time-sequence; the record of occupation and tyranny may continue, for is there not a threat in the phrase 'things to come'? There are forces in the world of many kinds beyond our control. Behind the passage lie the sufferings of Jewish history, which have been mentioned just previously:

> Who shall separate us from the love of Christ? shall tribulation, or distress, or persecution, or famine, or nakedness, or peril, or sword?

We may perceive a progression from the abstract to the concrete, the polysyllabic words shortening down to *peril*, to be gathered up as it were on the terrifying rhythmic climax *or péril, or sword.* The movement of the passage, now specific, advances to the closing verses of the chapter. We pass rapidly through a kind of circle set in space and time: to rest as it were on the simplicity of hope proclaimed in the final clause.

ii

An example of rhetoric, which is perhaps half-way between a public lecture and a sermon, is to be found in Luke's reporting of St. Paul's speech before the Areopagus at Athens.[2] It appears to follow the traditional pattern of an oration, through *exordium*, *narratio*, *divisio* (a dividing up into headings of the points at issue, and a discussion of them) and the *conclusio*. The philosophers of the city, 'always eager to hear or to tell some new thing', have asked Paul to lecture on the new faith. The Areopagus is both a gathering of scholars and a repository of tradition. It had condemned Socrates. Under the impact of the scrutiny of the philosophers the old Greek polytheism

---

[1] cf. Hamlet's "Angels and ministers of *grace* defend us".

[2] *Acts* 17:22 ff.

had collapsed, but the charge of teaching subversive doctrines of any kind was always a current danger in missionary work. The audience, cultivated and ready to recognize allusion and quotation, would include Stoics and Epicureans. Paul's problem was to make certain that his speech had at least some points of contact with them.

The Stoics accepted an immanent and material God, a universal soul of fire which permeates the whole universe, and of which the undivided soul is a part. This soul returns to the God who gave it, as a spark returns to find survival in unity, but not individuality, in a great central fire. In life it is imprisoned in the polluted body,[1] and longs to return to its maker. There is the hope of at least a limited kind of immortality. The other part of St. Paul's audience, the Epicureans, followed a different (and now much misunderstood) philosophy. Its finest expression is in Lucretius' great metaphysical poem, *De Rerum Natura*. There *are* gods, but they do not concern themselves with the world of men; they exist apart. The universe is governed by chance; its components are the atoms which collide fortuitously. Pleasure is not positive happiness, but rather the absence of pain. The soul is dissolved at death; there is therefore no immortality to hope for, no punishment to fear.

In the passage that follows there is, clearly, an appeal to whatever elements in the two philosophies might extend towards some common ground. There had been many 'known' gods, and they had passed; or, 'living', exacted no more than a conventional acknowledgement. And Stoicism had some meeting-point with Hebrew monotheism. All three philosophies denied the resurrection. But Paul is a Pharisee, and behind his thinking there is the massive authority of the Law.

Then Paul stood in the midst of Mars' hill, and said, Ye men of Athens, I perceive that in all things ye are too superstitious.	This is the standard *exordium*: Phillips has 'Gentlemen of Athens'. The 'too superstitious' of *A.V.* sounds like an insult; we should prefer the 'uncommonly scrupulous' of *N.E.B.*, or Phillips' 'an extremely religious people'.

[1] cf. Pope:

"Most souls, 'tis true, but peep out once an age
Dull sullen pris'ners in the body's cage."

or Plotinus' "The body is the garment of the soul"—together with the clay-mire (earth *plus* water) images.

For as I passed by, and beheld your devotions, I found an altar with this inscription, TO THE UN-KNOWN GOD.[1] Whom therefore ye ignorantly worship, him declare I unto you.

This is the second step in the rhetorical progress, the *narratio*. The speaker does not mean that he saw worship or men at prayer: rather, the many shrines and altars which he would have noticed. There is no specific inscription of this kind known to scholars, but there were possibly altars to unnamed deities. The inscription gives the perfect opening. 'Ignorantly worship' has again an almost insulting tone and is better translated 'Whom ye worship is unknown'.

God that made the world and all things therein, seeing that he is Lord of heaven and earth, dwelleth not in temples made with hands;

Neither is worshipped with men's hands, as though he needed any-thing, seeing he giveth to all life, and breath, and all things;

There were Jews among the audi-ence, and they would perhaps recognize the quotation from *Is-aiah*:[2] 'Thus saith God the Lord, he that created the heavens, and stretched them out . . . he that giveth breath unto the people upon it, and spirit to them that walk therein.'

And hath made of one blood all nations of men for to dwell on all the face of the earth, and hath determined the times before ap-pointed, and the bounds of their habitation;

Again, half-quotations from *Genesis* and from *Deuteronomy*. 'The times before appointed' will soon become a key-phrase in the argument. *N.E.B.* has 'the epochs of their history' and a footnote 'or fixed the ordered seasons'. Since these read-ings are contradictory in sense, we may accept *A.V.* and regard 'the times' as God's promise revealed in history.

That they should seek the Lord, if haply they might feel after him, and find him, though he be not far from every one of us;

'Feel after him' is a strange and vivid image, which is retained by *R.V.* The image is presumably that of a tentative groping, as of a man

---

[1] There are other renderings: *R.V.*, followed by *N.E.B.*, 'To an Unknown God'. Phillips has 'To God the Unknown', which suggests a wholly different meaning.

[2] 42:5. But it would be possible to make a composite quotation on this theme from many sources: cf. *Ps.* 50:12: 'If I were hungry, I would not tell thee: for the world is mine, and the fulness thereof.'

with outstretched hands feeling his way in a darkened room. *N.E.B.* has the same basic idea, though with a different emphasis: 'and, it might be, touch and find him'. Is there not something to be said for the seemingly archaic 'feel *after*', connoting both the tentative gesture, as in darkness, and the *pursuit* of a figure that is perhaps moving, receding?

For in him we live, and move, and have our being; as certain also of your own poets have said, For we are also his offspring.

Persuasion has now moved from the conditional 'if haply' to the assertion of the fact; the point being demonstrated or hammered home by the quotation from Aratus of Soli. (*Phenomena*, 5.)

Forasmuch then as we are the offspring of God, we ought not to think that the Godhead is like unto gold, or silver, or stone, graven by art and man's device.

This leads through the last emphasized word *offspring*, which is repeated to stress this Jewish conception. The offspring, the begotten, rejects the artefact; as in the Second Commandment. Paul is shortly to have trouble with the silversmiths of Ephesus on this very matter.[1] It requires some imagination to perceive the importance of this argument in the Greek world. We are, at least overtly, conditioned against the worship of idols; and we are probably unsympathetic with the ancient view that a statue may become the 'home' for a god, and so induce him to reside there.

And the times of this ignorance God winked at; but now commandeth all men every where to repent:

'Winked at': the *A.V.* phrase has, today, overtones of levity which it has acquired. *R.V.* has 'overlooked', which is hardly more satisfactory. The reason for the 'now' of His revelation is not the strongest point

---

[1] *Acts* 19:23. We may quote from Phillips '. . . this man Paul has succeeded in changing the minds of a great number of people by telling them that gods made by human hands are not gods at all.'

of the argument; but the rhetoric is moving towards the new and wholly Christian doctrines of repentance and judgment.

Because he hath appointed a day, in the which he will judge the world in righteousness by that man whom he hath ordained; whereof he hath given assurance unto all men, in that he hath raised him from the dead.

Here St. Paul comes to the first critical point, the *conclusio*. The first clause follows logically from the previous verse. It is assumed that there *will* be a Day of Judgment. But now follow the specific doctrinal assertions.

(i) it will be judged 'in righteousness', according to specific moral standards.

(ii) it will be judged by *that man*: the phrase of *A.V.* has a certain weight, perhaps mystery, in its rhythmic setting.

(iii) Christ has been ordained of God. The question of the Father and the Son has not been raised: either out of deference to the Jews present, or because of its incredibility.[1]

(iv) Christ has risen from the dead.

This close-packed paragraph is of special interest. Its complexity may be seen by quoting the Phillips version:

For he has fixed a day on which he will judge the whole world in justice by the standard of a man whom he has appointed. That this is so he has guaranteed to all men by raising this man from the dead.

The idea of a day of judgment, and of the prior repentance, would be familiar to the Jews in the audience, a quotation is embedded in the *A.V.* phrase,[2] one of many possible ones from *Psalms* and the prophets. It would have been obscure to the Greeks present, though they would have allowed the possibility of individual judgment of the

---

[1] Perhaps not so incredible to the Greeks in the audience if we remember the numerous children fathered by Zeus upon earthly mothers: or the children of goddesses begotten by heroes.

[2] 'He shall judge thy people with righteousness, and thy poor with judgement.' *Ps.* 72:2.

dead. But the Phillips version brings in the idea, which does not seem to be explicit elsewhere, of a specifically *Christian* judgment.

There follows the final point, which is 'stated, not inferred', from what has gone before. The judgment to come is assured by the fact of the resurrection. To this the whole speech or lecture has been leading. Until these last statements there is little that would have been wholly new to the Stoics. God's omnipotence and omnipresence might not have been inimical to their pantheism; so also Paul's cyclic survey of history and peoples, But—

And when they heard of the resurrection of the dead, some mocked; and others said, We will hear thee again of this matter.	Some impression has been made on the audience, but this is the familiar obstacle: "... We preach Christ crucified, unto the Jews a stumbling-block, and unto the Greeks foolishness."[1]

A few are converted. 'Certain men clave unto him'; among them Dionysius, a judge of the Areopagus, said to have become the first Bishop of Athens. Of 'a woman named Damaris' nothing more is known.

iii

The Sermon on the Mount as set out in Matthew 6:24 ff., is perhaps the most famous and cogent passage of 'persuasion' in the Gospels. It is clear that it impressed its hearers by its power and authority. The discourse is built on the household language; aphorisms, gnomic sayings, proverbs arise from the simplicities of everyday life and affairs. Even in a short passage we can see the easy and graceful progress of the rhetoric, the intermixing of question, precept, references to Jewish history, the reliance upon the perennial images of seed-time and harvest.

No man can serve two masters: for either he will hate the one, and love the other; or else he will hold to the one, and despise the other. Ye cannot serve God and mammon.	In the previous verses Jesus has been expounding the dichotomies of light-darkness, unity and division. Now he draws the argument into an authoritative statement; this final dichotomy is impossible. Mammon has itself become proverbial, almost a personification:

[1] *I Cor.* 1:23.

N.E.B. has 'Money' (capitalized); Phillips, 'the power of money'.

Therefore I say unto you, Take no thought for your life, what ye shall eat, or what ye shall drink; nor yet for your body, what ye shall put on. Is not the life more than meat, and the body than raiment?

The two threads of the argument are intertwined. 'Money' provides what is necessary for life—had Jesus in mind the petition in *Proverbs*, 'Give me neither poverty nor riches; feed me with the food which is needful for me?'[1]

Body and Soul are creatures of God, so that the next illustration is drawn from the world of God's nature.

Behold the fowls of the air: for they sow not, neither do they reap, nor gather into barns; yet your heavenly Father feedeth them. Are ye not much better than they?

Persuasion is reinforced by the device of the *demonstratio*. The homely image carries many overtones: from *Genesis*, from the Ark, perhaps from the desert ravens that fed Elisha. So also 'There's a special providence in the fall of a sparrow'.[2] There is a special force in the 'human' activities of the birds.

Which of you by taking thought can add one cubit to his stature?[3]

Into the middle of the 'demonstrations' comes this sudden spear-like thrust, perhaps a proverb, bringing the argument to the individual, demonstrably valid. It seems to prepare the way for the visual images that follow (stature—clothing).

And why take ye thought for raiment? Consider the lilies of the field, how they grow; they toil not, neither do they spin:[4]

N.E.B. gives as an "alternative witness" 'Consider the lilies; they neither card nor spin, nor labour', so that the imagery of the making of

[1] 30:8.   [2] *Hamlet*, V. 2. 220, quoting *Mt.* 10:31.
[3] *N.E.B.* gives as an alternative reading 'Add a day to his life'.
[4] The simplicity and dignity of *A.V.* is emphasized if we consider an eighteenth-century versification:
> "Observe the rising lilies' snowy grace,
>   Observe the various vegetable race.
> They neither toil nor spin, but joyful grow,
>   Yet see how bright they blush, how warm they glow."
>   (Tate and Brady)

raiment is completed by 'card'.[1] The lilies of the field are probably anemones of the plains, or possibly the martagon lily. The white lily, which has become such a common Christian symbol, is comparatively rare in Palestine.

And yet I say unto you, That even Solomon in all his glory was not arrayed like one of these.

Solomon is a name of power, evocative of past glory and of the completed Temple.

Wherefore, if God so clothe the grass of the field, which today is, and tomorrow is cast into the oven, shall he not much more clothe you, O ye of little faith?

The analogy is pressed home, and the general sense is clear enough: but alternative translations modify the details of the images: e.g. . . . 'the grass in the fields, which is there today and tomorrow is thrown on the stove' (*N.E.B.*) '. . . the flowers in the field, which are alive today, and burnt in the stove tomorrow' (Phillips). Behind the thought there is, surely, the memory of *Isaiah*: 'All flesh is grass, and all the goodliness thereof is as the flower of the field'.[2]

Therefore take no thought, saying, What shall we eat? or, What shall we drink? or, Wherewithal shall we be clothed?

Perhaps the commonest aspect of rhetoric is the device of returning to attack the subject from subtly differing angles. We are now ready to return to the assertions of the second verse quoted; and then to amplify them.

(For after all these things do the Gentiles seek:) for your heavenly Father knoweth that ye have need of all these things.

'Gentiles'—the sentence is interjected almost casually, but the heavy stress upon it suggests an overtone of scorn. They are the materialists; the chosen people alone can distinguish spiritual values.

[1] This word, once of the 'household language', would now be quite unfamiliar.
[2] 40:6 see p. 120, *infra*.

But seek ye first the kingdom of God, and his righteousness; and all these things shall be added unto you.	This is the over-riding priority; all else follows.
Take therefore no thought for the morrow: for the morrow shall take thought for things of itself. Sufficient unto the day is the evil thereof.	The details of the whole act of 'persuasion' are now gathered up into a single exhortation, with a startling personification of time: which is then clinched with a proverb which has passed into the language.

The passage has evoked an enormous amount of commentary, and some varied opinions. It remains a model of this kind of persuasion. Its place among the values is discussed in the final chapter.

iv

The Lesson for the Burial of the Dead, *1 Corinthians* 15, is probably less often read to-day than formerly. There are many possible reasons why alternative passages are so often used.[1] It is a long passage, of great intricacy, which contains some difficulties. It uses a wide spectrum of the classic devices of rhetoric: interrogation, irony, invective. It is both personal and abstract, individual and universal. Because of its exquisitely contrived modulations of tone and stress it remains one of the greatest pieces of writing in the Bible.

It is not primarily directed to problems of morality, or to a discussion of the nature of the divine. Its theme is the conquest of death, and with it the conquest of fear. Death, that had laid such strong hold on the medieval imagination, that was to be the subject of so many horrible and macabre speculations in the pulpits of the seventeenth century, and which underlay the noble melancholy of the Graveyard School in the eighteenth, has been a permanent subject for the most intense poetry. Many, like Keats, have been 'half in love with easeful death'. Meditation upon it had been sanctioned by the Church: we remember the aphorism 'Live to die, and die to live eternally',[2] and Saint Augustine's terrible exhortation:

"If you realize . . . that death itself will not turn aside for any plea; that it is not the end of sufferings, but only a passage: if you picture for

[1] Such as *1 Cor.* 13, *Rev.* 21, and, often for the funeral of an agnostic, Donne's 'No man is an Island . . .'
[2] As on the altar of Lucas de Heere's Marriage Painting, in the Dulwich Gallery.

yourself a thousand forms of punishment and pain, the noise and wailing of Hell, the sulphurous rivers, the thick darkness, and avenging Furies— in a word, the fierce malignity everywhere of that dark abode; and, what is the climax of its horror, that the misery knows no end, and the despair thereof itself is everlasting, since the time of God's mercy is passed by . . . then you may be assured that you have not meditated in vain."[1]

Christianity is the only religion that turns upon an empty tomb. The complexities introduced by the Resurrection have no place in the Old Testament. In the New there is a fresh crop of hopes and fears, untempered by Stoic or Epicurean thought, or the doctrines of the Sadducees.

I have used the word 'complexities'. Death-attitudes in literature are a blend of the emotional components of the human imagination with whatever may be gathered to confront it of faith, or rationalism, or pessimism. The sensations which the living attribute to the dead body, the process of corruption, the pictures of hell and purgatory, combine to exacerbate the horror. The passage from *Measure for Measure*,[2] in which Claudio contemplates his impending execution, is perhaps the most famous example of fear working upon the mind.

With memories of the sermons of Donne and Jeremy Taylor, and of Browne's *Urn-Burial*, we may turn to the Lesson; and, if we are to do any justice to its organic structure and its tonal variations, we must take a passage of some length.

Now if Christ be preached that he rose from the dead, how say some among you that there is no resurrection of the dead?

But if there be no resurrection of the dead, then is Christ not risen:

And if Christ be not risen, then is our preaching vain, and your faith is also vain.[3]

This is the core of St. Paul's message. Everything turns on the fact of the Resurrection. The rest of the passage is focused on this assertion.

---

[1] *The Third Dialogue.*   [2] *v.* p. 27 *supra.*

[3] That He did not rise, but was taken down alive from the Cross, is the basic situation in George Moore's *The Brook Kerith* and his play *The Apostle*. In the latter Jesus, who has been taken from the Monastery of the Essenes to recuperate by the sea (having been restored to partial health by the devoted women), meets St. Paul back from one of his missionary journeys. There is no evidence for this, and many cogent arguments against it.

Yea; and we are found false witnesses of God; because we have testified of God that he has raised up Christ: whom he raised not up, if so be that the dead rise not.

The startling phrase 'false witnesses of God' picks up as it were the Ninth Commandment. The logic is inexorable.

For if the dead rise not, then is not Christ raised:

And if Christ be not raised, your faith is vain; ye are yet in your sins.

Now the theme is attacked in a reverse direction, bringing in the new factor of the redemption.

Then they also which are also fallen asleep in Christ are perished.

And there is no hope for those who have died in the Christian faith.

If in this life only we have hope in Christ, we are of all men most miserable.

As relying on a fabric of belief whose essence is the resurrection: perhaps also as having lost the consolations of the traditional philosophies.

Now a new 'movement' begins: the tone changes from argument, from a statement of the logical consequences of reliance on a false hypothesis, to a series of assertions; with a simultaneous appeal to history:

But now is Christ risen from the dead, and become the firstfruits of them that slept.

A.V. renders this with four strong rhythmic beats, like hammer-blows. This seems preferable to *N.E.B.*: 'firstfruits of the harvest of the dead', which introduces a wholly different meaning: as suggesting that the dead are in some way reaped or garnered.[1] The reference, which would have produced an immediate response, is central. The Resurrection took place on the day when the priest offered the first-fruits of the temple. And 'slept' is not only the commonest of all images for death,[2] but is caught up from *v.* 18 of this passage.

[1] The image is familiar through the parable of the tares and wheat.
[2] Donne's 'For us that die now and sleep in the state of the dead . . .'; Hamlet's 'To sleep, perchance to dream . . .'; Catullus' 'Nox est perpetua una dormienda'.

For since by man came death, by man came also the resurrection of the dead.

The cycle begins: Adam and Christ, the beginning and the end: we remember Donne's:

'We think that Paradise and Calvary,
Christ's cross and Adam's tree, stood in one place.
Look, Lord, and see both Adams met in me . . .'[1]

Is it too recondite to perceive an image-cluster gathering to itself *fruits*, the fruit of the tree in the garden, the Cross and its fruit?

For as in Adam all die, even so in Christ shall all be made alive.

But every man in his own order: Christ the first-fruits; afterward they that are Christ's at his coming.

There is to be a pattern in all this. There are now three reference-points, Adam, Christ, the Second Coming. Throughout runs the motif of the *aparchê*, the first-fruits, with all its implications: harvest, sacrifice, dedication.

Then / cometh / the end, / when he shall have delivered up the kingdom to God, even the Father; when he shall have put down all rule and all authority and power. For he must reign, till he hath put all enemies under his feet.

The four words, heavily stressed, sound like drum-beats: and the rhythm quickens, gathering up the next clause. Again we have the often-quoted image from *Psalms*,[2] which is hammered home in the next verse.

The last enemy that shall be destroyed is death.
For he hath put all things under his feet. But when he saith, all things are put under him, it is manifest that he is excepted, which did put all things under him.

That is, the last of the three: Satan, Sin, Death.

The sense is clear enough, but for once the syntax of *A.V.* has failed to match the compression of the Greek.

And when all things shall be subdued unto him, then shall the

We may perhaps see this difficult and repetitious passage as 'enclosed'

[1] *Hymn to God my God in my Sickness.*
[2] e.g. *Ps.* 110:1 'Sit thou at my right hand, till I make thine enemies my footstool.'
and 8:6   'Thou madest him to have dominion over the works of thy hands; thou hast put all things under his feet.'
But underlying the thought there is, always, the hope of deliverance from some occupying tyranny.

Son also himself be subject unto him that put all things under him, that God may be all in all.	between two gnomic statements 'Then cometh the end . . .' 'That God may be all in all'

The end has been variously interpreted, but there is the idea of the 'last trump', when Christ the Son would render back earthly dominion and power to the Father, while retaining his Sonship. At the 'end', God's dominion will be universal.

Else what shall they do which are baptized for the dead, if the dead rise not at all? why are they then baptized for the dead?	We are told[1] that there are over sixty interpretations of this verse. It is perhaps best taken as referring to the custom of vicarious baptism, undertaken by the early Christians on behalf of dead friends. It may possibly be a reference to death by martyrdom, as the equivalent to baptism.
And why stand we in jeopardy[2] every hour?	We may take this in two senses: why do Christians continue to run the risk of persecution and death? Why do we all continue to reject the faith which will remove all sense of fear and danger?
I protest by your rejoicing which I have in Christ Jesus our Lord, I die daily.	
If after the manner of men I have fought with beasts at Ephesus, what advantageth it me, if the dead rise not? let us eat and drink; for tomorrow we die.	Paul's life is continually subject to danger of death. But the beasts are best taken metaphorically; as a Roman citizen he would not have been thrown into the arena.
Be not deceived: evil communications corrupt good manners.	The scornful interjection—perhaps aimed at the Epicureans?

[1] *Peake's Commentary*, p. 964.

[2] This famous sentence is almost a test-case for the modernization of language. Phillips has 'Why should I live a life of such hourly danger?' *N.E.B.* 'Why do we face these dangers hour by hour?' Rhythmically, *jeopardy* forms the nucleus of the sentence. Clearly, one reference, perhaps the immediate one, is to the risks of persecution of all the members of the early Church. But the word has two overtones which are not brought out in modern versions: the placing of the individual 'within danger of the law', and the sense of hazard, as in the act of gambling. If we are aware of these ambiguities, we lose the strong sense of the folly of gambling on the proposition that there may not be a future life.

Awake to righteousness, and sin not; for some have not the knowledge of God: I speak this to your shame.

But some man will say, How are the dead raised up? and with what body do they come?

This is the beginning of the final symphonic movement of the argument. (The anticipation of objections is almost the commonest of rhetorical devices.)

Thou fool, that which thou sowest is not quickened, except it die:

Scorn meets disbelief. Now he begins to develop the archetypal image of the sowing of the grain; death in winter, rebirth in spring: Eleusis, Persephone, and in innumerable literatures.

And that which thou sowest, thou sowest not that body that shall be, but bare grain, it may chance of wheat, or of some other grain:

The seed may differ from the plant: Each seed carries its own potentiality of mutation. Perhaps there is an allusion to the sowing of a mixed crop?

But God giveth it a body as it hath pleased him, and to every seed his own body.

All flesh is not the same flesh: but there is one flesh of men, another flesh of beasts, another of fishes, and another of birds.

'Paul, like Galen, thought there were different kinds of flesh of men, of beasts, birds or fish.'[1]

There are also celestial bodies, and bodies terrestrial: but the glory of the celestial is one, and the glory of the terrestrial is another.

Now begins a long series of antitheses: building up, hammering home, the perpetual *differences*, to make clear the essential distinctions between the corporeal and the spiritual body.

There is one glory of the sun, and another glory of the moon, and another glory of the stars; for one star differeth from another in glory.

We may note the image-links—
celestial—sun—moon—stars
glory—resurrection—incorruption, returning always to the image of the seed.

So also is the resurrection of the dead. It is sown in corruption; it is raised in incorruption:

---

[1] *Peake's Commentary*, p. 964.

115

It is sown in dishonour; it is raised in glory: it is sown in weakness, it is raised in power:

It is sown a natural body; it is raised a spiritual body. There is a natural body, and there is a spiritual body.

Between the two there is continuity, but no identity. Again it is a typical device of rhetoric to move round the circumference of the subject, thrusting inwards at different points; appealing to authority by quotation.

And so it is written, The first man Adam was made a living soul; the last Adam was made a quickening spirit.

'And man became a living soul' (*Gen.* 2:7). 'For as the Father raiseth up the dead, and quickeneth them; even so the Son quickeneth whom he will.' (*Jn* 5:21.)

Howbeit that was not first which is spiritual, but that which is natural; and afterward that which is spiritual.

'Natural' man is made spiritual by the Covenant and by the Sacraments.

The first man is of the earth, earthy: the second man is the Lord from heaven.

Earth—earthy develops from *natural*: both related to the seed; as well as to the making of Adam's body from clay, and his return to the dust. In 1611 there would also have been a reference to the basest of the four elements—earth, air, fire, and water.[1]

As is the earthy, such are they also that are earthy: and as is the heavenly, such are they also that are heavenly.

And as we have borne the image of the earthy, we shall also bear the image of the heavenly.

We have moved through a cycle of imagination which starts with the sown seed, and passes through the natural phases of corruption, dishonour and what Donne called the 'dispersion' of the grave.

Now this I say, brethren, that flesh and blood cannot inherit the kingdom of God; neither doth corruption inherit incorruption.

This leaves no room for doubt as to the problem of physical resurrection, and would appear to negate that sentence in the Apostles' Creed:

[1] Fire and air are of the spirit, earth and water of the body: cf. Cleopatra's
"I am fire and air; my other elements
I give to baser life." (*A. & C.*, V. 2. 287.)

which many Christians now understand as 'the survival of personality' rather than 'the resurrection of the body'. All the momentum of the previous persuasion is now gathered up in the tone of authority, leading to this climax.

Behold, I shew you a mystery;[1]

We should be aware of the implications of this simple assertion. The essence of a 'mystery' is that we approximate to a conception of it only by image and symbol; because it is the 'hidden thing'.

We shall not all sleep, but we shall be changed,

In a moment, in the twinkling of an eye, at the last trump: for the trumpet shall sound, and the dead shall be raised incorruptible, and we shall be changed.
For this corruptible must put on incorruption, and this mortal must put on immortality.

Here the image of the trumpet (embodied in countless pictures and poems) is apocalyptic. Then, out of deference, perhaps, to the Greeks in the audience, we move into abstraction. In translation the sentences seem to writhe and coil, clumsily, round the theme.

So when this corruptible shall have put on incorruption, and this mortal shall have put on immortality, then shall be brought to pass the saying that is written,

'Put on' is surely an image of a garment;[2] ('As a vesture shalt thou change them', the 'man clothed in white linen' in *Revelation*.) Again, *Isaiah* 25:8: 'He will swallow up death in victory'.

Death is swallowed up in victory.
O death, where is thy sting?
O grave, where is thy victory?
The sting of death is sin; and the strength of sin is the law.

Death himself is often personified as a devouring monster: *v. Hamlet*, V. 2. 364. There are, now, not quotations, but a triumphant assertion. But *R.S.V.* has an interesting 'reversal', which gives a new meaning:
'O death, where is thy victory?
'O death, where is thy sting?'[3]

[1] Phillips, 'Listen, and I will tell you a secret' which has a strangely childish ring, besides (in my view) missing the point. *N.E.B.* has the slightly pompous, 'Listen! I will unfold a mystery', which seems to miss the implications, as I have suggested, of *shew*. 'Unfold' seems a slightly 'tired' metaphor.

[2] cf. also Porphyry: 'The body is the garment of the soul'.

[3] The *A.V.* version not only gives us a different rhythm—the long syllables of *victory* contrasted with the monosyllabic *sting*—but gives us the 'grave' personified

But thanks be to God, which giveth us the victory, through our Lord Jesus Christ.

Therefore, my beloved brethren, be ye steadfast, immoveable, always abounding in the work of the Lord, for as much as ye know your labour is not in vain in the Lord.

After that dramatic assertion the whole passage modulates into a downward curve, a gentleness of completion; yet picking up the key-words: victory, and the labour that is not in vain.

It seemed necessary to give the passage at length, for only then is it possible to show the immense variety of tone, the patterning of the arguments, in relation to the assertions and to the overall rhythm. And part of this most famous exhortation is well summed up by Sir Thomas Browne, which we may quote (in part) for the sake of contrast in style:

"How shall the dead arise, is no question of my faith. To believe only possibilities is not faith, but mere philosophy. Many things are true in Divinity, which are neither inducible by reason, nor confirmable by sense; and many things in philosophy confirmable by sense, yet not inducible by reason. . . . I believe that our estranged and divided ashes shall unite again; that our separated elements, after so many pilgrimages and transformations into the parts of minerals, plants, animals, elements, shall at the Voice of God return into their primitive shapes, and join again to make up their primary and predestinate forms.

As at the Creation there was a separation of that confused mass into its species; so at the destruction thereof there shall be a separation into its distinct individuals. As at the Creation that we behold lay involved in one mass, till the fruitful Voice of God separated this united multitude into its several species; so at the last day, when those corrupted reliques shall be scattered in the Wilderness of forms, and seem to have forgotten their proper habits, God by a powerful Voice shall command them back into their proper shapes, and call them out by their single individuals."[1]

V

There is a type of rhetoric which verges on the lyric: whose method of persuasion is the 'lyrical cry' and which is organized for that end. For a last example, therefore, I propose to take a few verses from the famous chapter (40) of the Second Isaiah, of what we may call 'oracular rhetoric'.

---

into some sort of adversary. *Sting* carries us back to the serpent imagery, as of the Garden. For the bee-sting imagery, *v.* p. 68 *supra*.

[1] *Religio Medici*, I. xlviii. (*Proper habits*: original or *rightful* clothing.)

Comfort ye, comfort ye my people, saith your God.

The prologue or invocation; the repetition of *comfort* being a common intensifying device. First, the prophet speaks: then the people add their voices.

Speak ye / comfortably / to Jerusalem, / and cry unto her, that her warfare is accomplished, that her iniquity is pardoned: for she hath received of the Lord's hand / double[1] for all her sins.

The message is to an exiled people, not to the city: 'Jerusalem' is the symbol of the race. 'Cry unto her' is later interwoven into the lyric pattern. Then we slip into well-defined prose-rhythms: the first two lines forming classical cadences, the last two—shortening down to the key-word—have the 'English' cadence, that emphasizes the strong final beat.

The voice of him that crieth in the wilderness,

'The *voice*' is either a poetical equivalent for 'Thus saith the Lord' or, more concretely, the voice of a member of Jehovah's heavenly council.[2]

Prepare ye the way of the Lord, make straight in the desert a highway for our God.

We must record the alternative reading: 'The voice of one that crieth,
Prepare ye in the wilderness the way of the Lord'.[3]
The imagery is as striking as the rhythm. The desert highway suggests the return from exile, God leading his people from bondage. It has complex overtones. The return from exile, or the return to righteousness, is to be made direct, straight. We remember also 'I am the *way*, the truth and the light', the imagery, in many religions, of

[1] The *double* measure of punishment reads strangely.
[2] *Peake's Commentary*, p. 517.
[3] *R.V.* But 'highway' has connotations that 'way' has not; as of a broad, secure, even 'royal' road. *R.V.*, which is accurate, brings out the parallelism at the price of a familiar image: 'The voice of him that crieth:
In the wilderness prepare ye . .
In the desert prepare ye . . .'

the narrow and straight way. But there is additional power in the next verse when we think of the geography of Palestine: the traditional roads deflected by wadis and hills, following, with a few notable exceptions, circuitous valley routes.[1]

Every valley shall be exalted, and every mountain and hill shall be brought low:

and the crooked / shall be made / straight, and the rough places / plain:

And the glory of the Lord shall be revealed, and all flesh shall see it together;

for the mouth of the Lord hath spoken it.

The rhythm just fails to be a 'poetic' one: designed to shorten down, for emphasis, to the final sentence. We may be aware of a 'hover' or missed half-beat, after 'rough' and 'places': as well as the momentum given by the alliterations and by the falling tone.

The oracular opening is picked up to round the passage, and to prepare for the next 'movement':

The voice said, Cry.

And he said, What shall I cry? All flesh is grass, and the goodliness thereof is as the flower of the field:

What is the first of the three massively weighted accents: the oracular monotone contrasted with the tone—perhaps frightened or submissive?—of the response.

The grass withereth, the flower fadeth: because the spirit of the Lord bloweth upon it: surely the people is grass.

The archaic suffixes emphasize the cadences. The springing of the grass after the rain, its withering in drought or wind from the desert, is a natural image. We may not do wrong to read 'grass' as the image of the people as a whole, and remember the archetypal flower-imagery for woman.

The grass withereth, the flower fadeth: but the word of our God shall stand for ever.

Again, the repetitions for emphasis: resolved into ten separate stresses.

O Zion that bringest good tidings, get thee up into the high mountain; O Jerusalem, that bringest good tidings, lift up thy voice with

This is spoken as by a herald, who is Zion proclaiming the news. It is addressed to the cities of Judah (now in secession); but the procla-

[1] See any physical map of Palestine.

strength: lift it up, be not afraid; say unto the cities of Judah, Behold your God!

mation applies to all Israel. 'Be not afraid'; perhaps with memories of Sinai, and similar epiphanies?

Behold the Lord God will come with strong hand, and his arm shall rule for him: behold, his reward is with him, and his work before him.

The arm is—as in *Psalms* and elsewhere—the image of strength. God will return with the recompense of his labour.

He shall feed his flock like a shepherd: he shall gather the lambs with his arm, and carry them in his bosom, and shall gently lead those that are with young.[1]

The final pictorial image of the passage. We have had the images of power. Now the lyric is resolved into the image of the shepherd which will appear so often in the New Testament.

vi

That image is perennial; but we miss, perhaps, much of its significance to-day. For this, and many other passages, we may quote a single description:

"Judaea offers as good ground as there is in the East for observing the grandeur of the shepherd's character. On the boundless Eastern pasture, so different from the narrow meadows and dyked hillsides with which we are familiar, the shepherd is indispensable. With us sheep are often left to themselves; I do not remember to have seen in the East a flock without a shepherd. In such a landscape as Judaea, where a day's pasture is thinly scattered over an unfenced tract, covered with delusive paths, still frequented by wild beasts, and rolling into the desert, the man and his character are indispensable. On some high moor, across which at night hyenas howl, when you meet him, sleepless, farsighted, weather-beaten, armed, leaning on his staff, and looking out over his scattered sheep, every one on his heart, you understand why the shepherd of Judaea sprang to the front in his people's history; why they gave his name to their king, and made him the symbol of Providence; why Christ took him as the type of self-sacrifice.

Sometimes we enjoyed our noonday rest beside one of those Judaean wells, to which three or four shepherds come down with their flocks. The flocks mixed with each other, and we wondered how each shepherd would get his own again. But after the watering and the playing were over, the shepherds one by one went up different sides of the valley, and each called out his peculiar call; and the sheep of each drew out of the

---

[1] *R.V.* 'those that give suck'. *A.V.* gives a more perfect rhythmical close, and perhaps an ambiguity which contains both images.

crowd to their own shepherd and the flocks passed as orderly as they came. *The shepherd of the sheep, when he puts forth his own sheep, he goes before them and the sheep follow him, for they know his voice, and a stranger will they not follow. I am the Good Shepherd, and know Mine own, and am known of Mine.* These words our Lord spake in Judaea."[1]

[1] George Adam Smith, *The Historical Geography of the Holy Land* (1966 edn.), p. 210.

We admire 'the infection of dignity' which the Bible has given to the style, here and elsewhere, of this great book.

CHAPTER EIGHT

A Note on the Psalms

i

AT THE OUTSET it is necessary, even at the risk of stating platitudes, to outline certain aspects of the *Psalms*. Of all the books of the Bible this is the most heterogeneous. We have grown accustomed to regard it as a unity without, perhaps, being fully aware that this aspect of it is, in a sense, imposed from without; the welding together of a sequence of one hundred and fifty lyrics, greatly varying in length, under the pressure of the times and customs that have embodied them into Hebrew and Christian liturgies. The Greek word *psalmos* stands for the Hebrew *mizmor*, a 'song with musical accompaniment'. Of the ancient musical settings, as of the accompanying instruments, we know little. An examination of the headings in the Authorized Version makes it clear that these sub-titles indicated not only putative or traditional authorship (e.g. 'A Psalm of David', 'To' [or 'For'] The Chief Musician'), but descriptive titles such as 'A Prayer'[1] or 'A Praise'.[2] Others take their titles from the instruments; a concert of stringed instruments or on a single one;[3] one is possibly for flutes. Another 'Upon Alamoth',[4] is 'in the manner of maidens', that is, for soprano voices; yet another, 'Upon Sheminīth',[5] for tenor or bass.[6] There are other obscure sub-titles, taken from names of tunes from the first words of songs. Some of these are in themselves attractive: that of Psalm 22 is 'The hind of the morning', of Psalm 60 'The lily of testimony', of Psalm 56 'The silent dove of them afar'. These recall *The Song of Songs*. The meaning of the famous *Selah*, which occurs seventy-one times, remains obscure; it is commonly reckoned to be 'a musical term of great antiquity; a musical interlude, or a louder accompaniment'.

There are other titles of authorship: Psalm 90 is of 'Moses',

[1] 17, 86, 90, 102, 142.   [2] e.g. 145.   [3] 4, 6, 54, 55, 67, 76.
[4] 46.   [5] 6, 12.   [6] or, 'an instrument of eight strings'.

seventy-three are ascribed to David, two to Solomon, twelve to 'Asaph', one of David's principal musicians, eleven to 'the sons of Korah', and one each to two Hebrew sages.[1] There are traditional divisions:

Book	I	1–41
„	II	42–72
„	III	73–80
„	IV	90–106
„	V	107–150

A pleasant little psalm concerning the conquest of Goliath[2] that begins

I was little among my brethren

is not included in the Canon. Pieces of Psalmody are embedded in various portions of the Old Testament; in *Jeremiah*, in *Job*, the hymns of the Second *Isaiah*, the songs of praise from the Three Youths in the fiery furnace, and several others.

Within the Canon is the so-called 'Elohistic Group', 42–83, that substitute for the god Jahweh the term Elohim, or God. There is the group 120–134 known as the Psalms of Ascent (typically, 'I was glad when they said unto me, "We will go up into the house of the Lord"'),[3] presumed to be the pilgrim songs of those who were 'going up' to Jerusalem. The collection was in fact the hymn-book of the Second Temple Services. In them each day of the week had its own special psalms for the morning and evening sacrifices. Thus 92 was 'A Psalm or Song for the Sabbath Day': 38 and 70 'to bring to remembrance' may have been associated with the offering of incense, at thank-offerings.

When we attempt to classify the subject-matter the whole becomes even more complex. There are prayers of many kinds; for pardon for sin, Job-like outbursts under personal illness or trouble, prophet-like outcries for the nation in persecution or exile. Other prayers relate to public worship: yet others are declarations of the poet's own integrity; others, and (these are most numerous) his trust in God. There are many psalms of praise, declaring God's attributes;

---

[1] 88 and 89: to Heman and Ethan the Ezrahites.

[2] Added by the Septuagint, but excluded from the Hebrew text. The poem has now been found in the Dead Sea material.

[3] There is an untranslatable pun in vv. 6–9 between *shalom* (peace) and the name 'Jerusalem'.

power, majesty, glory, goodness, mercy. Others are 'Psalms of Instruction', in part gnomic or proverbial in character. God metes out blessings on His people, and misery to His enemies; or is at least exhorted to do so. The excellence of God's Law is stressed repeatedly. A small but important group stresses the vanity of human life,[1] the theme of *Ecclesiastes*. There are Psalms prophetical, and Psalms historical, recalling the salvations of an epic past.[2]

All that is clear is that this vast and varied collection, to which there seems no parallel in any other literature, took the name of David from its chief writer, embodying Psalms 1 and 2 as a preface or introduction, and amalgamated with Levitical and Temple Songs. The geological strata of the dates of compositions and provenance (certain of the psalms are post-exilic) need not concern us here.

ii

We have thus a collection of lyrics, in which are embedded from time to time fragments of epic and historical elements, adapted through a very long period to liturgical uses. Their scale of emotions is not a wide one. Most of them concentrate on the attributes of God in all His aspects; but mainly on His righteousness. The complaints against Him, and they are many, do not doubt His omnipotence, but cry out against the slow, sometimes infinitely deferred, processes of His justice. That concern may be national, as in the lamentations of the exiles; or social, as in the stress on the miseries of the poor; or personal, as in the outcries of the poet in depression, sickness, poverty. Much of this outcry is concerned with the problem of Job: Why do the wicked flourish? The answers oscillate between assurance in ultimate justice, and seeming despair:

> For I was envious at the foolish, when I saw the prosperity of the wicked.[3]

and

> I have been young, and now am old; yet have I not seen the righteous forsaken, nor his seed begging bread.[4]

The *righteous* and the *wicked* are set in a continuous antithetical conflict, which is expressed in a wide range of imagery. 'The

---

[1] 14, 39, 49, 53, 73, 90. [2] Here the most typical are 78, 105, 106.
[3] 73:3. [4] 37:25.

wicked watcheth the righteous to slay him',[1] or to 'beat him with rods'.

> I have seen the wicked in great power, and spreading himself like a green bay tree.[2]

but also

> The righteous shall flourish like the palm-tree: he shall grow like a cedar in Lebanon.[3]

The liberation of the Israelites from Egypt provides the theme for a remarkable passage of nature-imagery:

> Thou hast brought a vine out of Egypt: thou hast cast out the heathen, and planted it.
>
> Thou preparedst room before it, and didst cause it to take deep root, and it filled the land.
>
> The hills were covered with the shadow of it, and the boughs thereof were like the goodly cedars.
>
> She sent out her boughs unto the sea, and her branches unto the river.
>
> Why hast thou then broken down her hedges, so that all they which pass by the way do pluck her?
>
> The boar out of the wood doth waste it, and the wild beast of the field doth devour it.[4]

Israel's present enemies, and their past victories, are often celebrated in epic fashion.[5] But one of the dominant cries which echoes through time is that of despair:

> How long, Lord? wilt thou hide thyself for ever? shall thy wrath burn like fire?
>
> Remember how short my time is: wherefore hast thou made all men in vain?
>
> What man is he that liveth, and shall not see death? shall he deliver his soul from the hand of the grave?[6]

---

[1] The 'ambush' image is a frequent one: cf. the 'liers in wait' of *Jg.* 9:25.
[2] 37:35.   [3] 92:12.
[4] 80:8 ff. And cf. especially *Jer.* 2:21: 'Yet I had planted thee a noble vine, wholly a right seed: how then art thou turned into the degenerate plant of a strange vine unto me?' We remember the wild boar as an image of destruction; cf. Hercules, Venus and Adonis, Diarmuid and Grania. 'The wild beast of the *field*' does not refer to the cultivated areas, but to the desert and undergrowth, particularly of the Jordan Valley; a constant menace to the settlers and their cattle.
[5] e.g. 83.   [6] 89:46–48.

The unique character of Israel in its relationship with God is stressed again and again:

> If thy children will keep my covenant and my testimony that I shall teach them, their children shall also sit upon thy throne for evermore.[1]
>
> He hath not dealt so with any nation . . .[2]

Of all the great deliverances the most important, and the most frequently recalled, is that from Egypt. Psalms 105 and 106 provide a kind of synopsis of *Exodus*. Illness and suffering, depicted in Job with heart-rending detail, are the punishments for sin. As in *Job* and Aeschylus, suffering is learning.

The characteristics of the imagery of the Psalms are commensurate with the imaginative pressure of such lyrics. They range over a narrow but intense field. The tree by the waters, the chaff on the threshing-floor; the weapons of war, sword, spear and buckler; the snares of nets, and the concealed pit in which his enemies seek to entrap the poet. God's justice is like sudden arrows. There is the perennial fear of the chariots and horses of the hostile tribes that surround Israel. Iron stands for bondage, and perhaps for the fear of the iron chariots of the Philistines, since 'there were no smiths found in Israel'. Honey, as always in the desert, is the emblem of a rare sweetness: but oil and butter suggest the smoothness of the deceiver or calumniator, as well as the 'fatness' in which the soul delights. The struggle in mire, or in the 'deep waters', reminds us of Bunyan's adoption of those images in *The Pilgrim's Progress*; as well as their perennial appearance in dreams and nightmares. The bird is the archetypal image of the soul:

> O deliver not the soul of thy turtledove unto the multitude of the wicked.[3]

The familiar *unicorn*, with all its associated myths, is now usually translated by *wild oxen*. The *Psalms*, like *Job*, draw on the wonders of nature with a peculiar felicity and freshness; which comes, as always in poetry, from the sense of engagement with a living world. We may quote one of the loveliest of these passages:

> He sendeth the springs into the valleys, which run among the hills.

[1] 132:12.   [2] 147:20.
[3] 74:19. For the bird-soul emblem, see E. A. Armstrong, *The Folklore of Birds*; as well as W. B. Yeats' use of swan and curlew for that purpose.

They give drink to every beast of the field: the wild asses quench their thirst.

By them shall the fowls of the heaven have their habitation, which sing among the branches.[1]

So the pastoral imagery of Psalm 23, too familiar to quote; or the famous

He shall come down like rain upon the mown grass: as showers that water the earth.[2]

which recalls so vividly the intricate and lovely scents of the grass and the reviving land.

iii

The *Psalms* show, in a concentrated form, the qualities and defects of all Hebrew poetry when it is transcribed into any English poetic structure. We have to attune ourselves once more to the monotony of repetition, since the whole poetic involves this parallelism, and, at times, statements that seem to have little other value.[3] It has been said that the Hebrew is by nature poetic, contemplative and introverted.[4] The style develops in a pattern that is concentric, or sometimes, I think, spiral. A central point is often indicated in the middle of repeated statements which work and wind about it.[5] It is well to distinguish two larger parallelisms, the first of thought-rhythm, the second of phonetic rhythm, which are properly communicated only in the Hebrew. The phonetic rhythm is based on accents, commonly four in each half-line, known as the *stichos*. The accents thus float as it were on the half-lines, but they are sustained by the underlying thought structure rather than by any isometric pattern. The accents may be separated by any number of syllables,[6] a fact apparent in the constantly modulating chants. There is, of course, no rhyme, but some critics[7] speak of 'rhyming of thoughts'.

[1] 104:10–12. We should remember the peculiar geographical and climatic features of Syria; the dramatic vivifying effect of the rains, which bring springs and streams so rapidly to life.　　　　　[2] 72:6.

[3] e.g. '. . . the pit was empty, there was no water in it' (*Gen.* 37:24).

[4] I am indebted, here as elsewhere, to I. Drijvers, *The Psalms, their Structure and Meaning.*

[5] I have in mind Herbert's phrase in *Jordan*:
> "As flames do work and wind, when they ascend,
> So did I weave myself into the sense . . ."

[6] cf. Hopkins' 'sprung rhythm'.

[7] e.g. W. O. E. Oesterley, *A Fresh Approach to the Psalms* (1937).

Commentators on the Psalms usually distinguish five types of parallelism:

(a) *Synonymous*

Be wise now therefore, O ye kings: be instructed, ye judges of the earth.

(2:10)

O Lord, rebuke me not in thy wrath: neither chasten me in thy hot displeasure.

(38:1)

(b) *Antithetical Parallelism* (in which the original statement is balanced by a directly opposite one)

Some trust in chariots, and some in horses: but we will remember the name of the Lord our God.

(20:7)

(c) *Synthetic Parallelism* (an extension of a homogeneous statement)

O sing unto the Lord a new song: sing unto the Lord, all the earth.

(96:1)

(d) *Progressive Parallelism*

Except the Lord build the house // they labour in vain that build it: except the Lord keep the city // the watchman waketh but in vain.

(127:1)

(e) *'Stepped' Parallelism*: in which a refrain reinforces the progression, as in certain Scottish ballads[1]

Sihon king of the Amorites:
>   for his mercy endureth for ever:

And Og the king of Bashan:
>   for his mercy endureth for ever: (136:19, 20)

We might attempt to show the five types diagrammatically, thus

We may remember, as somewhat similar poetic devices, the subtle shifting of the positions of noun, verb, adverb and adjective in the structure of the heroic couplet at its best, as in the hands of Pope; as

[1] We may, for example, recall the double refrain of 'A Lyke-Wake Dirge',
—*Every nighte and all . . .*
—*And Christ receive thy saule.*

well as the classic method of varying the monotony of the blank-verse line by caesura-shifts and by varied additions of extra-metrical syllables, or by 'reversed' feet.

iv

No parts of the Bible have been so much versified, paraphrased or used for the bases of poetic meditation. A study of the translations alone would fill a book. We can do no more than offer some examples from different ages. As a sample, let us consider the opening of the Vulgate version of Psalm 38 (39 in the Authorized Version) and set opposite to it a fine translation into modern idiom by Father Ronald Knox:[1]

Dixi: custodiam vias meas,	It was my resolve to live watchfully
Ut non peccem lingua mea;	and never use my tongue amiss;
Frenum apponam ori meo,	still, while I was in the presence
dum impius est coram me.	of sinners,
Obmutui silens, bono carens,	I kept my mouth gagged, dumb and
sed dolor meus recruduit.	patient, impotent for good.
Incalcuit cor meum intra me;	But indignation came back, and
cum consideravi, exarsit ignis:	my heart burned within me, the
locutus sum lingua mea.	fire kindled by my thoughts, so that
	at last I kept silent no longer.

We may admire the balance maintained between the demands of popular speech, and the sonorous strength of the Latin; though 'never use my tongue amiss' is surely less happy than 'ut non peccem lingua mea': 'impotent for good' seems brilliant for 'bono carens'. We now turn to the *A.V.*, perhaps unfamiliar because of our memories of Coverdale in the Cranmer Prayer Book.

> I said, I will take heed to my ways, that I sin not with my tongue: I will keep my mouth with a bridle, while the wicked is before me.
> I was dumb with silence, I held my peace, even from good; and my sorrow was stirred.
> My heart was hot within me, while I was musing the fire burned: then spake I with my tongue.

These last verses show up something of the limitations of Tudor English: as in the obsolescent 'I will take heed to my ways', 'I held my peace'. But even in an age unfamiliar with horses there is some force in 'I will keep my mouth with a bridle' (we remember Plato's

---

[1] One volume edition, 1961.

charioteer) instead of Knox's 'gagged'. It is not easy to choose between 'my heart burned within me' and 'my heart was hot within me', but we may recall this common fire-imagery for the coming of poetic or prophetic inspiration.

Let us look next at Sir Philip Sidney's version:

> "Thus did I thinck, I well will marke my way
>   Least by my tongue I happ to stray;
> I musle[1] will my mouth while in the sight
>   I do abide of wicked wight.
> And so I nothing said, I muett[2] stood,
>   I silence kept, even in the good.
>
> But, still, the more that I did hold my peace,
>   The more my sorrow did encrease,
> The more, me thought my heart was hott in me;
>   And as I mus'd such world to see,
> The fire tooke fire, and forcibly out brake;
>   My tongue would needes and this I spake: . . ."

Beside these we may set an early eighteenth-century version, the well-known Nahum Tate and Nicholas Brady:

> "Resolv'd to watch o'er all my ways,   I kept my tongue in awe;
> I curb'd my hasty words when I   the wicked prosp'rous saw.
> Like one that's dumb I silent stood   and did my tongue refrain
> From good discourse; but that restraint   increas'd my inward pain,
> My heart did glow with working thoughts   and no repose could take,
> Till strong reflection fann'd the fire,   and then at length I spake . . ."

We are made unpleasantly aware of the manipulations necessary to find rhymes (*awe—saw, take—spake*), the otiose adjectives (*strong reflection*), the heavy alliteration—which is almost a cliché—of *fann'd the fire*.

Or we may watch Addison making a wholly new poem on the familiar Nineteenth Psalm ('The heavens declare the glory of God, and the firmament showeth his handiwork').

> " The Spacious Firmament on high
> With all the blue Etherial Sky,
> And spangl'd Heav'ns, a Shining Frame,
> Their great Original proclaim:

[1] *muzzle.*   [2] *mute.*

Th' unwearied Sun, from Day to Day,
Does his Creator's Power display,
And publishes to every Land
The work of an Almighty Hand."

We have lost the 'tabernacle of the sun', the bridegroom coming out of his chamber, the sun as the runner of the race; all submerged in the resonant abstractions of Deism. In the second stanza Addison moves even further from the Psalm:

"Soon as the Evening Shades prevail,
The Moon takes up the wondrous Tale
And nightly to the list'ning Earth
Repeats the Story of her Birth:
Whilst all the Stars that round her burn,
And all the Planets in their turn,
Confirm the Tidings as they rowl
And spread the Truth from Pole to Pole."

But in fact this particular Psalm seems to have become widespread as a source of inspiration. Here is part of an adaptation by the Neo-Platonist poet, Henry More (1614–87):

"Sing aloud His praise rehearse
Who hath made the Universe.
He the boundlesse Heavens has spread
All the vital orbs has kned;[1]
He that on *Olympus* high
Tends his flocks with watchfull eye,
And this eye has multiplide
Midst each flock for to reside.
Thus as round about they stray
Toucheth each with out-stretch'd ray,
Nimble they hold on their way,
Shaping out the Night and Day,
Summer, Winter, Autumne, Spring,
Their inclined Axes bring.
Never slack they; none respires,[2]
Dancing round their Centrall fires.

In due order as they move
Echo's sweet be gently drove
Through Heaven's vast Hollownesse,
Which into all corners presse:

---

[1] *kned*: knitted together.   [2] *respires*: pauses for breath.

Musick that the heart of *Jove*
Moves to joy and sportfull love.
Fills the listning saylers ears
Riding on the wand'ring Sphears.
Neither Speech nor Language is
Where their voice is not transmisse . . ."[1]

Strange things are happening here. God and Jove, Olympus and the firmament are blended; perhaps we remember that synthesis of the decorations of the Sistine Chapel. Jove seems to converge on the Shepherd of Psalm 23, and the description of the Music of the Spheres in Plato's myth; and the 'list'ning saylers' we have an echo of

"These see the works of the Lord, and his wonders in the deep."[2]

In the last two lines we return to the direct words of the Psalm:

There is no speech nor language, where their voice is not heard.

Cowper is among the great hymn-writers; we may attempt to show his characteristic use of a number of passages from the Psalms in the 'weaving' of a single poem:[3]

"God of my life, to thee I call,
Afflicted at thy feet I fall;
When the great water-floods prevail,
Leave not my trembling heart to fail!

(i) Save me, O God, for the waters are come in unto my soul. I sink in deep mire, where there is no standing: I am come into deep waters, where the floods overflow me. (69:1–2)

(ii) Let not the waterflood overflow me, neither let the deep swallow me up . . . (69:15)

(iii) I am afflicted very much: quicken me, O Lord, according to thy word. (119:107)

Friend of the friendless, and the faint!
Where should I lodge my deep complaint?
Where but with thee, whose open door
Invites the friendless and the poor!

(i) But I am poor and sorrowful: let thy salvation, O God, set me up on high. (69:29)

(ii) For the needy shall not alway be forgotten: the expectation of the poor shall not perish for ever. (9:18)

[1] *The Philosophical Poems of Henry More*, "The Philosophers' Devotion", *ed.* Geoffrey Bullough, Manchester, 1931. 'The tyranny of rhyme' is well illustrated in the clumsy final conflict.   [2] 107:24.
[3] *Olney Hymns*, Bk. III, XIX: 'Looking upwards in a Storm'.

Did ever mourner plead with thee
And thou refuse that mourner's
   plea?
Does not the word still fix'd remain,
That none shall seek thy face in
   vain?

(i) (Perhaps) Psalm 27:8
   When thou saidst, Seek ye my
   face; my heart said unto thee,
   Thy face, Lord, will I seek.

Fair is the lot that's cast for me!
I have an advocate with thee;
They whom the world caresses
   most,[2]
Have no such privilege to boast."

(i) The lines[1] are fallen unto me in
   pleasant places; yea, I have a
   goodly heritage. (16:6)
(ii) 'For we have an advocate with
   the Father . . .'
(iii) (Perhaps) 'The rich he hath
   sent empty away'.

v

There are, of course, obscure passages. For an example we may take some familiar, even proverbial, verses of Psalm 58:4 ff. In *A.V.*:

> Their poison is like the poison of a serpent: they are like the deaf adder that stoppeth her ear.

> Which will not hearken to the voice of charmers, charming never so wisely.

> Break their teeth, O God, in their mouth: break out the great teeth of the young lions, O Lord.

> Let them melt away as waters which run continually: when he bendeth his bow to shoot his arrows, let them be as cut in pieces.

> As a snail which melteth, let every one of them pass away: like the untimely birth of a woman, that they may not see the sun.

> Before your pots can feel the thorns, he shall take them away as with a whirlwind, both living, and in his wrath.

It is clear that the Psalmist is calling down miscellaneous curses on the enemy. Job noted the terror of the lion's teeth;

> The roaring of the lion, and the voice of the fierce lion, and the teeth of the young lions, are broken.[3]

The difficulties begin at verse 7. In *R.S.V.* we have:

---

[1] Coverdale: 'the lot is fallen'; so proverbially.

[2] Note the eighteenth-century paraphrases; in this instance a particularly clumsy one.

[3] *Job*, 4:10. cf. Browning's image of the Judaean Hills—'like an old lion's cheek-teeth' ('Karshish').

> Let them vanish like water that runs away; like
> grass let them be trodden down and wither.

The first image seems to be that of a water-channel that is broken or leaking. But the image of the trodden and withered grass is something quite new, wholly unrelated to the *broken arrows* of *A.V.*: an excellent instance of the variations possible when we have a footnote 'Meaning of the Hebrew uncertain'. Clearly, the images of the drying water-course and the withered grass combine very much better than the broken arrows of the *A.V.*

So, too, the obscure 'snail that melteth'. Sir Philip Sidney in his verses saw the image as that of a snail robbed of its shell, shrivelling in the sun. To others there may be an overtone of the shell as an empty tomb. *R.S.V.* has

> Let them be like the snail which dissolves into slime

which we can at least visualize. The 'untimely birth' is not unfamiliar: we may think of Shakespeare's

> Abortive be it, prodigious and untimely[1]

—also of a curse. Verse 9 also presents difficulties; *R.S.V.* has

> Sooner than your pots can feel the heat of thorns,
> whether green or ablaze, may he sweep them away!

which is less clear than *R.V.*

> Before your pots can feel the thorns,
> He shall take them away with a whirlwind,
> the green and the burning alike.

The image is presumably that of the traveller in the wilderness, lighting his fire of desert thorn and coarse bents of grass; with the overtones of

> For as the crackling of thorns under a pot, so is the laughter of the fool:
> this also is vanity.[2]

We then have a sort of transference from the image to the accursed enemy; he is foolish, he is to be frustrated in his attempt to cook his meal; and the agency that scatters his fire is to be the whirlwind, like that out of which God speaks to Job. Again, we may note the

---

[1] *Richard III*, I. 2. 21. I am informed that 'dissolves into slime' means 'a miscarriage': which brings it still closer to Elizabethan usage. *v.* also *Love's Labour's Lost*, I. 1. 104.　　　　[2] *Eccl.* 7:6.

climatic conditions of the Holy Land; the sudden sand-laden winds from the desert.

vi

A minor but interesting aspect of the *Psalms* is in the adjustments that have been made in order to bring out their singable qualities in English. Clearly, a compromise has been necessary; between the directness of *A.V.* based on a text that is often uncertain, the Prayer Book version based on Coverdale, the *R.V.* and *R.S.V.*, and lastly the Revised Psalter of 1966. It will be remembered that the terms within which the most recent revision took place were to keep so far as possible to the Coverdale version (so as not to impair the traditional modifications made to enable it to be chanted) and at the same time to apply the most modern scholarship to the interpretation of some of the obscurities. I have space for no more than a single example: let us choose one of the greatest of all the poems, Psalm 90, and set together, in the first instance, *A.V.* and the normal Prayer Book version.

A.V.	*P.B.*
1. Lord, thou hast been our dwelling place in all generations.	Lord, thou hast been our refuge: from one generation to another.
2. Before the mountains were brought forth, or even thou hadst formed the earth and the world, even from everlasting to everlasting, thou art God.	Before the mountains were brought forth, or ever the earth and the world were made: thou art God from everlasting, and world without end.
3. Thou turnest man to destruction: and sayest, Return, ye children of men.	Thou turnest man to destruction: again thou sayest, Come again, ye children of men.
4. For a thousand years in thy sight are but as yesterday when it is past, and as a watch in the night.	For a thousand years in thy sight are but as yesterday: seeing that is past as a watch in the night.
5. Thou carriest them away as with a flood: they are as a sleep: in the morning they are as grass which groweth up.	As soon as thou scatterest them they are even as a sleep: and fade away suddenly like the grass.
6. In the morning it flourisheth and groweth up: in the evening it is cut down, and withereth.	In the morning it is green, and groweth up: but in the evening it is cut down, dried up, and withered.

7. For we are consumed by thine anger, and by thy wrath are we troubled.

For we consume away in thy displeasure: and are afraid at thy wrathful indignation.

8. Thou hast set our iniquities before thee, our secret sins in the light of thy countenance.

Thou has set our misdeeds before thee: and our secret sins in the light of thy countenance.

9. For all our days are passed away in thy wrath: we spend our years as a tale that is told.

For when thou art angry all our days are gone: we bring our years to an end, even as a tale that is told.

10. The days of our years are threescore years and ten: and if by reason of strength they be fourscore years, yet is their strength labour and sorrow; for it is soon cut off, and we fly away.

The days of our age are threescore years and ten, and though men be so strong that they come to fourscore years: yet is their strength then but labour and sorrow; so soon passeth it away, and we are gone.

11. Who knoweth the power of thine anger: even according to thy fear, so is thy wrath.

But who regardeth the power of thy wrath: for even thereafter as a man feareth, so is thy displeasure.

12. So teach us to number our days, that we may apply our hearts unto wisdom.

O teach us to number our days: that we may apply our hearts unto wisdom.

13. Return, O Lord, how long? and let it repent thee concerning thy servants.

Turn thee again, O Lord at the last: and be gracious unto thy servants.

14. O satisfy us early with thy mercy; that we may rejoice and be glad all our days.

O satisfy us with thy mercy, and that soon: so shall we rejoice and be glad all the days of our life.

15. Make us glad according to the days wherein thou hast afflicted us, and the years wherein we have seen evil.

Comfort us again: now after the time that thou hast plagued us: and for the years wherein we have suffered adversity.

16. Let thy work appear unto thy servants, and thy glory unto their children.

Show thy servants thy work: and their children thy glory.

17. And let the beauty of the Lord our God be upon us: and establish thou the work of our hands upon us; yea, the work of our hands establish thou it.

And the glorious majesty of the Lord our God be upon us; prosper thou the work of our hands upon us, O prosper thou our handy-work.

It will be clear that the Prayer Book version does not make alterations, other than very minor ones, whenever the *A.V.* text has in itself a singable quality, as in verses 3, 12. It has cut off the obsolete verb endings; *hadst* in v. 2, *flourisheth, withereth,* in v. 6, the second part of the original verse providing a different cadence ending. This care for the cadence is also apparent, often finding its mould through the polysyllables:[1]

1 . . . in all generations	. . . from one generation to another.
7 . . . by their wrath we are troubled	. . . are afraid at thy wrathful indignation.
11 . . . so is thy wrath	. . . so is thy displeasure
14 . . . be glad all our days	. . . be glad all the days of our life
16 . . . thy glory unto thy children	. . . and their children thy glory

Verse 4 presents an interesting problem:

> For a thousand years in thy sight are but as yesterday when it is past, and as a watch in the night.
>
> Thou carriest them away as with a flood: they are as a sleep . . .

The Prayer Book has

> Seeing that is past as a watch in the night. As soon as thou scatterest them they are even as a sleep . . .

which changes the meaning little.

But the Revised Psalter has something rather different:

> For a thousand years in thy sight are but as yesterday *even as it were a day that is past.*
>
> As a night watch that cometh quickly to an end thou scatterest them: *they are even as a dream and fade away.*

R.V. has a different version:

> For a thousand years in thy sight
> Are but as yesterday when it is past,
> And as a watch in the night.
> Thou carriest them away like a flood; they are as a sleep:

We may feel that to expand a *watch in the night* to *as a night watch that cometh quickly to an end* has lost something in conciseness as well as

---

[1] It seems in general as if *A.V.* favoured the English cadences, with the strong accent on the first syllable; the Prayer Book version tending more to the classical type, with the stress on the penultimate.

rhythm: that *scatterest* is different in meaning from *carriest away* and that *they are even as a dream* is rather more pedestrian than *as a sleep*.

At this point I must record the interpretation put forward by the Regius Professor of Hebrew[1] at Cambridge:

"Psalm 90:5 is almost impossible to translate (as are 4 and 5) as they stand. If, as is thought by some, the psalmist's theme is the unclean origin of men in procreation and birth,[2] the Hebrew text, with the transposition of only one letter, yields the sense 'from (as a result of) emission of seed in sleep ($=concubitus$) are they' (this translation takes the place of 'thou carriest them away like a flood')."

The same authority has pointed out to me that the last clause of Psalm 127:2

"for so he giveth his beloved sleep."

refers to the sexual act, so that the Revised Psalter has adopted C. S. Lewis' proposal

"for he blesseth his beloved in their beds."

We need not cavil at, or deprecate out of prudery, such readings. The euphemisms 'sleep' and 'death' are familiar in literature, and we may recall Yeats' exquisite *Lullaby*:

"Belovéd, may your sleep be sound
That have found it where you fed."

Be gracious unto thy servants (v. 13) is clearly lighter and more graceful than the archaic and clumsy *let it repent thee concerning thy servants* of *A.V.*, though the equally archaic *tarry not* has appeared in the latest version, instead of the simple, and more profound, *Turn thee, O Lord, at the last.*

vii

Within the terms which I have proposed, the Psalter is clearly the most difficult book to assess as literature, without falling into *hubris* or what some might consider blasphemy. The *Psalms* have been sung or recited, for centuries, in many languages, settings, metrical versions. Their familiarity for the common reader is probably greater than that of any portion of the Bible, with the exception of the Four Gospels and the opening chapters of *Genesis*. They are the source of many phrases, idioms, proverbs and images which still live in the

---

[1] Professor D. Winton Thomas; to whom my debt is great. *v.* his article on this subject in *Vetus Testamentum* 18 (1968), pp. 267 ff.   [2] cf. 52:5, *infra*.

language. It would be tedious to rehearse them. They are frequently quoted in the New Testament; Jesus appears to have been specially fond of them. And, at one point or another, they epitomize most, perhaps all, of the major themes and wisdoms of the Old Testament.

But these things alone do not make the *Psalms* significant as literature. Let us examine, for a moment, the negative side of the picture.

This, we repeat, is a collection of lyrics, of widely varying dates, embodying fragments rooted in the poems of other nations, and deriving something from the music-loving Egyptians.[1] They are full of borrowings from the surrounding literatures of the Middle East.[2] The conception of God is frequently primitive. He is frequently given human attributes, which we must, of course, construe in a figurative sense. There are few passages which emphasize monotheism. God is the creator of all things, and there is some ground for attributing to Him a profound mind:

O Lord, how great are thy works! and thy thoughts are very deep.[3]

There is a constant recapitulation of Jewish history, the deliverance from Egypt, the conquests of Canaan. God is invoked continually: to pardon the backsliding of His people, to assist them against their enemies and oppressions. The evils which the poet suffers are the consequences of his own sin; both actively by his own wrong-doing, but also as a predestined fate:

Behold, I was shapen in iniquity; and in sin did my mother conceive me.[4]

Sin (as with Job) may be unrecognized:

Who can understand his errors? cleanse thou me from secret faults.[5]

God is all-knowing—

Thou hast set our iniquities before thee, our secret sins in the light of thy countenance.[6]

and yet—

He hath not dealt with us after our sins; nor rewarded us according to our iniquities.[7]

---

[1] *v.* especially *Ps.* 104.

[2] The lovely phrase 'Hide me under the shadow of thy wings' (17:8) is, we are told, taken from the idea of the wings of the Sun-God (Oesterley, *op. cit.* p. 208).

[3] 92:5. [4] 51:5. [5] 19:12. [6] 90:8. [7] 103:10.

The wicked are, sooner or later, subject to divine retribution. In the perfect world of God's justice and omniscience, the wicked should not flourish. If they appear to do so, this is only temporary:

> For they shall soon be cut down like the grass, and wither as the green herb. (37:2)

But the great problem of the *Psalms* as literature seems to be implicit in the fact that they are lyrics which were designed for musical accompaniments of many kinds. What seems to be their central deficiency, that of repetition and monotony, is implicit in these poetic structures, and is in any event submerged in their musical statements. Perhaps all liturgies are open to criticism because of their repetitions; which may be justified on various grounds, but become doubly monotonous when read. And too many of the *Psalms* seem to follow a kind of formula. The poet describes his own state of misery, depression, sickness; he bewails the attacks of his enemies, 'the wicked', whether these are personal (they often appear to be so) or national. He asserts his own righteousness, or his repentance, and calls for God's vengeance upon his enemies. The formulation of individual troubles, the assertion of a faith in ultimate justice, may indeed have significant value for the individual; we should not minimize, in the face of literary history, the strong cathartic value of the 'complaint' or 'lament', and the recognition that such outcries can become, in some measure, anodynes for suffering. We should not deny that pessimism is on occasion, valuable; as inculcating the virtues of humility, patience, faith, courage. But, taken in bulk, and without the supporting music and the strong compulsion to worship, the reader may well feel baffled and a little depressed.

Such an effect is mitigated a little by detailed exegesis of each text; of the historical setting of each; and our knowledge of the traces of other and older faiths that illuminate certain aspects of the imagery.[1]

It is, perhaps, those *Psalms* which are of most concern to-day—always within the terms which I have postulated—are those which communicate, with vitality and simplicity, the poet's intense joy in nature. We may name some of them:

> As the hart panteth after the water brooks . . .   (42)
>
> God is our refuge and strength . . .   (46)

---

[1] e.g. the complexities of angelology and demonology, *v.* Oesterley, *op. cit.* ch. xv.

Give the king thy judgements, O God . . .   (72)

Give ear, O Shepherd of Israel . . .   (80)

He that dwelleth in the secret place of the most High   (91)

Bless the Lord, O my Soul . . .   (104)

We should include the Love Song or Epithalamium (45) for its exquisite imagery; together with the incomparable nineteenth and twenty-third. But is there not room for a small selection of these and other of the greatest psalms? purified, perhaps, of what we are told may be interpolations, textual corruptions and the dark places of the 'uncertain Hebrew'.

CHAPTER NINE

The Book of Job

Canst thou by searching find out God?
(11:7)

i

No book of the Old Testament, with the exception of the early chapters of *Genesis*, and the *Psalms*, is better known than that of *Job*. Its title and theme and gnomic sayings have passed into the language, its poetic images into the consciousness of many nations. It does not fit into any literary category. It has a remarkable range and intensity of imagery, more especially that drawn from the natural world.

It is nearly but not quite a tragedy, though it is sometimes written of as such. It offers a supreme opening for the agnostic, on several grounds, for it seems to be a refutation of the familiar text:

> I have been young and now am old; yet have I not seen the righteous forsaken, nor his seed begging bread.[1]

and, from another viewpoint, a denial of the many assertions that this 'forsaking' is a punishment on a nation or individual for some estrangement from God. (This is a constant theme of the prophets.) Here is, on the face of it, a monstrous narrative. As a result of a boastful statement to Satan,[2] there is a kind of wager between Satan and Jehovah. To justify himself, Jehovah delivers Job into Satan's hands, with the one reservation that sounds ironic in view of Job's subsequent tortures:

> Behold, all that he hath is in thy power; only upon himself put not forth thy hand.[3]

---

[1] *Ps.* 37:25.
[2] It has been noted that, in the writings before *Amos*, Jehovah can be moody and capricious, subject to violent outbursts of wrath.
[3] 1:12.

This same permission is repeated later:

> And Satan answered the Lord, and said, Skin for skin, yea, all that a man hath will he give for his life.
>
> But put forth thine hand now, and touch his bone and his flesh, and he will curse thee to thy face.
>
> And the Lord said unto Satan, Behold, he is in thy hand; but save his life.[1]

To prove God's point, the whole patriarchal household is, one by one, destroyed: herds and flocks, camels, the young men and women of his household, in a series of catastrophes, narrated by messengers as in a Greek play. For these there is not the slightest justification; they are in no sense the 'sacrifices' of a tragic pattern. Job himself is afflicted, as part of the 'trial' with the most horrible and painful diseases. His response to his 'trials' and the speculations of his friends on their causes, is the theme of the book.

ii

It is first of all necessary to place this dramatic dialogue in some kind of perspective, and to do so it is essential to take advantage of the findings of modern textual criticism.

The book is the result of a conflation of two works; the popular prose prologue in Chapters 1 and 2—which explains the repetitive elements in them—and an extrinsic Epilogue, with fairy-tale qualities of magical restitution, in Chapter 42:7–17. It was probably written in the fourth century B.C. (a little after the period of Aeschylus) and is the product of mature Hebrew thinking. It has been divided into five distinct parts:

The Prologue, 1 and 2
The Dialogues 3–31
The Speeches of Elihu, 32–37, which are
    probably a later interpolation
The Speech of Jehovah, 38–42:6
The Epilogue 42:7–17

Nor is there any unanimity of critical opinion as to detail. Chapter 28, of which a great part is a poem on Wisdom built on analogy from the mining of metals and precious stones, is believed by some scholars to be of secondary origin. The ending of Chapter 27 appears

---

[1] 2:4 ff.

to fade out, perhaps because of a *lacuna*. There are many textual difficulties and uncertainties.[1]

We have therefore two narratives, not one. The 'popular' one teaches that a pious man may, in spite of his utmost piety and care for ritual, fall into misfortune, but that Jehovah will restore the balance of his prosperity, suitably multiplied, at the end of the 'trial'.

We do not ask what has happened to his dead children. His wife remains a witness, usually passive, of his sufferings. His family and herds are restored, almost laconically, at the end, by a miraculous extension of life and virility. The unknown poet of the central part of the book views the matter very differently. The misfortunes and suffering of the good and pious are a fact of human experience. He appeals to this experience, as against the ordinary Jewish belief that God always, *in the end*, rewards the righteous and punishes the wicked: even without our memory of the New Testament version of Dives and Lazarus. Sin, and its reward in some form of temporary chastisement, are forgotten; this is a more profound problem, perhaps the most profound and intractable in literature. We can at least postulate some of the causes of Lear's sufferings, both in events and in character; but none for those of Job.

The poem is not a theodicy;[2] it does not set out to justify the ways of Jehovah to man. It probes continually, through the chorus-figures, for possible explanations. Job's sin may be some secret one, of action or of thought; against unconscious neglect of ritual, or of some unknown sin, he has, as he thinks, insured by his sacrifices. Jehovah may assert that man's spirit is equal to any trial; Job is not so certain, either of his own power, or of Jehovah's goodness and wisdom in permitting it. The Three Friends, who put forward the current theory of just though obscure causation, are effectively silenced by Job. The young man, Elihu, who approaches the problem from a slightly different angle, is no more successful; he is arrogant in his approach, and even more tedious in his repetitions.

I have said that it is nearly, but not quite, a tragedy. It follows the familiar trajectory of prosperity passing through loss to the extremity

---

[1] 'When the Old Testament part of the New English Bible appears, *Job* will read like a new book.' (F. F. Bruce, *op. cit.*, p. 146.)

[2] Pfeiffer (*Introduction to the Old Testament*, London, 1952) quotes Kant's definition: 'Theodicy is the defence of the most exalted wisdom of the creator of the world against the accusations presented against it by reason, on account of the anomalies of the world.'

of personal suffering, to a state approaching death. If there had been some hint of causation, some past evil or some motion to trigger off the tragedy, and if it had then ended with Job's death, and Jehovah's great *apologia* become a lyric Chorus,[1] we might have had something close to the classical tragic pattern. The Epilogue of the restoration, shocking in its improbabilities and abruptness, softens and blunts any possible edge of tragedy.

We may discuss, briefly, two aspects which may be thought to converge on, or at least gesture towards, a solution.

The first is the prophetic statement of faith, one of the rare instances in the Old Testament where an after-life is involved. It is too famous not to require quotation:

> For I know that my redeemer liveth, and that He shall stand at the latter day upon the earth:
> And though after my skin worms destroy this body, yet in my flesh shall I see God.[2]

It is well to look at the Revised Version:

> But I know that my redeemer (or, *vindicator*) liveth, and that he shall stand up at the last upon the earth (or, *dust*):
> And after my skin hath been thus destroyed, yet from (or *without*) my flesh shall I see God.

The 'redeemer' appears to be God seen as a 'champion', who will 'defend' Job's soul after his death.

> Yea, his soul draweth near unto the grave, and his life to the destroyers.
> If there be a messenger with him, an interpreter, one man among a thousand, to show unto man his uprightness:
> Then he is gracious unto him, and saith, Deliver him from going down to the pit: I have found a ransom.[3]

iii

It is the statement of the second dilemma that is the reason for the book's greatness. In this poetic epiphany there is no explanation of the problem of evil or of suffering, apprehended through multiplex experience and finding expression through poetry, that enables us to

---

[1] Perhaps like that of *Samson Agonistes*. We know that Milton regarded *Job* as a 'brief' epic.　　　　　[2] 19:25, 26.
[3] 33:22–24. The pit is Sheol, the country of the dead.

approach to an acceptance of the aspect, perhaps the single most important one, of the human situation. As general propositions:

Pain and suffering are not to be regarded as punishment, but as redemptive and sacramental. God also suffers.[1]

Life is a spiritual pilgrimage, beyond all manifestations of orthodox theology, towards faith and hope.

God's essential and ultimate goodness is exemplified in the *poetry* of his creation, which is to be perceived in the expression of ultimate power, order, *phusis*.

This is a poetic assertion, not susceptible to argument or even to apprehension. Or, if we choose, ultra-rational.

As a poetic assertion it underlies some of the greatest literature. It is sufficient to quote from certain of the more famous statements into which it has been compressed:

> "For good comes in evil's traces,
>   And the evil the good displaces,
>   And life 'mid the changing faces
>   Wandereth weak and blind."[2]

> "Suffering is permanent, obscure and dark,
>   And shares the nature of infinity."[3]

> "Wilt thou, I pray, demand that demi-devil
>   Why he hath thus ensnared my soul and body?"[4]

> "My soul, like to a ship in a black storm,
>   Is driven, I know not whither."[5]

> "The President of the Immortals had finished his sport with Tess."[6]

>   "No, no, no life!
>   Why should a dog, a horse, a rat have life,
>   And thou no breath at all? Thou'lt come no more,
>   Never, never, never, never, never!"[7]

The indictment of the justice of the world is as old as *The Songs of the Harper* and the Babylonian *Dialogue with a Servant*.[8]

---

[1] I am indebted to Kazoh Kitomoro, *The Theology of the Pain of God* (in Japanese, 1946; first British edn. 1966). The theology is controversial.

[2] Euripides, *Hippolytus*, tr. Gilbert Murray.

[3] Wordsworth, *The Borderers*.   [4] *Othello*, V. 2. 302.

[5] Webster, *The White Devil*.   [6] Hardy, *Tess of the D'Urbervilles*.

[7] *King Lear*, V. 3. 306.

[8] cf. *Documents from Old Testament Times*, *loc. cit.*

iv

The dilemma of the author is expressed simply by the Three Friends, who each state and re-state the problem, even to the point of weariness. Jehovah is ultimately the embodiment of justice. Affliction must imply sin, overt or hidden, at some period in the sufferer's life. Prosperity is the outward sign of righteousness. (We may remember countless instances of the principle demonstrated, often pharisaically, in Victorian morality.) To deny the principle of justice in God's dealing is wholly against the current of Hebrew thought. That desert monotheism gave no opportunity for dispersed or irrational causation, such as was readily provided by divine rivalries like those within the Greek Pantheon, or the ambivalent and menacing thunderclouds of curse or oracle.

Job's torments, physical and mental, appear to increase steadily through the book. We may divide the dialogue into cycles. The first is 4:1 to 19:22.[1] Eliphaz, who opens it, states the normal case. He is a little pompous, even complacent. God is all beneficent, all-wise. Therefore Job *must* have sinned. Therefore he must regard his present misfortunes as a just punishment. If he does this, all will yet be well. But Job makes the obvious point. Why should he repent when he does not know what he is to repent of? He is not conscious of any sin, or even of ritual neglect. The Prologue has stated the ultra-precautionary measures he has taken against some unconscious sin. And he parodies a Psalm.[2] 'What is man that thou art mindful of him, and the son of man that thou so regardest him?' His own strength, his power to bear pain, has its limitations. His friends—he implies this—are treacherous: and in a magnificent simile

> He who withholds kindness from a friend
>   forsakes the fear of the Almighty.
> My brethren are treacherous as a torrent-bed,
>   as freshets that pass away.
> which are dark with ice,
>   and where the snow hides itself.[3]

The terrors of God do set themselves in array against me.[4]

Bildad the Second Friend is equally futile. Job is wrong to attribute injustice to God. God *must* be right. Job's children, he says, must

---

[1] I am indebted to William Neill's *Commentary.*
[2] 8:4.   [3] 6:14–16 (*R.S.V.*).   [4] 6:4.

have sinned; that is why they were all killed. (We remember Job's sacrifices to avert just this contingency; in case the children had sinned inadvertently. There is not the slightest hint that they did.) The fact that Job himself was not struck down in the early catastrophes is a proof that Job's sin was only moderate. Let him endure, and then:

> Behold, God will not reject a blameless man,
>   nor take the hand of evildoers.
> He will yet fill your mouth with laughter,
>   and your lips with shouting.
> Those who hate you will be clothed with shame,
>   and the tent of the wicked will be no more.[1]

Job's reply reaches the height of despair. The whole world is unjust. Might is right. God, who has created him, is now hunting him.[2]

> And if I lift myself up, thou dost hunt me like a lion.

Why cannot God leave him alone?

> . . . Let me alone, that I may find a little comfort
> before I go whence I shall not return,[3]
>   to the land of gloom and deep darkness,
> the land of gloom and chaos,
>   where light is as darkness.[4]

The second cycle of speeches begins at chapter 15. It is clear that tempers are rising. The three Comforters seem to find their patience wearing thin. Eliphaz becomes rather specious.[5] Even if the wicked *seem* to prosper they surely suffer in their consciences. Job (rightly) dismisses this as sophistry. Bildad renews his attack, and again implies that Job *must* have sinned. He draws a violent picture of the fate of the wicked,[6] to which Job replies with equal violence:

> How long will ye torment me,
>   and break me in pieces with words?[7]

It seems as if the symptoms of the disease, and his pain, are growing steadily worse; as we should expect from his rising exasperation with

---

[1] 8:20–21 (*R.S.V.*).
[2] 10:16 (*R.S.V.*) cf. Francis Thompson, *The Hound of Heaven*.
[3] *v. Hamlet*: 'The undiscovered country, from whose bourn/No traveller returns.'
[4] 10:20–22 (*R.S.V.*).
[5] It is pleasant to note that 'comforters' probably means 'wind bags'.
[6] Ch. 18.   [7] 19:1 (*R.S.V.*).

the Comforters. He is becoming, as we should expect, obsessed with death:

> I am repulsive to my wife,
> loathsome to the sons of my own mother . . .
> My bones cleave to my skin and to my flesh,
> and I have escaped by the skin of my teeth.[1]

Zophar—his character is emerging as a rather stupid, bitter, self-righteous rationalist—returns to his stock argument. Now they are trying to extort from Job *some* confession of guilt, otherwise all their arguments fall to the ground. Job is reduced to questioning the whole moral order. His experience is wholly contrary to the ultimate redressing of the balances that the friends have urged as the very basis of their philosophy. *It is not so.*

> Why do the wicked live,
> reach old age, and grow mighty in power?
> Their children are established in their presence,
> and their offspring before their eyes. . . .[2]

There is no justice in this random universe:

> One dies in full prosperity,
> being wholly at ease and secure,
> his body full of fat,
> and the marrow of his bones moist.[3]
> Another dies in bitterness of soul,
> never having tasted of good.
> They lie down alike in the dust,
> and the worms cover them.[4]

We may remember Shirley's 'The glories of our Blood and State':

> . . ."Sceptre and Crown
> Must tumble down,
> And in the dust be equal made
> With the poor crooked scythe and spade."

as well as Donne's terrible sermon on 'Vermiculation'.[5]

In the third movement or cycle Eliphaz, having exhausted his gentler arguments for God's providence, descends to abuse. In an

---

[1] 19:17, 20 (*R.S.V.*).   [2] 21:7, 8 (*R.S.V.*).
[3] cf. the image 'My strength is dried up like a potsherd'.
[4] 21:23–26 (*R.S.V.*).
[5] Based on 17:14. 'I have said to corruption, Thou art my father: to the worm, Thou art my mother, and my sister.'

incredible passage he accuses Job—without the slightest pretext that we can see—of sheer wickedness. 'There is no end to your iniquities.' He has stripped the naked of their clothing, and sent widows away empty. The only things left for Job is to 'agree' with God, and he will immediately be rewarded. After the middle of Chapter 24 the text becomes confused. There are no new arguments. Chapter 28 contains the magnificent *excursus* on wisdom; its hidden attributes, its existence uniquely in the understanding of God. All this is developed through a series of progressive imagery in terms, first of gold mining and metallurgy, and passing through a kind of cosmic dialogue to celebrate God Himself. Once more Job asserts his righteousness, and curses His injustice, His cruelty and persecution. It is difficult to refrain from quoting:

> Thou liftest me up on the wind,
>   thou makest me to ride on it,
>   and thou tossest me about in the river of the storm.[1]
> Yea, I know that thou wilt bring me to death
>   and to the house appointed for all living.[2]

We expect much from the coming of the young man, Elihu, and it is disappointing to find that he has nothing new to say. 'I am young and ye are very old.' It is, at first, the exultant arrogant challenge of youth to age. He has listened in respectful silence while his elders spoke (it is one of Job's complaints that now, in his affliction, he, an elder, is interrupted by children) but he merely repeats the old stereotyped arguments. It is some little consolation to know that Chapters 32–37 are generally held to be a later interpolation, inserted to confirm orthodox doctrine. We may note that this 'Elihu' passage is far more abstract, less rich in forceful imagery, than the rest of the book; as such, it is a poetic foil to Jehovah's first speech in Chapter 38.

V

One way by which we may perceive the 'peaks', as it were, of this Book is to examine the sequence of Blake's illustrations for it.[3] No one but a great poet and artist could have compassed such a

---

[1] cf. *Measure for Measure* (*cit.* p. 27): and the compelling imagery of wave and flood.   [2] 30:22, 23 (*R.S.V.*).
[3] Better, perhaps, what Foster Damon, to whom all Blake scholars are profoundly indebted, calls Blake's 'invention'.

subject; no other book could have stirred so profoundly Blake's powers as visionary and a prophet. It is illuminating to consider the series in outline.

We begin with the text 'Thus did Job continually . . .;' offering the sacrifice of prayer for himself and his family. He has seven sons and three daughters; the proper number for a patriarch, since sons should out-number daughters. There are sheep sleeping in the foreground; the sun is setting; a crescent moon rises behind. On the tree at Job's back are hanging musical instruments, but no one plays on them; probably derived from Psalm 137: 'As for our harps we hanged them up: upon the trees that are therein.' In the background there is a *gothic* church, a symbol of Christianity which Blake opposes to the *classical* structure of paganism. The next, 'When the Almighty was yet with me, when my children were about me', shows Job and his family on the lowest of three tiers in the picture: in the middle tier, above a cloud-layer are the weeping angels, one poised on either side of Satan: the topmost, God Himself, with an open book on His knees,[1] set against the disc of the sun, and surrounded by two 'whirlwind' spiral clouds. There are many marginal illustrations and texts.

The third is the catastrophe of the falling house; the young men and maidens overwhelmed by the crashing columns and lintels. Satan hovers, like a black bat,[2] above the falling ruin. In the fourth a messenger—'and I only am escaped to tell thee'—comes running to where Job and his wife sit in a sort of stone alcove; sheep grazing quietly beside them. In the far distance another messenger can be seen running, with the second news of misfortune.[3] Job's wife has her hands clasped above her head in horror.

The fifth is a very strange vision: 'Then went Satan forth from the presence of the Lord.'[4] At the top, God sits on his throne, still framed against the disc of the sun. But the sun now has darkened edges, and God seems to turn his face aside in a gesture of infinite weariness and frustration, even annoyance: as if He had been tricked into some

---

[1] There are more books that Job's family are reading: this is the Law, the 'letter that killeth'.

[2] As in Meredith's 'Lucifer in Starlight'—

'And now upon his western wing he lean'd,
Now his huge bulk o'er Afric's sands careen'd,
Now the black planet shadowed Arctic snows . . .'

[3] Both messengers have the left foot forwards, to signify news of ill-omen.

[4] I:I–13.

action of which He now repented. On either side of the throne are the female angels, set in the curved flowing patterns that Blake often used for the illustrations to Dante. Below them Satan is beginning to dive through the clouds of heaven to where Job sits with his wife, while he gives alms (but with his *left* hand) to an old man on crutches: two angels watch the scene, pitying Job's coming fate. In the next picture, the sixth, is 'Satan smiting Job with boils'.

No detail of this horror is spared. Again and again, throughout the adjurations of the Comforters, Job refers to the physical tortures that he is suffering: bones, blood, sinews, bowels. We have the tempera painting (as contrasted with the engravings) of the series: and we may describe the picture of which the composition is similar to that of the engraving. Satan, with his bat-wings outspread, stands on the loins and knees of Job, whose middle is covered with a matting-like cloth. The red of his wings is contrasted with dark dramatic clouds. From Satan's right hand the four arrows of disease[1] are shooting toward Job, signifying the death of the four senses of sight, hearing, taste and smell; from his left he is emptying a phial of poison upon him. Job's head is thrown back as the poison falls on his breast; his hands are bending at the wrists in his agony. The sun is painted in brilliant crimson and gold. In the middle ground, faintly suggested, are the houses of a Palestinian village. At Job's feet, her features obscured in her hair, Job's wife is crouching in a posture beyond grief.

In the engraved version we have the strange associated patternings of Blake's imagination: a broken shepherd's crook rests on stone steps: beside it the grasshopper and broken pitcher from *Ecclesiastes* 12: a hint of the fish with dragon-pointed fins that is to become Leviathan: and a spider at the end of a long single thread, presumably recalling

> So are the paths of all that forget God; and the hypocrite's hope shall perish:
> Whose hope shall be cut off, and whose trust shall be a spider's web.[2]

The next episode engraved is on the text 'And when they lifted up their eyes afar off, and knew him not, they lifted up their voice, and wept.'[3] Job sits, half-reclining, on a stone bench; his wife behind him

[1] See also Blake's illustration to Milton's '*The Lazar House*' (*Paradise Lost*, XI. 477).   [2] 8:13, 14.   [3] 2:12.

supports his head. The three friends approach with hands uplifted in horror at his state. Then Job, his hands uplifted in the traditional attitude,[1] curses his fate:

> Let the day perish wherein I was born, and the night in which it was said, There is a man child conceived.[2]

We remember the speech of his wife.

> Then said his wife unto him, Dost thou still retain thine integrity? curse God and die.
>
> But he said unto her, Thou speakest as one of the foolish women speaketh. What? shall we receive good at the hand of God, and shall we not receive evil? In all this did not Job sin with his lips.[3]

But this is not Blake's view; just as his own wife had supported him in misfortune, so does Job's. Blake then selects (typically, for he can convey his own characteristic impression of the numinous), verses from the speech of the First Comforter, Eliphaz the Temanite. He has suggested that Job will be angry at his reproof. God is not unjust. There must be some reason for Job's misfortune. He has helped others with his words, he himself cannot endure these trials. The whole passage is strange, and must be quoted:

> Now a thing was secretly brought to me, and mine ear received a little thereof.
>
> In thoughts from the visions of the night, when deep sleep falleth on men,
>
> Fear came upon me, and trembling, which made all my bones to shake.
>
> Then a spirit passed before my face; the hair of my flesh stood up:
>
> It stood still, but I could not discern the form thereof: an image was before mine eyes, there was silence, and I heard a voice, saying,
>
> Shall mortal man be more just than God? shall a man be more pure than his maker?[4]

It is a strange composition. Across the top of it, by the side of the speaker (Eliphaz) who half-sits up in bed, God passes, the sun behind his head, the shell-like hollow of the thunder cloud at his back. Below are the three Comforters, of whom Eliphaz is pointing upwards

---

[1] I am not wholly in agreement with Foster Damon, who makes the attitude of the uplifted hands to contrast significantly with the posture of crucifixion.

[2] 3:3; cf. the almost identical language of *Jer.* 20:14, 15.

[3] 2:9, 10.   [4] 4:12 ff.

as he recounts his vision. Job and his wife are also looking upwards towards this roof of cloud. The last verse is surely the key to the whole dialogue.

But Job too is afflicted with this vision, and for him it has a more terrible quality. He lies on his left side, his face turned towards us. Below, there are demons emerging out of a fiery lake: hands with long hooked nails reach up to clutch at his loins and thighs.[1] Above him floats a nightmare figure, hair matted into points, which seems to press upon him; and round the figure a serpent writhes. As the text—

> When I say, My bed shall comfort me, my couch shall ease my complaint;
> Then thou scarest me with dreams, and terrifiest me through visions:
> So that my soul chooseth strangling, and death rather than my life.[2]

The next episode is Job's reply to Zophar the Naamathite:

> No doubt but ye are the people, and wisdom shall die with you.
> But I have understanding as well as you; I am not inferior to you: yea, who knoweth not such things as these?
> I am as one mocked of his neighbour, who calleth upon God, and he answereth him: the just upright man is laughed to scorn.[3]

It is these last words that Blake seized on. Job, his wife beside him, kneels, an expression on his face between bewilderment and anger. On his left, the Comforters stretch out their hands towards him in a uniform gesture of contempt: Job feels that they are 'laughing him to scorn'.

Blake's next illustration is out of tone, graphically, with the rest: it is a quotation from *Psalms*, and not from the book, though it is quoted again in *Hebrews*:[4]

> What is man, that thou art mindful of him? and the son of man, that thou visited him?[5]

—which Blake takes to be central to the argument. Two of the Comforters, and Job's wife, are set in a crowded composition, a

---

[1] cf. Yeats, *The Countess Cathleen*:
> 'Behind her a host heat of the blood made sin,
> But all the little pink-white nails have grown
> To be great talons.'

[2] 7:13–15.   [3] 12:1–4.   [4] 2:6.   [5] *Ps.* 8:4.

jagged lightning-stroke in the background. All three are gazing at Job, who is looking upwards: his face (for the first time) irradiated by a kind of saintliness.

It is possible that Blake felt the protracted dialogues after Chapter 12 to be repetitive and lacking in drama. His next episode is the arrival of Elihu; he is the angry young man who has listened patiently while his elders spoke. Now for five chapters he speaks, again accusing Job. Our expectations have been aroused; have the young something genuinely new to contribute to the problem? Blake sees his arrival as a dramatic moment. The naked young man, superbly vigorous,[1] hair flowing, appears as on a stage. Above and behind him there is a glittering array of stars; his left hand points upwards towards them, his right to the four figures. Job's wife hides her face in a posture of despair: the three Comforters are crouching, against the pattern of that heavy squared masonry which Blake so often uses as a background. Job himself, a little more serene, is prepared to listen.

The young man's 'wrath is kindled'; both against Job and his three friends:

> And Elihu the son of Barachel the Buzite answered and said, I am young, and ye are very old; wherefore I was afraid, and durst not shew you mine opinion.
>
> I said, Days should speak, and multitude of years should teach wisdom.
>
> But there is a spirit in man: and the inspiration of the Almighty giveth them understanding.
>
> Great men are not always wise: neither do the aged understand judgement.[2]

But we are, in fact, disappointed. Elihu does little more than repeat the old arguments from a slightly different angle. He too relies on inspiration in dreams:

> For God speaketh once, yea twice, yet man perceiveth it not.
>
> In a dream, in a vision of the night, when deep sleep falleth upon men, in slumberings upon the bed;
>
> Then he openeth the ears of men, and sealeth their instruction.
>
> That he may withdraw man from his purpose, and hide pride from man.[3]

---

[1] Compare Blake's water-colour, *Glad Day* (B.M.).
[2] 32:6–9. [3] 33:14–17.

After the long gap in his sequence Blake has one illustration of no great interest on a theme that he has treated before—'But thou hast fulfilled the judgement of the wicked.'[1] He then selects, very rightly, the supreme dramatic moment, God's sudden appearance, the opening of the great hymn which is the justification of the whole book, the resolution of the dialogue with God:

> Then the Lord answered Job out of the whirlwind, and said, Who is this that darkeneth counsel by words without knowledge?
>
> Gird up now thy loins like a man; for I will demand of thee, and answer thou me.[2]

God appears, venerable and almost benevolent, with arms outstretched, in Blake's favourite shell-like structure. Job and his wife contemplate Him in amazement, their hands raised in the gesture of prayer, or of mercy. Beneath the cloud of God's presence the Comforters are suggested, crouching in fear, now opaque (as in Blake's symbolism) because of their failure to achieve spiritual vision. The hymn continues, and Blake immediately seizes on its next great lyric moment:

> Who hath laid the measures thereof, if thou knowest? or who hath stretched the line upon it?[3]
>
> Whereupon are the foundations thereof fastened? or who laid the corner stone thereof;
>
> When the morning stars sang together, and all the sons of God shouted for joy?[4]

At the base of the picture, as in a cave below the roof of heaven, we see five protagonists. Above them God stretches out His arms in the gesture of creation. Beneath His right arm is a woman's figure; below his right, an angel, a serpent and a crescent moon. Above, and on either side of the disc of the sun against which God's head is outlined, are four of what is clearly a whole row of angels with uplifted arms; the spaces between and above them are patterned with stars.

It is now that Blake's imagination takes wing upon the text:

> Behold now behemoth, which I made with thee; he eateth grass as an ox.

---

[1] 36:17.　　　　[2] 38:1–3. (This is repeated at 40:7.)
[3] cf. the engraving known as *The Ancient of Days* where, with a compass, the earth is being measured.　　　　[4] 38:5–7.

Lo now, his strength is in his loins, and his force is in the navel of his belly.

He moveth his tail like a cedar: the sinews of his stones are wrapped together.

His bones are as strong pieces of brass; his bones are like bars of iron.

He is the chief of the ways of God . . .[1]

Here God, attended by two angels, and with a background pattern of stars, points downwards as it were through a break in the circular roof of the world; pointing out the marvels of His creation: to Job, his wife and a third figure who follow His pointing arm. In the circular pattern there are the two monstrous beasts. Behemoth is half-elephant, half-rhinoceros, perhaps with a hint of lion about the quarters and tail: the hippopotamus shortened and transformed.

Below Behemoth is one of Blake's favourite designs, the dragon-crocodile Leviathan, open-jawed, writhing in the flood. Blake has disregarded Leviathan's whale-aspects,[2] and has taken from the next chapter the terror of the crocodile.[3]

This epiphany of Creation's power in relation to man seems to be the climax of the book. But it is difficult to account for its effect as poetry unless we are prepared to allow some depth-symbolism in the whole passage. Leviathan is the term for the monster whom God overcame at, or before, creation. Behemoth, we are told, is 'a sort of plural of majesty: 'The Beast.'[4] Alternatively, Behemoth may be the crocodile, and Leviathan the whale. Leviathan was identified with Egypt and Babylon. In *Revelation*, Satan, the Serpent and Leviathan seem to converge. Does this turmoil of beasts, these mysterious and terrifying animals that wanton in the waters that are the matrix of all life, suggest the fallen yet vital dark agencies, which Satan may still control?

From it we move to the resolution. God blesses Job and his wife. The Three Comforters again shown darkly because of their spiritual failure, turn their backs on the scene that is lit by a radiance of the

---

[1] 40:15–19. We remember Christopher Smart's *Jubilate Agno*: as for example—
'Let Andrew rejoice with the Whale, who is arrayd in
beauteous blue and is a combination of bulk and activity.
Let James rejoice with the skuttle-fish, who foils his foe
by the effusion of his ink . . .'
—and his Cat Jeffrey who also is 'the chief of the ways of God'.
[2] As in *Ps*. 104:26.   [3] See pp. 70–71, *ante*.   [4] *Peake's Commentary*, p. 406.

sun. It is a picture that is related, I believe, to Blake's own theory of four-fold vision; of the senses, the senses and the mind, these two added to the heart, and, finally, the compound vision of the spirit. At the base of the design an angel exhibits the scrolls and books of the Law; above, in the crests of hills, there is also a pattern of texts. We may quote what are, in fact, the words of the reconciliation; or of the surrender.

> Then Job answered the Lord, and said,
> I know that thou canst do every thing, and that no thought can be withholden from thee.
> Who is he that hideth counsel without knowledge? therefore have I uttered that I understood not; things too wonderful for me, which I knew not.
> Hear, I beseech thee, and I will speak: I will demand of thee, and declare thou unto me.
> I have heard of thee by the hearing of the ear: but now mine eye seeth thee.
> Wherefore I abhor myself, and repent in dust and ashes.[1]

In quick succession Blake illustrates this 'restoration' of the next ten verses. Job offers sacrifice upon an altar of squared stones, for the three friends, who are now out of favour with God

> for ye have not spoken of me the thing that is right, as my servant Job hath.[2]

The smoke of the sacrifice rises in a pear-shaped structure towards heaven, symbolized by the sun.[3] The three friends crouch in humility beside. Then a patriarchal figure, with his wife, and two maidens approach Job, seated with his own wife under a leafy tree:

> every man also gave him a piece of money, and every one an earring of gold.[4]

Next, Job seated on a kind of throne, stretches out his hands over three women who nestle against him:

> And in all the land were no women found so fair as the daughters of Job.[5]

There are seven sons and three daughters—the number of the original family 'restored'. Jemima, Kezia, and Kerenhappuch

cluster round their father above a lower border of music instruments
—are they now 'the daughters of music' of *Ecclesiastes*?—with a
border and lintel of vine-leaves. Presumably the reference to the
Psalm:

> Thy wife shall be as a fruitful vine by the sides of thy house: thy children
> like olive plants round about thy table.[1]

Blake ends with a sort of musical tableau to illustrate the verse

> So the Lord blessed the latter end of Job.

Job himself appears to be playing a harp: one daughter has a viol,
and another a cither: two young men are playing trumpets, and
another some stringed instrument. Beneath them are a collection of
sheep.

Blake's solution to the problem of Job is consistent with his own
views throughout his work: but it is unique. Briefly, Job *has* sinned, by
his devotion to the letter of the Law instead of its spirit. Blake shows
him in the first illustration as reading in the book of the law, while
the musical instruments hang unused on the wall. His charity is
ceremonial only. He must learn through trial and suffering the path
of experience to the mystic revelation of God out of the whirlwind.
After such a vision, and the epiphany of creation, he has achieved
full and inward knowledge, and his final sacrifice, with its complex
symbolism of altar, flame, signifies his spiritual knowledge and his
union with the divine.

In this section, and in the illustrations, Blake selects from the story
what is consonant with his philosophy. Job's wife, so far from exhort-
ing him to 'curse God and die', is his helper and support. There are
vast gaps that he does not attempt to illustrate, and we may suspect
that he grew impatient with the interminable monologues. The first
nine illustrations cover the first four chapters; there are two significant alterations in the order that the book gives,[2] and the last eight
illustrations are based on the last six chapters. The illustrations are

---

[1] 128:3.
[2] No. 10 ('The just upright man is laughed to scorn'—12:4).
No. 11 ('With dreams upon my bed thou scarest me'—7:14).
No. 16, 'Thou has fulfilled the judgment of the wicked' (36:17) comes after No.
15, 'Behold now Behemoth' (40:15), presumably because Blake wanted this latter
plate to follow the lyric illustration of 'When the morning stars sang together'
(38:7).

significantly augmented by the complex symbolic decorations in the margins.[1]

vi

I have found it difficult to realize an aesthetic unity in the Book. It begins rapidly and dramatically, and then seems to founder in the interminable speeches of the Three Comforters, and Job's replies. Among many flashes of gnomic wisdom there is an infinity of repetition, which does not appear to be differentiated as to any of the characters. The splendour of the book is in God's speech out of the whirlwind. It is an epiphany, a manifestation. It offers no explanation of *why* God has inflicted these trials; nor is there any preparation for Job's sudden collapse.

The hymn is an exposition of the absolute power of God, the mystery of His immanence in every aspect of creation. Man is in comparison impotent and ignorant. In the *lusis*, the resolution, of the drama there is no solution. The reason for Job's suffering is still wholly mysterious. All that has happened is that, quite suddenly, complete acceptance has come:

> I have heard of thee by the hearing of the ear—

(is not this the endless debate about God's attributes, the tangential aspects of His wisdom and omnipotence?)

> —but now mine eye seeth thee.

This *sight* is a metaphor for a new and complete knowledge.

From another point of view we might see the book as a terrible, even monstrous parable. Virtue is *not* necessarily correlated with prosperity. Calamity is not certainly the result of misdeeds. The Cartesian world of causality breaks down before the infinite. Man must fall back, as the poets have done, on the burthen of the mystery. He can curse God and die; the road of many who take their own lives for this, or some slighter reason. It is not easy to dismiss the casual cruelty that may be implicit in this non-Cartesian universe:

> Master, who did sin, this man, or his parents, that he was born blind?[2]
> Or those eighteen, upon whom the tower in Siloam fell, and slew them, think ye they were sinners above all men that dwelt in Jerusalem?[3]

---

[1] The *locus classicus* for this is Foster Damon's *William Blake*, ch. xxx; following Joseph H. Wicksteed's *Blake's Vision of the Book of Job*.

[2] *Jn.* 9:2.   [3] *Lk.* 13:4.

CHAPTER TEN

Proverbs and Prophecy

i

At first sight no literary category could be more alien to the modern consciousness, and few whose very title carried a greater possibility of revulsion. Proverbs are too often associated with the laborious assimilation, sometimes by punitive copying, of platitudinous and sometimes questionable or pointless *exempla*: 'A stitch in time saves nine', 'A bird in the hand is worth two in the bush'. It is true that we have probably been intrigued by

Cast thy bread upon the waters: for thou shalt find it after many days

and speculated on various possible interpretations other than the correct one.[1] And we may reflect that no English writer, with the possible exception of Blake, has worked with distinction in this form. Our revulsion may well be increased if we have read Martin Tupper's *Proverbial Philosophy*,[2] in its day the most popular example of didactic verse. At the same time it is well to recall the great historic collections: the Icelandic Hávamál, the proverbs of Alfred, the *Adages* of Erasmus; as well as the frequent incorporation into Elizabethan and Jacobean drama, of Senecan-type *gnomai*.

Again we must try to look with fresh eyes. The 'wisdom' literature occurs at many points in the Bible and the Apocrypha, mainly in *Proverbs, Ecclesiastes, Job, Ecclesiasticus*, and *Wisdom*; as well as being largely dispersed, as gnomic utterances, throughout the *Psalms*. The meaning of the word 'proverb' is a good deal wider than that suggested by the English translation. We may see it as the product of a long chain of transmitted wisdom. God is the source of all things, wisdom one of His attributes. Those who have meditated on, and synthesized, their experience of the world, record and transmit this wisdom. *Proverbs* itself is composed of five groups of sayings, two of

[1] *Eccl.* 11:1. The image is of sowing seed, or planting seedlings, in flooded ground. [2] Martin Farquhar Tupper, 1810–89.

them described as 'Sayings of the Wise', two as 'Proverbs of Solomon'. The fifth, and the group that is the most vivid in its imagery, are Chapters 30 and 31 : 10–31, which is an acrostic poem on the Virtuous Woman.

For any Eastern people the proverbs are pillars of social intercourse. The ability of the stranger to quote aptly, and if possible humorously, is an invaluable aspect of his resources of communication: not unlike the once-valued ability to quote appositely from the Classics, whether in private or in public life. Proverbs become a kind of index of the speaker's wit, poise, and experience of the world. They cover an infinite number of situations and problems of conduct. Their imagery can be pungent, picturesque; at times 'metaphysical' in the linking of heterogeneous ideas. In language they have the virtues of vividness, compression, and a capacity for being easily memorized. For Western parallels we can turn to innumerable authors: from Bacon, Montaigne, Pascal through Swift and Johnson to Wilde and Shaw. As random examples—

"All rising to great place is by a winding stair."

(Bacon)

"A man knows his companion in a long journey and a little inn."

(Fuller)

"We have just enough religion to make us hate, but not enough to love one another."

(Swift)

"Know then thyself, presume not God to scan:
The proper study of mankind is man."

(Pope)

But the Hebrew conception is different. Behind it is the fact of a godhead, a living and omnipotent will, that manifests itself in every imaginable activity. This world is moral in essence, hierarchical in structure. 'There is a general beauty in the works of God',[1] underlying the infinite differences in the manifestations of that beauty. It is for the Wise to perceive, mediate, record the distillations of experience that give the *exempla* of these unchallenged facts. The Hebrews made no attempt to deduce, from a mass of observed instances, the principles that underlie the universe. They were already accepted in the totality of the Creation. It was the *exempla* that mattered; compressed, made memorable in metre and imagery,

[1] Sir Thomas Browne, *Religio Medici*, I, xvi.

163

nailed, in the memorable phrase of *Ecclesiastes* 12, to vitalize and guide morality and conduct; or, at worst, to inculcate a philosophic pessimism. There are analogies with the reflective hedonism of Fitzgerald's *Rubá'iyát*, and parallels may be readily adduced from *Ecclesiasticus*.

> The words of the wise are as goads, and as nails fastened by the masters of assemblies, which are given from one shepherd.[1]

'Wisdom' literature, whether explicit or incidental, is found in many parts of the Bible.

'The Wise'—those who distilled and formulated wisdom after due meditation—were as well-known as the prophets and the priests. 'For the law shall not perish from the priest, nor counsel from the wise, nor the word from the prophet.'[2] The form was not peculiar to the Jews. We may quote one or two instances from the Assyrian sage Ahikar:[3]

> "My son, draw not near to a woman that is a whisperer, nor to one whose voice is loud." (VIII)
> "My son, I have carried iron and removed stones, and they were not more burdensome upon me than when a man dwells in the house of his father-in-law." (XVII)
> "To him that doeth good, what is good shall be recompensed, and to him that doeth evil, what is evil shall be repaid. And he that diggeth a pit for his neighbour filleth it with his own body." (XXXVIII)

ii

The Hebrew word for proverb is *máshál*, meaning comparison or 'parable', and we find in them an extensive range of simile and occasionally metaphor. But there are two roots: (1) mashal (*represent, be like*) and (2) mashal, (*to rule*). They are in fact compressed highly-polished aphorisms, following the general structure of Hebrew poetry: based on antithesis, parallelisms, repetition and incremental repetition: usually[4] set in a distal of which the first half contains three accents, the second two.

> Understanding is a wellspring of life unto him that hath it: but the instruction of fools is folly.[5]

[1] 12:11.   [2] *Jer.* 18:18.
[3] Quoted from *Documents from Old Testament Times (op. cit.)*.
[4] The so-called Hezekian Collection—XXV–XXIX—also contains quotations.
[5] *Prov.* 16:22.

We can perceive certain *dramatis personae*. There is the speaker, the sage or teacher, whose tone to his listener is usually that of a father to a son. The wise are contrasted with the fools (which means literally 'the fat ones'), the righteous with the wicked. If the exhortations are disregarded, judgment will follow. The loose woman is the embodiment, and the cause, of folly.

The choice between Wisdom and Folly is one for each individual. Wisdom is something which can be obtained by study, experience and a certain humble receptivity to the experience of the old: the relationship of a scholar to his master. In the relationship of wise parents and their children one aspect of the discipline of wisdom is seen. Morality is in the main prudential, though above and beyond it is the providence of God, the justice of His hand. It has been pointed out that the attitude to the poor is ambivalent. On the one hand, they are to blame for their state because of their idleness and folly; on the other, it is (as in all Eastern countries) a supremely charitable act to relieve them:

> He that hath pity upon the poor lendeth unto the Lord; and that which he hath given will he pay him again.[1]

There is much advice on self-discipline, particularly in the matter of speech.

> The heart of the righteous studieth to answer: but the mouth of the wicked poureth out evil things.[2]
>
> He that is soon angry dealeth foolishly . . .[3]
>
> He that is slow to anger is better than the mighty; and he that ruleth his spirit than he that taketh a city.[4]

The mouth that speaks is of decisive importance, and a variety of images are used to emphasize the importance of the spoken word. Words are 'deep waters' or 'sword thrusts': the standard images of net and pitfall, fire and tower, ointment and honeycomb, of wild beasts, occur continually. Wisdom is regarded as a sort of object of traffic, a valued currency circulated among responsible men:

> For the merchandise of it is better than the merchandise of silver, and the gain thereof than fine gold.[5]

[1] 19:17. Compare the familiar and justly-condemned hymn:
"Whatever, Lord, we lend to thee
Repaid a thousandfold will be."
[2] 15:28. The same sentiment is repeatedly emphasized: cf. 15:2; 10:14.
[3] 14:17.   [4] 16:32.   [5] 3:14.

The foolish and the wicked are condemned in various picturesque phrases:

For they eat the bread of wickedness, and drink the wine of violence.[1]

It has been pointed out that much of the difficulty of the 'Wisdom' literature, and perhaps some of its 'flatness' to our generation, consists in its use of a precise vocabulary of morality, which uses such terms as *knowledge, correction, understanding, discretion, scorners, froward*; whose full meaning is apparent only to those who can relate them to the Hebrew and Greek.

iii

But one of the most interesting aspects of the proverbs is the continual return to the subject of woman, her qualities and deficiencies. The theme is older than Juvenal, who set the model, and the tone, of perennial satire on this subject. We have already seen the reasons for the outbursts throughout the Bible against the 'outland' woman, the harlot, the danger of 'whoring after strange gods', the seductions of the fertility cults. Here is a spirited and dramatic description of the young man going furtively to his doom:

For at the window of my house I looked out through my casement,

And beheld among the simple ones, I discerned among the youths, a young man void of understanding,

Passing through the street near her corner; and he went the way to her house,

In the twilight, in the evening, in the black and dark night:

And, behold, there met him a woman with the attire of an harlot, and subtil of heart.

(She is loud and stubborn; her feet abide not in her house:

Now she is without, now in the streets, and lieth in wait at every corner.)

So she caught him, and kissed him, and with an impudent face said unto him,

'I have peace-offerings with me; this day have I payed my vows.

Therefore came I forth to meet thee, diligently to seek thy face, and I have found thee.

I have decked my bed with coverings of tapestry, with carved works, with fine linen of Egypt.

[1] 4:17.

I have perfumed my bed with myrrh, aloes, and cinnamon.

Come, let us take our fill of love unto the morning: let us solace ourselves
with loves . . .'[1]

Besides this we may set an extract from the Babylonian *Counsels of
Wisdom* (? 1500–1000 B.C.):

Do not marry a prostitute, whose husbands are legion,
A temple harlot, who is dedicated to a god,
A courtezan, whose favours are many.
In your trouble she will not support you,
In your dispute she will be a mocker;
There is no reverence or submissiveness with her.
Even if she dominate your house, get her out,
For she has directed her attention elsewhere.[2]
(*Variant*: She will disrupt the house she enters, and her partner will not
assert himself)

Pictures of the virtuous woman recur at intervals:

Let thy fountain be blessed: and rejoice with the wife of thy youth.

Let her be the loving hind and pleasant roe; let her breasts satisfy thee
at all times; and be thou ravished always with her love.[3]

and again:

It is better to dwell in a corner of the housetop, than with a brawling
woman in a wide house.[4]

It is better to dwell in the wilderness, than with a contentious and an
angry woman.[5]

She enters into the group of the four 'disquieting' things:

For three things the earth is disquieted, and for four which it cannot
bear:

For a servant when he reigneth; and a fool when he is filled with meat;

For an odious woman when she is married; and an handmaid that is
heir to her mistress.[6]

But the most famous description of the virtuous woman is in the
final chapter, verse 10 onwards. It is in the form of an acrostic poem,
on successive letters of the Hebrew alphabet. It illustrates admirably
the domestic side of a large household, and is not unlike the accounts
of the lives of Greek women of substance. Both had few legal rights;

[1] 7:6–18. We need not be surprised at the similarities to *The Song of Songs*.
[2] *Documents from Old Testament Times*, op. cit., p. 106.
[3] *Prov.* 5:18–19.   [4] 21:9.   [5] 21:19.   [6] 30:21–23.

industry, the concern for her husband's standing and reputation, are all the more praiseworthy since they are disinterested. We may quote a few verses:

Who can find a virtuous woman? for her price is far above rubies.[1]

We may make two comments here. The book has used the same image as Wisdom personified in woman, in an early chapter:

She is more precious than rubies: and all the things thou canst desire are not to be compared unto her.[2]

and, there is, perhaps, an oblique allusion in Marvell's *To his Coy Mistress*:

"Thou by the Indian *Ganges* side
Should'st rubies find . . ."

that is, acquire even more precious attributes of virtue.

The heart of her husband doth safely trust in her, so that he shall have no need of spoil.[3]

She will do him good and not evil all the days of her life.

She seeketh wool, and flax, and worketh diligently with her hands.

She is like the merchants' ships; she bringeth her food from afar.

She riseth also while it is yet night, and giveth meat to her household, and a portion to her maidens.

She considereth a field, and buyeth it; with the fruit of her hands she planteth a vineyard.

. . . . .

She layeth her hands to the spindle, and her hands hold the distaff.

She stretcheth out her hand to the poor; yea, she reacheth forth her hands to the needy.[4]

. . . . .

Her husband is known in the gates, when he sitteth among the elders of the land.

. . . . .

Favour is deceitful, and beauty is vain: but a woman that feareth the Lord, she shall be praised.

[1] *Prov.* 31:10 ff.   [2] 3:15.

[3] We might think that this implied plunder from war, as in the poem of Sisera's mother; but in this context it means 'wool'; the virtuous lady never lacks wool to spin.

[4] We may compare the economy of a late medieval household in England: as depicted, say, in *The Paston Letters* or in Thomas Tusser's rhymes.

Give her of the fruit of her hands; and let her own works praise her in the gates.

We may the better appreciate the calm lucidity of the description in *Proverbs*—monotonous though it can become—by setting beside a piece of Jacobean prose, in the style deriving from Euphuism, roughly contemporary with the prose of the *A.V.*:

"A GOOD WIFE is a world of wealth, where just cause of content makes a kingdom in conceit: she is the eye of weariness, the tongue of silence, the hand of labour, and the heart of love: a companion of kindness, a mistress of passion, an exercise of patience, and an example of experience: she is the kitchen physician, the chamber comfort, the hall's care, and the parlour's grace: she is the dairy's neatness, the brewhouse wholesomeness, the garner's provision, and the garden's plantation . . . she is her husband's jewel, her children's joy, her neighbour's love, and her servants' honour: she is poverty's praiser, and charity's praise, religion's love and devotion's zeal: she is a case of necessity, and a course of thrift, a book of huswifery, and a mirror of modesty. In sum, she is God's blessing, and man's happiness, earth's honour, and heaven's creature."[1]

Compression, abstraction, antithesis, and alliteration, have combined to rob the passage of vitality. The 'minute particulars', the details of the household economy, give the seminal passage a certain simple cogency, which are choked by striving for epigrammatic 'wit'.

iv

Yet I think we must indicate the limitations of this form. *Proverbs, Ecclesiastes, The Wisdom of Solomon* are, in the main, monotonous, even to the point of tedium. The same sins of Middle Eastern life are emphasized again and again: false witness, slander, drunkenness, gluttony, cheating by false weights and measures, injustice, slothfulness. The tone of the instruction is of the elder, or the parent, to the young. It does not sound as if the relationship were any less difficult than it always has been: there is, perhaps, some humour in the description:

And say, How have I hated instruction, and my heart despised reproof;

[1] Nicholas Breton (1545–1626): *The Good and the Badde, or Descriptions of the Worthies and Unworthies of this Age. Where the Best may see their Graces, and the Worst discern their Badness.*" (1616)

And have not obeyed the voice of my teachers, nor inclined mine ear to them that instructed me![1]

The 'flashes' of poetic perception are relatively few, and they, for the most part, have passed into the language. It is when we look at them in parallel with some of the proverbs of, say, Blake, that their limitations appear:

> "A robin redbreast in a cage
> Puts all Heaven in a rage."

> "A dog starv'd at his master's gate
> Predicts the ruin of the State."

> "He who the ox to wrath hath mov'd
> Shall never be by woman lov'd."[2]

Here we are participating in a series of imaginative leaps into the depths of meaning, invited to project our minds into metaphysical comparisons with the most terrifying implications. There are, of course, such expansive insights in *Proverbs*, but they are not many:

> Better is a dinner of herbs where love is, than a stalled ox and hatred therewith.[3]

Or a famous passage (echoed by many moralists):

> Remove far from me vanity and lies: give me neither poverty nor riches; feed me with food convenient for me.

> Lest I be full, and deny thee, and say, Who is the Lord? or lest I be poor, and steal, and take the name of my God in vain.[4]

and the familiar

> Boast not thyself of tomorrow; for thou knowest not what a day will bring forth.[5]

Sometimes the similes are especially cogent:

> A continual dropping in a very rainy day and a contentious woman are alike.[6]

and for the fool in his folly:

> Though thou shouldest bray a fool in a mortar among wheat with a pestle, yet will not his foolishness depart from him.[7]

---

[1] *Prov.* 5:12–13. [2] From *Auguries of Innocence.* [3] *Prov.* 15:17.
[4] 30:8, 9. [5] 27:1. [6] 27:15. [7] 27:22.

V

The word 'prophecy' can also be misleading, for the popular conception of it includes a strong, perhaps predominant, element of foretelling the future—'We have known too many prophets'; the astrologers, soothsayers, the sects which prophesy from time to time the imminence of the Last Judgment, or some convulsion preparatory to it: these have been sufficiently discredited in our present civilization, whether by astrologers or by certain of the 'jarring sects', for the whole question of 'prophecy' to be under a cloud of contempt. Again, we must look at the literary material in a different light.

Prophecy is sometimes spoken, or written down, at the time of composition, but more usually much later, under certain specific conditions. The overriding one is that the writer or speaker should be, or believe himself to be, the vehicle for some power outside and above himself:[1]

> Who hath believed our report? and to whom is the arm of the Lord revealed?[2]

> The word that came to Jeremiah from the Lord, saying, Stand in the gate of the Lord's house, and proclaim there this word, and say, Hear the word of the Lord . . .[3]

> And he said unto me, Son of Man, stand upon thy feet, and I will speak unto thee.

> And the spirit entered into me when he spake unto me, and set me upon my feet, and I heard him that spake unto me.[4]

Prophecy is in fact a complex and varied literary genre. In the first place it must be seen in terms of the personalities, often well-defined, of the prophets themselves. In the second their emergence and ministries must be seen against the varying social, political and religious backgrounds of their particular times. Thirdly, the prophecies must be seen as intimately connected with the Law: suggested in the phrase, The Law and the Prophets. They, with the priests, are the mediators of God's word, but they are also commentators upon it in the situation in which Israel or Judah find themselves at each stage of history. The purely prophetic element, the

---

[1] Donne's 'Secretaries of the Holy Ghost', as applied to the Prophets, gives part of this conception.

[2] *Isa.* 53:1.   [3] *Jer.* 7:1.   [4] *Ezek.* 2:1, 2.

forecasting of future events, has two elements: the warnings of imminent punishment for sin, the promise of the coming of a golden age, or the prediction of such an event as the destruction of Jerusalem, which was widely believed to be under the special protection of God, and hence impregnable for ever. The second element is what we might call that of retrospective interpretation: the drawing of parts of the prophetic writings into the whole unity of the Bible by quotation and allusion in the New Testament. We should not be contemptuous of this activity, nor regard it as a mere instance of hindsight. All prophetic or oracular utterances are, by their very nature, ambiguous; whether because of the different interpretations which can be placed upon their imagery, which ranges from the humble to the esoteric; and the ambivalences, the riddles, so prevalent among the oracles of the classical world.

Such retrospective interpretation is seen most strikingly in the subsequent history of the churches: whether by allegory, by the exegetical interpretation of the thing said into a parallel but wholly new structure of ideas; or by typology, which builds upon the incident (rather than on the words and imagery) in interpretative structure. A classic instance is that of Jonah and the Whale, where the three days are explained as typifying Christ's sojourn in the tomb.

We may attempt some brief characterization of the poetic styles of the four major prophets. They are, as we should expect, children of their ages. The book which we know as 'Isaiah' falls into three groups, which obtain to some extent their characteristic unity from subsequent redactions. Thus Chapters 1–39 is accepted as the First, 40–55 as the Second, and the remainder the Third, 56–66. The time, as commonly with the prophets, is one of crisis; the Assyrian invasion is imminent. Therefore one object is to stiffen the national will, and to give various political counsels. Among them were advice to Ahaz not to approach Tiglath-Pileser for aid, and to advise Hezekiah not to appeal to Egypt for help. Only this last piece of advice was followed.

In these conditions we may perceive a pattern that recurs constantly. Judah has been rejected for her sins; God is both the accuser, and the judge, of a people who have forgotten His past acts of salvation, who have engaged in every kind of moral and religious corruption, who have degraded the Law to empty ritual, who have made unjustifiable foreign alliances ('they strike hands with foreigners'). Drunkenness and extortion are common. The women are vain and immoral. The land is divided, and its rulers are corrupt opportunists. Yet one day God's justice will reassert itself; Assyria and Egypt will be destroyed.

Here, as elsewhere, many fragments of cultic oracles, and some suspected interpolation, make it difficult to quote whole poems. We may refer to the Song of the Vineyard and its parabolic interpretation,[1] the vision of the seraphim bearing the live coal to purify the prophet's lips;[2] the Messianic prophecies—ever debated in interpretation—of 7:14 and 9:2 ff. with the notorious mistranslation of verse 3:

A.V. Thou hast multiplied the nation, and not increased the joy.

R.V. Thou hast multiplied the nation, thou hast increased their joy.[3]

We should remember the slight but exquisite psalm embedded in Chapter 13. Of the classic indictments of nations and cities we may recall the ending of 'the Burden of Damascus'[4] with its superbly imaginative imagery:

In that day shall his strong cities be as a forsaken bough, and an uppermost branch, which they left because of the children of Israel: and there shall be desolation.

Because thou hast forgotten the God of thy salvation, and hast not been mindful of the rock of thy strength, therefore shalt thou plant pleasant plants, and shalt set it with strange slips:

In the day shalt thou make thy plant to grow, and in the morning shalt thou make thy seed to flourish: but the harvest shall be a heap in the day of grief and of desperate sorrow.

Woe to the multitude of many people, who make a noise like the noise of the seas; and to the rushing of nations, that make a rushing like the rushing of mighty waters![5]

[1] 5:1 ff.
[2] 6:6; cf. Yeats: *The Soul.* Isaiah's coal, what more can man desire?
　　　　　　　　The Heart. Struck dumb in the simplicity of fire.
[3] Better,"Thou hast multiplied gladness,
　　　　　Thou hast increased joy."
[4] *Prov.* 17:9–14.
[5] We may note the recurrent mingling of waves, floods, water-spouts; as being of peculiar interest for peoples cut off from the sea. So, too, the power of the hot dust-storms from the desert.

The nations shall rush like the rushing of many waters, but God shall rebuke them, and they shall flee far off, and shall be chased as the chaff of the mountains before the wind, and like a rolling thing before the whirlwind.

And behold at eveningtide trouble; and before the morning he is not. This is the portion of them that spoil us, and the lot of them that rob us.

Several matters are worth attention here. There is the image of the forsaken bough and the branch,[1] which has perennial overtones. The image of the 'slips' which are cuttings of the vine, cults of a strange god, we remember from *A Winter's Tale*.[2] We pause on the phrase *a heap of grief* and find in *R.V.* the weaker phrase 'but the harvest fleeth away in the day of grief and of desperate sorrow'. The images are constantly shifting in their perspective. We now have the ebb and flow of the great empires, dispersion, and captivity: from the storm images we pass to that of the *chaff*,[3] at once the image of lightness, worthlessness; and, obliquely, to the practice of Israel of taking refuge in the remote hills from the raids and invasions. The same thought is projected in a fresh image in the dust-devils, the *rolling thing*, with the image of the whirlwind,[4] one embodiment of divinity, to give it further depth.

vi

But the 'great' poems are in the Second or Deutero-Isaiah, 40–55. I have already quoted part of Chapter 40, and referred to Chapter 55. They are those connected with what is known as The Suffering Servant. Their relevance to the New Testament need not be stressed here, but we may quote part of what is perhaps the most famous of all of them, Chapter 53:

Who hath believed our report? and to whom is the arm of the Lord revealed?

[1] cf. Shakespeare, *Sonnet* 73:
  . . . "Upon those boughs which shake against the cold,
    Bare ruin'd choirs, where late the sweet birds sang."
[2] cf. (e.g.) IV. 3. 99.
[3] cf. Shelley, 'Ode to the West Wind':
      "Thou from whose unseen presence the leaves dead
        Are driven, like ghosts from an enchanter fleeing."
See Dante's *Inferno*, esp. Cantos V, IX, for other uses of this image.
[4] 'Then the Lord answered Job out of the whirlwind' (38:1).

For he shall grow up before him as a tender plant, and a root out of a dry ground: he hath no form nor comeliness; and when we shall see him, there is no beauty that we should desire him.[1]

He is despised and rejected of men; a man of sorrows,[2] and acquainted with grief: and we hid as it were our faces from him; he was despised, and we esteemed him not.

Surely he hath borne our griefs, and carried our sorrows: yet we did esteem him stricken, smitten of God,[3] and afflicted.

But he was wounded for our transgression, he was bruised for our iniquities: the chastisement of our peace was upon him; and with his stripes we are healed.

All we like sheep have gone astray; we have turned every one to his own way; and the Lord hath laid upon him the iniquity of us all.

He was oppressed, and he was afflicted, yet he opened not his mouth:[4] he is brought as a lamb to the slaughter, and as a sheep before her shearers is dumb, so he openeth not his mouth.

He was taken from prison and from judgement, and who shall declare his generation?[5] for he was cut off out of the land of the living: for the transgression of my people was he stricken.

And he made his grave with the wicked, and with the rich in his death;[6] because he had done no violence, neither was there any deceit in his mouth.

Yet it pleased the Lord to bruise him; he hath put him to grief: when thou shalt make his soul an offering for sin, he shall see his seed, he shall prolong his days, and the pleasure of the Lord shall prosper in his hand.

He shall see of the travail of his soul, and shall be satisfied: by his knowledge shall my righteous servant justify many; for he shall bear their iniquities.

Therefore will I divide him a portion with the great, and he shall divide the spoil with the strong; because he hath poured out his soul unto death: and he was numbered with the transgressors; and he bare the sin of many, and made intercession for the transgressors.

[1] A difficult phrase, *v. Peake's Commentary*: pp. 527–528.
[2] The phrase will be familiar: among other reasons, for Dürer's picture of that title, and Handel's *Messiah*.
[3] Perhaps we remember Job: and *Ps.* 69:26.
[4] Note *R.V.*: 'He was oppressed, yet he humbled himself'. . .
[5] *R.V.* is still difficult: 'Who among them considered that he was cut off out of the land of the living?'
[6] We need not stress the thieves at the Crucifixion, or the tomb of Joseph.

vii

With Jeremiah we see the outcome of the situation depicted by Isaiah. We are now in the second half of the seventh century B.C. Assyria is falling, the empire eroded by the Scythians. Babylon is about to assume leadership and has become the new enemy to Josiah. Egypt descends like a vulture, and tries to push northwards, defeats Judah at the Valley of Megiddo, and makes her a vassal state. But at Carchemish (605 B.C.) Babylon utterly routed the Egyptian army, and Judah became a vassal of Babylon. Part of Jeremiah's teaching, and one reason for his unpopularity, was his advocacy of the need to compromise with the occupying power.

Jehovah has rejected Israel because of her backsliding, Judah because she has 'played the harlot'. Israel and Judah have both behaved treacherously. Salvation is in Jehovah only, not in the idols, the Baals of the high places, or in alliances with the multitude of nations to whom she might turn in desperation:

> Truly in vain is salvation hoped for from the hills, and from the multitude of mountains: truly in the Lord our God is the salvation of Israel.[1]

Idolatry and deceit are everywhere:

> We looked for peace, but no good came; and for a time of health, and behold trouble![2]

The people live in luxury, the tabernacle is deserted:

> The sin of Judah is written with a pen of iron, and with the point of a diamond: it is graven upon the table of their heart, and upon the horns of your altars;

> Whilst their children remember their altars and their groves by the green trees upon the high hills.[3]

The popular image of Jeremiah as the supreme pessimist, the writer of unrelieved gloom, is in some part due to the erroneous ascription to him of the authorship of *Lamentations*. But apart from that his reputation is not ill-earned. His ministry covers few critical decades of Judah's history, 626–586 B.C. His personality is not less interesting than the ethical, political and sociological background against which he writes. He was called to the role of prophet at an

[1] 3:23.   [2] 8:15.   [3] 17:1, 2.

early age; a shy, reserved man, mistrustful of himself, a poet caught inexorably by God:

> Then the Lord put forth his hand, and touched my mouth. And the Lord said unto me, Behold I have put my words in thy mouth.
>
> See, I have this day set thee over the nations and over the kingdoms, to root out, to pull down, and to destroy, and to throw down, to build and to plant.[1]

The process was to be, first, one of purgation. Every imaginable image is pressed into service to denounce the wickedness of Israel:

> For my people have committed two evils; they have forsaken me the fountain of living waters, and hewed them out cisterns, broken cisterns, that can hold no water.[2]

Idolatry has reached its extremities. The Baals are worshipped 'upon every high hill and under every green tree'.[3] Idols, 'stocks and stones' are set up. Even families 'make cakes for the queen of heaven'.[4] One consequence is theft, injustice, murder, adultery. In consequence, retributory evil is imminent, first in the raiders from the north:

> The snorting of his horses was heard from Dan: the whole land trembled at the sound of the neighing of his strong ones . . .[5]

Into this maelstrom of corruption within and invasion from without, the prophet is driven to his task: 'the long struggle between his native reserve and the ecstatic compulsion to heroism'.[6] He wrestles with his despair; like Job, he curses the day of his birth:

> Wherefore came I forth out of the womb to see labour and sorrow, that my days should be consumed with shame?[7]

Like Job, he reproaches God (15:18, 20:7). He is repeatedly under threat of death: he is placed in the stocks, imprisoned, flees for his life. He has to contend with the false prophets; he becomes unpopular through his advocacy of submission to the invader; his advice that the deported people should make a home in Babylon, and the promise that a remnant would one day return, must have exacerbated those who heard his denunciations. He pronounces

---

[1] 1:9, 10.
[2] 2:13. For a projection of the image, cf. Blake, 'The Cistern contains, the Fountain overflows'.   [3] 2:20.   [4] Astarte.
[5] 8:16. cf. 'the mighty ones', the war-stallions, in the Song of Deborah and Barak.   [6] Pfeiffer, op. cit., p. 494.   [7] Jer. 20:18.

'oracles' against the enemies that surround Israel: Moab, Egypt, Philistia and the peoples of the desert. He weeps over the ruins of his people, as Jesus wept over the fate of Jerusalem.

Jeremiah is a poet, a man of the countryside from a village called Anathoth, a few miles north of Jerusalem. Under the terrible pressure of his spiritual suffering, for himself and for his people, he returns again and again through multiplex imagery to the known experiences of the countryside and of rural life. The dreaded North shows as a vision of a boiling cauldron about to spill over.[1] All life ceases where the invading armies have passed:

> I beheld, and, lo, there was no man, and all the birds of the heavens were fled.[2]
> —neither can men hear the voice of the cattle.[3]

There is the tears-fountain imagery, memorable and often abused in Petrarchan and metaphysical verse, but perhaps at its best in Donne.

> Oh that my head were waters, and mine eyes a fountain of tears, that I might weep day and night for the slain of the daughters of my people![4]

So Donne's "Twickenham Gardens:"

> "Make me a mandrake, that I may groan here,
> Or a stone fountain, weeping out my year."

There is the image of death the reaper, familiar in so many icons and images:

> For death is come up into our windows, and is entered into our palaces, to cut off the children from without, and the young men from the streets.[5]

There is a terrible picture of the drought in this waste land of evil, and the vision moves outwards from the city to the surrounding countryside. Children are sent to bring water from the pits and find them dry; the ground is 'chapt' (giving, superbly, the senses of hardened, cracked, crusted), so that men cannot plough; the calving hinds as well as the wild asses on the heights can find no grass.[6] The denunciations are illustrated by allegories: as of the potter and the clay figure,[7] the basket of figs,[8] 'the wine cup of this fury'[9] (that

---

[1] 1:13.
[2] 4:25. cf.: "The sedge is withered from the lake,
And no birds sing."
Keats, 'La Belle Dame Sans Merci.'
[3] 9:10.   [4] 9:1.   [5] 9:21.   [6] 14:1–6.
[7] 18:2 ff.   [8] 24:1 ff.   [9] 25:15.

perennial image of pain and desolation), the burning of the roll.[1]
There are oracles against Egypt, the Philistines, Moab, the Ammonites, and above all, Babylon. It is worth while quoting an extract here:

> A sound of a cry cometh from Babylon, and great destruction from the
> land of the Chaldeans:

> Because the Lord hath spoiled Babylon, and destroyed out of her the
> great voice; when her waves do roar like great waters, a noise of their
> voice is uttered:

> Because the spoiler is come upon her, even upon Babylon, and her mighty
> men are taken, every one of their bows is broken: for the Lord God of
> recompences shall surely requite.

> And I will make drunk her princes, and her wise men, her captains, and
> her rulers, and her mighty men: and they shall sleep a perpetual sleep,
> and not wake, saith the King, whose name is the Lord of hosts.[2]

Jeremiah's world is one of conflict, national and international.
Within his denunciation we can trace the progress of the 'dark night
of the soul', and an emergence to a consciousness of authority and
power. Sin is omnipresent; idolatry has produced an atrophy of the
national will, and a formalism in the interpretation of the Law has
dulled their religious conscience so that evil and injustice multiply
at every turn. Yet there are gleams of hope. Jehovah is still the
guardian of His people if they will but turn to Him. In the dialogue
with Jeremiah He recalls, time after time, His past mercies and
deliverances; but it is clear that a vital tradition of His mercy has
been lost and can only be recovered by a change of heart, a moral
reawakening of rulers and people alike. Always there is the threat of
raids, of destruction, as part of God's punishment:

> Behold, I will send for many fishers, saith the Lord, and they shall fish
> them; and after that will I send for many hunters, and they shall hunt
> them from every mountain, and from every hill, and out of the holes
> of the rocks.[3]

It is a strange pair of images: the fishers for the invading armies, the
hunters for the mopping-up troops who pursue the fugitives into the
wilderness.

There are high passages in *Ezekiel*: we remember the allegory of
the foundling girl who becomes a bride,[4] the building and manning

---

[1] 36:20 ff.   [2] 51:54 ff.
[3] 16:16. We may think of David's description of himself as 'hunted like a
partridge in the mountains'.   [4] 16.

of the ship in the 'lamentation for Tyre',[1] the descriptions of Egypt and her Pharoah in terms of the dragon or crocodile of her rivers,[2] and the dragon which is a survival from Babylonian myth. There is the perennial image of the great tree, for the fallen kingdom, or for man:

> Upon his ruin shall all the fowls of the heaven remain, and all the beasts of the field shall be upon his branches . . .[3]

Above all there is the poem of the Valley of Dry Bones, the most familiar of all dramatic visions.

It is not until we read the visions of *Zechariah* that we become aware of a new mass of imagery, some of which is to become archetypal. There is the mysterious Rider upon the red horse that appears among the myrtle-trees[4]—a patrol of the Parthian Army?—and the symbolic conjunction of the seven-branched golden candlestick between the two olive-trees,[5] the flying scroll embroidered with curses that is sent out over the land,[6] the four chariots, with their different-coloured horses that go out from between the mountains of copper to patrol the earth;[7] the flashes of poetry that again suggest Blake's Innocence and Experience:

> Thus saith the Lord of hosts; There shall yet old men and old women dwell in the streets of Jerusalem, and every man with his staff in his hand for very age.

> And the streets of the city shall be full of boys and girls playing in the streets thereof.[8]

Perhaps *Daniel* is the most unified, and the most dramatic of all the books; Nebuchadnezzar and his dreams, the writing on the wall, the fiery furnace, the composite Beasts that are to shape so much medieval and renaissance imagery, and have given rise to much wild speculation as to their bearing on world affairs, and their *dramatis personae*, throughout the ages.

viii

It is not easy to assess the work of the prophets, singly or in bulk, as literature. Not even Blake offers any standards with which to compare the national and apocalyptic visions towards which they so constantly converge. As prose, they contain large areas of dullness.

---

[1] 27:5, 26 ff.   [2] 29:3.   [3] 31:13 (see also *Dan.* 4:14).
[4] 1:8.   [5] 4:2, 3.   [6] 5:1.   [7] 6:1–8.
[8] 8:4, 5. We may contrast the picture of desolation in the last chapter of *Ecclesiastes.*

The denunciations of wrong-doing, the perpetual imagery of harlots and whoredoms, become monotonous and (as various critics have pointed out) a little nauseating. So, too, the incessant turgid accounts of slaughter and destruction, present or to come, of friends or enemy. One difficulty for the reader is the need to master, at least in outline, the historical backgrounds of the prophets, the effects of the international situation, the response of the people to their own inconstant rulers. Such a background is not easy to absorb; and, for the common reader, there may be some revulsion from unintelligently-taught scripture lessons in school; where somewhat arid historical tables can become a substitute for more intelligent and critical reading. For a somewhat comparable illustration from English literature we might think of the need to consider the history of the Commonwealth as a background for the work of Marvell and Milton, or that of the French Revolution for Blake, Shelley, Wordsworth.

Out of this massive confusion there emerges a picture which is not without its relevance to us. Every age has, it seems, lamented its own decadence, its loss of standards. 'Hora novissima, tempora pessima sunt.' Housman may place the blame on the stars:

> "The signal fires of warning
> They blaze, but none regard:
> And so through night to morning
> The world runs ruinward."[1]

Yet it would be wrong to regard the work of the prophets as having no more than a historical value. Through them we can see the growth of human personality under the terrible compulsion of God's calling: even to the height of spiritual agony—such as Jeremiah's—that man can bear. It is one aspect of the *furor poeticus*, the divine energy communicated in its most intense form. The denunciation of a civilization because of its lost values is an activity of all moralists, the hoped-for prelude to all kinds of reform. Because conversion can and must be through the spirit, every means of communication is used to touch that spirit to new issues. Another part is the perpetual hope. A child will be born, a king shall reign and prosper, the remnant will return from exile, men will once again build houses and own fields. Some such hope has sustained all prisoners, all the displaced victims of war.

[1] *More Poems.*

A noble verse of Jeremiah looks forward to a millennium in words which are valid to-day:

> And they shall teach no more every man his neighbour, and every man his brother, saying, Know the Lord: for they shall all know me, from the least of them unto the greatest of them, saith the Lord: for I will forgive their iniquity, and remember their sin no more.[1]

The work of Amos is of special interest. 'I was no prophet, neither was I a prophet's son: but I was an herdsman, and a gatherer of sycamore fruit.'[2] Much of the imagery is therefore based upon a shepherd's life; as in that graphic passage where the paws and ears of a lamb are recovered from the lion's mouth.[3] Fire is called down upon the walls of outland cities and tribes, but the denunciation soon shifts to Jerusalem. Again the prophet is the man caught inexorably by God to be His mouthpiece: to denounce evil, to assert the divine omnipotence, to bring promise of judgment and salvation:

> But let judgment run down as waters, and righteousness as a mighty stream.[4]

God is all-powerful: He controls the evils of the crops, the locust plagues, the sending of the rain. The rhetorical imagery is picturesque and violent:

> Shall horses run upon the rock? Will one plough them with oxen? for ye have turned righteousness into gall, and the fruit of righteousness into hemlock.[5]

And we end up with the lovely promise of fertility:

> Behold the days come, saith the Lord, that the plowman shall overtake the reaper, and the treader of grapes him that soweth seed, and the mountains shall drop sweet wine, and the hills shall melt.[6]

[1] *Jer.* 31:34.

[2] 7:14. Amos was a poor man, and the tending of the sycamore trees was his off-season occupation.

[3] 3:12. If a shepherd could show that a wild beast had killed in his flock, he was not liable for the loss.

[4] 5:24.

[5] 6:12. We may be aware of the overtones of gall and of hemlock.

[6] 9:13.

CHAPTER ELEVEN

Character and Action

"For life consists in action, and its end is a mode of action, not a quality."

(Aristotle, *Poetics*)

i

THE CHARACTERS of the Bible are, in Aristotelian terms, 'inferred' rather than stated. We are given little clue to personal appearances; there is, clearly, a stock and uninformative diction like that of the Scottish ballads. David, son of Jesse, is a 'comely' person.[1] The heroine of the Song of Songs is 'black but comely'.[2] The Nazarites were 'more ruddy than rubies'.[3] Of women, 'fair' is the standard adjective: we may remember that it is applied to Sarah, Rebekah, Tamar, Vashti, the Daughters of Job, and occurs in a description of Egypt in which that country is described as 'a very fair heifer'.[4] Warriors are commonly 'men of valour', though the accounts of Goliath and David afford rare instances of vivid personal descriptions. It is probable that many of our own impressions of Biblical character are refracted through iconography. For example, we may find it difficult to separate Moses from Michelangelo's statue of him, and we remember that St. Peter is commonly portrayed with curly hair, while St. Paul is bald.[5] Imaginative portraiture has had the most fertile ground in countless episodes of the Bible: we may recall the great Annunciations, Nativities, Crucifixions, Entombments. The painters and sculptors of every age have taken their models from the civilizations within which they worked.

We remember how paganism and Christianity converge in the Sistine Chapel, and how the same model served Michelangelo for

---

[1] *1 Sam.* 16:18.   [2] 1:5. Sunburned from her work in the fields.
[3] *Lam.* 4:7.   [4] *Jer.* 46:20.
[5] Understandably of Elisha, but less clear in others.

Bacchus and for St. John.[1] And the all-powerful statement, 'God made man in his own image', needs no emphasis in iconography. Even the very sheep acquired a Biblical character in the vision of Samuel Palmer; 'The sheep of God, Sir!'

ii

The second great method of portraying character, through the tone, rhythm, and accent of speech, leads us to more dangerous ground: for here we are dealing, of necessity, with the shadow of a shadow, speech long ago reported, edited, and finally refracted in translation. Yet it is perhaps neither fanciful nor misleading to perceive, in the simple directness of the book of *Ruth*, a peculiar rippling rhythm like that of Shakespeare's Cordelia:

> And Ruth said, Intreat me not to leave thee, or to return from following after thee: for whither thou goest, I will go; and where thou lodgest, I will lodge: thy people shall be my people, and thy God my God.
>
> Where thou diest, will I die, and there will I be buried: the Lord do so to me, and more also, if ought but death part thee and me.[2]

Even the tone of Naomi seems to reflect this gentleness of woman-hood:

> . . . Sit still, my daughter, until thou know how the matter will fall; for the man will not be in rest, until he have finished the thing this day.[3]

It is not altogether fanciful to find something of this kind (for who can doubt that the translators of all ages have entered to some degree into their characters?) in such rhythms as these:

> Therefore Sarah laughed within herself, saying, After I am waxed old shall I have pleasure, my lord being old also?
>
> And the Lord said unto Abraham, Wherefor did Sarah laugh, saying, Shall I of a surety bear a child, which am old?[4]

So Jonah in his anger:

> And God said unto Jonah, Doest thou well to be angry for the gourd? And he said, I do well to be angry, even unto death.[5]

We remember the tension in the voice of David: the twice repeated agony of

> Is the young man Absalom safe?

[1] In the Louvre.   [2] 1:16, 17.   [3] 3:18.   [4] *Gen.* 18:12.
[5] 4:9. 'Unto death' is a rhetorical intensification: 'very angry indeed'.

and the lament that follows, with the sobbing repetitions:

> And the king was much moved, and went up to the chamber
> over the gate, and wept: and as he went, thus he said,
> O my son Absalom, my son, my son Absalom! would God I
> had died for thee,
> O Absalom, my son, my son![1]

The tones of Jesus himself have been noted so often that it would be impertinent to attempt any recapitulation; it is enough to note the authority of the Sermon on the Mount, the tension of

> Then said Jesus unto him, That thou doest, do quickly.

> Little children, yet a little while I am with you.[2]

Martha and Mary seem to be differentiated by rhythm and a querulous tone; both have grown into type-figures:

> But Martha was cumbered about much serving, and came to him, and said, Lord, dost thou not care that my sister hath left me to serve alone? bid her therefore that she help me.

> And Jesus answered and said unto her, Martha, Martha, thou art careful and troubled about many things:

> But one thing is needful: and Mary hath chosen that good part, which shall not be taken away from her.[3]

The Old Testament characters are a little rounder. Moses comes down from the second visit to Sinai with his face shining from that terrible experience on the mountain; we remember his peremptory and ironical outburst against Jehovah:

> And Moses besought the Lord his God, and said, Lord, why doth thy wrath wax hot against thy people, which thou hast brought out of the land of Egypt with great power, and with a mighty hand?

> Wherefore should the Egyptians speak, and say, For mischief did he bring them out, to slay them in the mountains, and to consume them from the face of the earth? Turn from thy fierce wrath, and repent of this evil against thy people.[4]

Rebekah is faintly delineated—she too is 'very fair' to look upon—by the quick generosity of her action in watering the camels; the most perfect descriptions of an eastern courtship coming alive

---

[1] *2 Sam.* 18:33. 　　　　　[2] *Jn.* 13:27, 33.

[3] *Lk.* 10:40–42. Notice the tone given by the repetition of Martha's name.

[4] *Ex.* 32:11–12. It is a question that reverberates through the journeys in the Wilderness, but which is never answered.

through the grace and tact of tiny, almost casual descriptions, as in the meeting with Abraham's servant:

And when she had done giving him drink, she said, I will draw water for thy camels also, until they have done drinking.

And she hasted, and emptied her pitcher in the trough, and ran again unto the well to draw water, and drew for all his camels.

And the man wondering at her held his peace, to wit whether the Lord had made his journey prosperous or not.[1]

iii

One of the most fully-delineated characters-in-action is Jezebel; behind the laconic and brutal story there moves a living woman, individual yet true to her type in history and in literature. We may recall her most dramatic rôle, as well as the vividness of the woman herself, in the intense simplicity and energy of the descriptions.

The 'plot' is simple.[2] Naboth owns a vineyard adjoining the palace of Ahab, King of Samaria. Ahab wants the land for a herb-garden, and offers to buy it outright, or to exchange it for a better vineyard. Naboth refuses:

The Lord forbid it me, that I should give the inheritance of my fathers unto thee.

This is typical of Israelite practice, as in so many peasant countries. Land has a sacred character; inherited land is a trust of a special kind. Ahab sulks like a spoilt child. Then Jezebel—

Why is thy spirit so sad, that thou eatest no bread?

Ahab repeats what Naboth has said, but, significantly, makes it a flat refusal, without repeating to Jezebel the cogent plea that the land is a family inheritance. Jezebel rallies him scornfully, and the tones of her voice come strongly through the rhythms:

Dost thou now govern the kingdom of Israel? arise, and eat bread, and let thine heart be merry: I will give thee the vineyard of Naboth the Jezreelite.[3]

---

[1] *Gen.* 24:19-21. The form '*wist*' is familiar, but the Anglo-Saxon *to wit* is strange but effective: perhaps suggesting the servant's puzzlement as to the outcome of the meeting by the well. We do not lose if we meditate on the archetypal symbolism of the well, and of other such meetings there.

[2] *1 Kgs.* 21, *2 Kgs.* 9.

[3] Jezebel was a Phoenician woman, who understood only tyranny. She would have no sympathy with the more democratic traditions of Israel.

186

So Jezebel plots; writing letters in Ahab's name, and sealed with his seal, to the elders of Naboth's city. They are to proclaim a fast, a sign that some member of the community has committed a monstrous sin. They are to bring Naboth before a court, and set up two false witnesses, 'sons of Belial', to accuse him.

> And there came in two men, children of Belial, and sat before him: and the men of Belial witnessed against him, even against Naboth, in the presence of the people, saying, Naboth did blaspheme God and the king. Then they carried him out of the city, and stoned him with stones, that he died.

We can reconstruct the scene. False accusation and perjury is a constant trouble in all courts of justice, but is peculiarly vicious in the Middle and Far East.[1] The law required two witnesses. The power of their testimony, and the difficulty of refutation, may be assessed by the prohibition in the Decalogue. We recall the alleged blasphemy in the trial of Christ; but there Pilate had been able to exercise the Roman power of cross-examination.[2]

Jezebel is told of Naboth's death, and gives Ahab the news, with a further subtle twist, making Naboth's action seem still more capricious:

> Arise, take possession of the vineyard of Naboth the Jezreelite, which *he refused to give thee for money*: for Naboth is not alive, but dead.

The affair has become notorious, in the way such things do; we can recall instances in recent history. The prophet Elisha is ordered to confront Ahab:

> Thus saith the Lord, Hast thou killed, and also taken possession? And thou shalt speak unto him, saying, Thus saith the Lord, In the place where the dogs licked the blood of Naboth shall dogs lick thy blood, even thine.

It seems that this instance of Ahab's wickedness is one of many. Evil is to come on him and on his posterity.

> And of Jezebel also spake the Lord, saying, The dogs shall eat Jezebel by the wall of Jezreel.[3]

---

[1] Even to production of evidence of murder, including the corpse and all needful witness, which is not uncommon.   [2] *Lk.* 23:14.

[3] We must remember the unclean horror of the scavenging dogs of Middle East villages; and 'Deliver my soul from the sword: my darling from the power of the dog.' (*Ps.* 22:20.)

Then Jezebel vanishes from the narrative for a time, but we have the strange episode of the prophets and the battle of Ramoth-gilead against the Syrians. Here we are involved with the prophet Micaiah: who first advises battle, and then, being adjured to tell the truth, prophesies defeat. But this does not suit Ahab, and we have a curious insight into his mind. It is best given in the words of *A.V.*:[1]

> And the king of Israel said unto Jehoshaphat, Did I not tell thee that he would prophesy no good concerning me, but evil?
>
> And he said, Hear thou therefore the word of the Lord: I saw the Lord sitting on his throne, and all the host of heaven standing by him on his right hand and on his left.

(We remember many pictures of such a scene—Michelangelo, Blake, Doré—and think of the meaning of *Sabaoth*, the hosts, the armies of God; for He commands the angels and the warriors of Israel, and, by later tradition, the 'stars in their courses'.)

> And the Lord said, Who shall persuade Ahab, that he may go up and fall at Ramoth-gilead? And one said on this manner, and another said on that manner.
>
> And there came forth a spirit, and stood before the Lord, and said, I will persuade him.
>
> And the Lord said unto him, Wherewith? And he said, I will go forth, and I will be a lying spirit in the mouth of all his prophets. And he said, Thou shalt persuade him, and prevail also: go forth and do so.

This accounts in Ahab's mind for the 'lying spirit' among the prophets other than Micaiah, who is imprisoned on his orders for his forthright speaking. The two kings go up to battle; Ahab disguises himself, whereas Jehoshaphat wears his royal robes. The enemy commander orders the Syrian chariots to 'fight neither with small or great, save only with the king of Israel'. At first they pursue the wrong king, because of the robes. Then Ahab is mortally wounded by a random shot, the bow drawn 'at a venture', struck between the joints of his armour.[2] For a time his charioteers or armour-bearers tie him upright or support him, so that the armies should not see that he was wounded: much as the Celtic hero Cuchulain, mortally wounded in his last battle, had himself tied to the stump of a tree.[3]

---

[1] *1 Kgs.* 22:18 ff.

[2] or, 'between the lower armour and the breastplate'. All armour is vulnerable to arrow-fire; a favourite mark was the arm-pit.

[3] As in Oliver Sheppard's bronze statue in the General Post Office in Dublin.

But Ahab dies in the evening; the Syrians rout the combined forces of Israel and Judah. Ahab is buried in Samaria; his chariot and armour are washed out in a pool, and the dogs lick up his blood.

So the first part of the prophecy is fulfilled; there remains the doom on Ahab's children. This is reasserted by Elisha: 'the whole house of Ahab shall perish':

> And the dogs shall eat Jezebel in the portion of Jezreel, and there shall be none to bury her. And he opened the door and fled.

Gradually the curse is fulfilled. Jehu the son of Jehoshaphat conspires against Joram. Jehu's driving has become proverbial for its fury: but he emerges in the narrative as a bitter, ironic, powerful man, economical of phrase, rapid and ruthless in action. He confronts Joram, who is accompanied by Ahaziah; three kings in their chariots:

> And it came to pass, when Joram saw Jehu, that he said Is it peace, Jehu? And he answered, What peace, so long as the whoredoms[1] of thy mother Jezebel and her witchcrafts are so many?

Joram turns to flee: Jehu shoots him through the chest. By Jehu's order the body is flung into the plot of ground that had been Naboth's. Ahaziah flees 'by the way of the garden house', but the charioteers overtake him, and he dies of his wounds at Megiddo. Now comes the final act of the drama, the prophecy on Jezebel:

> And when Jehu was come to Jezreel, Jezebel heard of it; and she painted her face, and tired her head, and looked out at a window.[2]
> And as Jehu entered at the gate, she said, Had Zimri peace, who slew his master?

Here is the taunt, the warning against the nemesis that follows rebellion. As to Jehu—

> And he lifted up his face to the window, and said, Who is on my side? who? And there looked out to him two or three eunuchs.[3]

---

[1] This is clearly idolatry, as set out in *2 Chron.* 21:13; but some additional point is given subsequently by the description of Jezebel's painting.

[2] This too is part of the picture of the prostitute. In view of what follows, was her house, like Rahab's, on the wall?

[3] Perhaps household servants, terrified of the conqueror's approach. Eunuchs were traditionally timorous.

And he said, Throw her down. So they threw her down: and some of her blood was sprinkled on the wall, and on the horses; and he trode her under foot.

And when he was come, he did eat and drink,[1] and said, Go, see now this cursed woman, and bury her, for she is a king's daughter.

And they went to bury her: but they found no more of her than the skull, and the feet, and the palms of her hands.

Wherefore they came again and told him. And he said, This is the word of the Lord, which he spake by his servant Elijah the Tishbite, saying, In the portion of Jezreel shall dogs eat the flesh of Jezebel:

And the carcase of Jezebel shall be as dung upon the face of the field in the portion of Jezreel; so that they shall not say, This is Jezebel.[2]

Jehu's picture is completed in the next chapter.[3] He slaughters the seventy sons of Ahab, puts their heads in two baskets and lays them at the gate of Jezreel.[4] Then he speaks to the assembled people in the morning, and we can hear the ironic tones:

Ye be righteous: behold, I conspired against my master, and slew him: but who slew all these?

The policy of extermination is pursued with ruthless laconic efficiency:

Jehu met with the brethren of Ahaziah king of Judah, and said, Who are ye? And they answered, We are the brethren of Ahaziah; and we go down to salute the children of the king and the children of the queen.

And he said, Take them alive. And they took them alive, and slew them at the pit of the shearing-house, even two and forty men; neither left he any of them.

The culmination of Jehu's work is the great purge of Baal. He proclaims a solemn assembly or synod; they fill the house of Baal 'from one end to the other'. The worshippers are invited to check their own numbers, to make sure that there are no 'servants of the Lord' among them. The priests of Baal then proceed with ritual sacrifice.

[1] Perhaps a deliberately-assumed carelessness, like that of Coriolanus? (cf. his treatment of the 'poor host' of Corioli, I, 9. 81–91), or delaying to take action in order to show his greatness? In either event, another aspect of Jehu's character.
[2] 2 *Kgs.* 9:30 ff.   [3] *Ibid.*, 10.
[4] The *samadh*, the pile of severed heads, has various precedents as a battle trophy, a memorial or a warning. *v.* Kipling's ballad, 'The Grave of the Hundred Dead'.

Jehu has prepared a band of picked men, stationed outside the temple, each under threat of death if he allows anyone to escape alive. It is possible that Jehu himself goes in to make the sacrifice of burnt offering, which is the signal for the armed men to go in and massacre the priests. The images are brought out of the temple and destroyed, with the image of Baal himself.

But Jehu himself later becomes a worshipper of 'the golden calves that were in Beth-el, and that were in Dan'.

iv

Of all the leaders of the Old Testament, there is only one whose whole life-span from birth to death is covered by the narratives. It has been pointed out[1] that the pattern of his life corresponds almost exactly with the typical trajectory, the rise and fall, of the tragic heroes of mythology. His parents were of the principal family of the Levites, and near relatives. He was reputed to be of royal lineage, the son of Pharaoh's daughter. Pharaoh attempted to kill him at birth, but he was spirited away, and reared secretly. We know nothing of his childhood. On reaching manhood he kills an overseer who is afflicting his countrymen, and flees to Midian, where he marries the ruler's daughter. He returns to Egypt, and, as a Magus, gains magical victories over Pharaoh (the staff turned into a serpent, the leprous hand healed, the water turned to blood). He becomes a leader, ruler and law-giver, but later loses the favour of Jehovah and is removed from his leadership. He disappears mysteriously from the top of a mountain. In all this there is a close correspondence with the pattern shown by such diverse figures as Oedipus, Theseus, Romulus, King Arthur, Robin Hood.

Against this broad backcloth we can turn our attention to some of the details of Moses' life. As a refugee from Pharaoh's revenge he travels some two hundred miles across the desert into Midian, and meets his bride by a well. There he brings his flock to Sinai, and we have the first meeting with Jehovah; the episode of the burning bush, the order to lead Israel out of Egypt, and to 'serve God upon this mountain'. Moses is reluctant to obey. He is provided with the three magical signs to impress Pharaoh: Jehovah is in open competition with the Egyptian gods. We then have the first of many dialogues with God, and we note that Moses is the only character,

---

[1] e.g. Lord Raglan, *The Hero*, London, 1936, ch. xvi.

191

other than Job, who achieves this, repeatedly and at length. Uniquely also, there is some self-analysis:

> And Moses said unto the Lord, O my Lord, I am not eloquent, neither heretofore, nor since thou has spoken unto thy servant: but I am slow of speech, and of a slow tongue.[1]

This is the first of several such difficulties:

> And Moses spake before the Lord, saying, Behold, the children of Israel have not hearkened unto me; how then shall Pharaoh hear me, who am of uncircumcised lips?[2]

Both objections are over-ruled:

> And the anger of the Lord was kindled against Moses, and he said, Is not Aaron the Levite thy brother? I know that he can speak well.[3]

Two very strange incidents follow:

> And it came to pass by the way in the inn,[4] that the Lord met him, and sought to kill him.[5]

This is the first sign that we are dealing with the attempt to describe the attributes of Jehovah in their non-rational form. The ascription to deity of emotions such as 'wrath' and 'jealousy' we must take in the first place as primitive aspects of what Otto calls 'daemonic dread': secondly as an attempt, within the limitations of figurative language, to describe attributes of the divinity which, because they are of a wholly different *kind*, can only be perceived in approximate and hence misleading terms.[6]

The rest of Moses' epic is too familiar to require recapitulation. Only we may note certain points in the great journey. The bones of Joseph are carried with the host out of Egypt. Moses and Aaron his lieutenant are faced with the continuous, inevitable complaints:

> Because there were no graves in Egypt, hast thou taken us away to die in the wilderness?[7]

---

[1] *Ex.* 4:10.

[2] *Ibid.*, 6:12. The image is sometimes used of moral defects: cf. *Ezek.* 44:7, 'uncircumcised in heart'.   [3] *Ibid.*, 4:14.

[4] *Ibid.*, 4:24. R.V. has 'lodging place' for 'inn'.

[5] Some commentators read this as no more than a circumlocution for 'he fell ill'; others, that the cause for Jehovah's wrath is Moses' failure to circumcise his son. Zipprah his wife proceeds to do this, with the flint knife of ritual.

[6] See Otto, *The Idea of the Holy*, esp. ch. viii.   [7] *Ex.* 14:11.

Would to God we had died by the hand of the Lord in the land of Egypt, when we sat by the flesh pots, and when we did eat bread to the full; for ye have brought us forth into this wilderness, to kill this whole assembly with hunger.[1]

Wherefore is this that thou hast brought us up out of Egypt, to kill us and our children and our cattle with thirst?[2]

Sometimes (as Moses protests to Jehovah) the people are ready to stone him. When Moses lingers on Sinai, they demand 'gods which shall go before us'. Aaron makes a faltering and naïve apology for the episode of the Golden Calf:

And I said unto them, Whosoever hath any gold, let them break it off. So they gave it me: then I cast it into the fire, *and there came out this calf*.[3]

Only the repeated dialogue of Moses with the Lord saves, again and again, this 'stiff-necked people'. Slowly the complex Law is unfolded, the ark and the tabernacle prepared, the precautions for hygiene, sanitation, sexual conduct are codified. There are the prohibitions which are become the common law of Western Europe, and the superstitions that are to cause so much misery and bloodshed:

A man also or woman that hath a familiar spirit, or that is a wizard, shall surely be put to death: they shall stone them with stones: their blood shall be upon them.[4]

Through so much that is tedious, repetitious, cliché-ridden, we have the impression of an immense integrity, relieved by outbursts of very human despair at Moses' terrible responsibility:

And Moses said unto the Lord, Wherefore hast thou afflicted thy servant? and wherefore have I not found favour in thy sight, that thou layest the burden of all this people upon me?[5]

Rebellion, transgression, intercession, pursue their oscillating courses. Even Aaron and Miriam engage in a plot, and are confronted by Jehovah in person, and Miriam is smitten with leprosy.[6] Again the congregation mutiny: 'Would God that we had died in the Land of Egypt! or would God we had died in this wilderness!'[7] It is not difficult to imagine the horrors of that life, the punishment of

---

[1] *Ibid.*, 16:3.   [2] *Ibid.*, 17:3.   [3] *Ibid.*, 32:24.
[4] *Lev.* 20:27. Consider, for example, the terrible *Malleus Maleficarum*, the text book on the 'examination' of witchcraft.
[5] *Num.* 11:11.   [6] *Ibid.*, 12.   [7] *Ibid.*, 14:2.

'this evil congregation' by thirst, by raids from the Amalekites and Canaanites.[1]

Yet it is not all gloom. There are lyric fragments, such as the digging of the well:

> And from thence they went to Beer: that is the well whereof the Lord spake unto Moses, Gather the people together, and I will give them water.
>
> Then Israel sang this song, Spring up, O well; sing ye unto it:
>
> The princes digged the well, the nobles of the people digged it, by the direction of the lawgiver, with their staves.[2]

Many dramatic incidents in the story are familiar. It is wholly human, and would become even more perspicuous and vital if it could be purged of much that we now consider irrelevant. At the end, in the mysterious death-scene on the mountain top of Pisgah that looks over Jordan to the Promised Land, we have the impression of a complex and noble figure. It is less, perhaps, the image of the stern-faced hornéd prophet of Michelangelo's vision, burdened with the Stone Tables; but rather a great and versatile leader, infinitely provoked with all the problems that any leadership involves; human in his despair at the fallibility and petulance of the chosen people; unwearying in his terrible doom of incessant confrontation with God on their behalf. The patience of Job has become proverbial; it seems pale beside that of Moses. A few great men in time to come were to multiply the roles of military leader and lawgiver; none were to combine them with this mysterious dialogue that left his face shining, so that none could bear to look on it. The epilogue, or rather *lusis* of his tragedy is the great hymn that concludes the recapitulation of the action.[3] The 'song'[4] is at once a prophecy, a promise, a threat. Then the tribes receive his blessing, and we may conclude by quoting the end of that benediction:

> The eternal God is thy refuge, and underneath are the everlasting arms: and he shall thrust out the enemy from before thee; and shall say, Destroy them.
>
> Israel then shall dwell in safety alone: the fountain of Jacob shall be upon a land of corn and wine; also his heavens shall drop down dew.[5]

[1] *Num.* 14:45.   [2] *Ibid.*, 21:17.   [3] *Deut.* 1–31.
[4] *Ibid.*, 32:1–43.   [5] *Ibid.*, 33:27, 28.

V

But the fullest, and probably the most famous chronicle of characters-in-action is contained in the drama of which the main actors are Samuel, David, Jonathan, and Saul. It is a story of war, intrigue loyalty, perfidy; witchcraft and idolatry; magnanimity, jealousy, and the extremities of deceit. We may outline the story as told in the two books of *Samuel*.

Hannah is given a son, after suffering the indignities and taunts flung at childless women in the East. The child Samuel is 'lent' by her to the Lord, and becomes a servant in the temple, under the priest Eli. Hannah lives in the song which is the precursor of the *Magnificat*[1] and for the strange passage after she has taken her vow:

> Now Hannah, she spake in her heart; only her lips moved, but her voice was not heard: therefore Eli thought she had been drunken.

> And Eli said unto her, How long wilt thou be drunken? put away thy wine from thee.[2]

The reply gives the full dignity of the woman, and a metaphor for all sorrow:

> And Hannah answered and said, No, my lord, I am a woman of a sorrowful spirit: I have drunk neither wine nor strong drink, but have poured out my soul before the Lord.

There follows the story of the call in the night to Samuel; the accusation of the evil done by Eli's sons with the temple prostitutes; Samuel's reluctance to discuss his vision with Eli, for Samuel is to be the instrument of the Lord:

> And the Lord said to Samuel, Behold I will do a thing in Israel, at which both the ears of every one that heareth it shall tingle.[3]

The scene shifts to one of the interminable wars. Israel is defeated with heavy loss. Why has the Lord smitten them? A hurried conference of the Elders decides that the ark of the Covenant must be fetched from Shiloh. The Philistines hear the shout of jubilation that greets its arrival in the camp, and speak of it in words that echo, a little confusedly, those used so often by Israel:

> Woe unto us! who shall deliver us out of the hand of these mighty Gods? these are the Gods that smote the Egyptians with all the plagues in the wilderness.

[1] See p. 94, *supra*.　　　　[2] *1 Sam.* 1:13.　　　　[3] *Ibid.*, 3:11.

Be strong, and quit yourselves like men, O ye Philistines, that ye be not servant unto the Hebrews, as they have been to you: quit yourselves like men, and fight.[1]

But even the ark is useless as a talisman; Israel is again defeated, with still greater loss.[2] Eli's two sons and the ark are captured; Eli falls at the news, and dies. The Philistines bring the ark in triumph to Ashdod, but they find it too troublesome to retain; its hidden indwelling deity has a kind of personal tournament with their own corn-god,[3] Dagon; and Dagon becomes in Milton's verse

> ". . . That twice-batter'd god of Palestine."

Then the Philistines are smitten with boils. Clearly the ark is too strong a magic to be retained with comfort or safety. They return it to Israel with trespass-offerings, including golden models of the boils and of the mice that have plagued them. But the men of Bethshemesh look into the ark, and are smitten by the Lord (50,070 of them, a wholly ridiculous number), so that they hand it over hastily to the men of Kirjath-jearim. Samuel exhorts Israel to mend their ways, departing from the 'strange gods' and Ashtaroth (Astarte). They demand that Samuel shall give them a king to judge them. Samuel does his utmost to dissuade them, pointing out the certain extortions and oppressions that will be exercised by a king. But the people will not be persuaded; they would be familiar with kingship in the surrounding hostile tribes, and it seems possible that they anticipate more decisive leadership in battle. The Lord advises Samuel:

> Hearken unto their voice, and make them a king.

Samuel records the election and anoints Saul with the ritual that was to set a Christian precedent, and initiates the dilemma which is at the centre of Shakespeare's history plays:

> "Not all the water in the rough rude sea
> Can wash the balm from an anointed king;
> The breath of worldly men cannot depose
> The deputy elected by the Lord."[4]

---

[1] *1 Sam.* 4:8, 9.

[2] 4,000 in the first battle, 30,000 in the second. The numbers are much exaggerated, as are all the 'orders of battle' in the subsequent narratives.

[3] Formerly described as a fish-god; through a combination of false etymology, and the closeness of the Philistines to the sea.

[4] *Richard II*, III. 2. 54.

The principle of kingship implies a rejection of Jehovah, but divine help is promised if both king and people continue to obey Him. Yet the act is hardly completed before we hear the first warnings of the ealous storms that are to occupy so much of the succeeding narrative:

> But the children of Belial said, How shall this man save us? And they despised him, and brought him no presents. But he held his peace.[1]

Saul's first kingly action is to react violently to a threat by the Ammonites, who demand as the price of a peace treaty that they shall thrust out the right eyes of the Israelites. After begging for time to discuss the terms, time which the Ammonites (curiously) grant, Saul sends out the fiery cross in the form of dismembered oxen, raises an army, and defeats the Ammonites with great slaughter. The dissidents who have attacked Saul's kingship are threatened with death by the people because of their lack of faith, but Saul shows, once again, his magnanimity:

> And Saul said, There shall not a man be put to death this day: for to day the Lord hath wrought salvation in Israel.[2]

Saul reigns for two years, and raises a force against the ever-turbulent Philistines. Part of it is under the command of Jonathan, who leads a successful expedition against the Philistines in Geba. The latter, enraged, muster a very large army, 'as the sand of the sea-shore in multitude', and encamp at Michmash. The Israelite army disperses in a panic. Saul in desperation offers burnt and peace offerings; this is a usurpation of the spiritual powers of Samuel, who, as the king-maker, is the divine agent for ritual. The ageing Samuel comes to visit him; Saul has fallen from grace, and his kingdom will not endure.[3] The classic trajectory, the rise and fall of the Hero, is now apparent. From their base at Michmash the Philistines send out raiding parties in three large detachments. The weapons of the Israelites are in a poor state because of the lack of smiths, but Saul and Jonathan at least seem to have effective weapons. Jonathan goes off on a counter-raid, without informing his father, and defeats the Philistines, who panic in their turn. Saul pronounces a curse on anyone who touches food until the rout of the Philistines is completed.[4]

---

[1] *1 Sam.* 10:27.   [2] *Ibid.*, 11:13.   [3] *Ibid.*, 13:14.

[4] Such quasi-magical prohibitions are not uncommon: cf. the Celtic *gedsa*. But, as Jonathan says, it is clearly the height of military incompetence. The problem of completing an initial rout is one of the commonest in warfare; cf. the episode of Gideon on Mt. Gilboa.

Jonathan unwittingly transgresses the edict by tasting honey. This prohibition is clearly so foolish that Jonathan protests, and this marks the beginning of the schism, perhaps even of Saul's psychic illness:

> Then said Jonathan, My father hath troubled the land: see, I pray you, how mine eyes have been enlightened, because I tasted a little of this honey.
>
> How much more, if haply the people had eaten freely to day of the spoil of their enemies which they found? for had there not been now a much greater slaughter among the Philistines?[1]

The famished troops make matters worse by slaughtering the captured sheep and cattle 'on the hoof', and eating the meat with the blood.[2] Saul threatens Jonathan with death, but his exploits against the Philistines have made him into a national hero, and the people refuse to allow Jonathan to be put to death.[3]

From now on Saul falls into error after error. This is the classic sequence of tragedy, and we may again consider Shakespeare's histories. After an expedition against the southern raiders, the Amalekites, he disobeys the divine injunction to put them all to the sword, including their flocks and herds.[4] He spares the latter, and justifies his action on the feeble grounds that the people have insisted on sacrificing the animals. This brings out Samuel's classic reproof, which marks, perhaps, a turning point in the theology of the Old Testament:

> And Samuel said, Hath the Lord as great delight in burnt offerings and sacrifices, as in obeying the voice of the Lord? Behold, to obey is better than sacrifice, and to hearken than the fat of rams.
>
> For rebellion is as the sin of witchcraft, and stubbornness is as iniquity and idolatry. Because thou hast rejected the word of the Lord, he hath also rejected thee from being king.[5]

vi

The stage is now set for a series of familiar episodes; the choice and anointing of David, the 'evil spirit from God' that begins to trouble

---

[1] *1 Sam.* 14:29, 30.

[2] The blood is sacred to Jehovah. It must be drained into the earth to restore the life-force. This is one of the commonest of beliefs.

[3] *1 Sam.* 14:45.　　　　　　　　[4] This is the *cherem*, the ban of God.

[5] *1 Sam.* 15:22, 23. An alternative reading of *witchcraft* is *divination*: which links up with Saul's despairing visit to the Witch of Endor, and recalls the astrological practices of other leaders in their decline.

Saul, the temporary exorcising of that spirit by David's music, the duel with Goliath, the covenant of friendship between David and Jonathan that is become proverbial. There follows the notorious often-quoted ballad:

> Saul hath slain his thousands, and David his ten thousands.

Saul is clearly falling a victim to intermittent mania, shown by the attempts on David's life with the javelin.[1] The king's instability grows; he first promises his daughter Merab as David's wife, then gives her to another. A second daughter, Michal, is in love with David:

> . . . and they told Saul, and the thing pleased him.
> And Saul said, I will give him her, that she may be a snare to him, and that the hand of the Philistines may be against him.[2]

The plot grows and ramifies, like an Elizabethan play. Saul, through the agency of his servants, suggests that David would be an acceptable son-in-law. David protests his unworthiness and humble birth. Again Saul sends an 'inspired' message through his servants that David need produce no dowry: only the foreskins of a hundred Philistines. David goes on a raid, and returns with two hundred; Saul's ineffective plot to cause David's death is to be repeated ironically when David uses somewhat the same means to have Uriah killed, so that he may take Uriah's wife, Bathsheba.[3] In spite of attempts at reconciliation by Jonathan, enmity and suspicion increase. Another victory by David is followed by another attempted javelin murder by Saul. Michal his wife warns David and he escapes. Michal has bought time by a strange device:

> And Michal took an image, and laid it in the bed, and put a pillow of goat's hair for his bolster, and covered it with a cloth.[4]

The 'image' is mysterious; the Hebrew word, *teraphim*, is also used of divinatory practices. If it were indeed a life-sized figure, there seems to have been little value in its delaying effect, for David had already escaped. It is possible that it may have been some magical object to discourage the messengers of the king, who had been ordered to bring David to him 'in his bed'.[5]

---

[1] Browning's poem on the episode is familiar.
[2] *I Sam.* 18:20, 21.   [3] *2 Sam.* 11.   [4] *I Sam.* 19:13.
[5] *Ibid.*, 19:15. But we remember the function of such a simulacrum in Celtic myth: as in Yeats' *The Only Jealousy of Emer*.

David now becomes an outlaw. He absents himself from the king's table, and through Jonathan sends a message asking leave on his behalf to go to Bethlehem to a family sacrifice. Now the evil starts to multiply; Saul turns on Jonathan:

> Then Saul's anger was kindled against Jonathan, and he said unto him, Thou son of the perverse rebellious woman,[1] do not I know that thou hast chosen the son of Jesse to thine own confusion, and unto the confusion of thy mother's nakedness?

> For as long as the son of Jesse liveth upon the ground, thou shalt not be established, nor thy kingdom. Wherefore now send and fetch him unto me, for he shall surely die.[2]

It is an archetypal situation. Jonathan by his loyalty to David is breaking the strongest bond, that of the family; the breach more terrible because of the sanctity of the royal line.

There follows the incident of the transmission of information between Jonathan and David by the dramatic shooting of the arrows.[3] David flees for his life, comes to Nob, and asks for help from Ahimelech the priest, who receives him fearfully. At David's instance he gives him the hallowed shewbread, and the sword of Goliath, which has been kept as a trophy in the sanctuary:

> There is none like that; give it me.

The help given by Ahimelech costs that priest his life. David comes to Gath and is recognized by the Philistines as the hero of the ballad

> Saul hath slain his thousands, and David his ten thousands.

Achish the king of Gath is obviously interested—perhaps because David would be a valuable hostage in negotiations with Saul—but David anticipates treachery, and feigns madness. He escapes to Adullam, and becomes the leader of a band of outlaws, who finally take up their position in the forest of Hareth. There, as one would expect, an informer brings news of him to Saul: Doeg the Edomite, a member of that ill-omened tribe, also tells Saul the story of Ahim-

---

[1] Even more vividly, 'Thou son of perverse rebellion'. Again we are reminded of Shakespeare: of Aumerle in *Richard II*, Edmund in *Lear*, Prince Hal of *Henry IV*.
[2] *Ibid.*, 20:30.
[3] *1 Sam.* 20:35–40. It is pleasant to note the *A.V.*'s term for the bows and arrows: 'And Jonathan gave his *artillery* unto his lad, and said unto him, Go, carry them to the city'. So also in the Elizabethan 'classic' on archery, Ascham's *Toxophilus*.

elech and the shewbread. The latter is summoned, and we have a graphic picture of the oriental tyrant, the threat, and Ahimelech's defence:

> And who is so faithful among all thy servants as David, who is the king's son in law, and goeth at thy bidding, and is honourable in thine house? . . .
>
> And the king said, Thou shalt surely die, Ahimelech, thou, and all thy father's house.
>
> And the king said unto the footmen that stood about him, Turn, and slay the priests of the Lord; because their hand is also with David, and because they knew when he fled, and did not shew it to me. But the servants of the king would not put forth their hands to fall upon the priests of the Lord.[1]

It is a terrible and common happening in war, this reprisal for concealment. Saul's likeness to Macbeth increases steadily

> "I am in blood
> Stepp'd in so far, that, should I wade no more
> Returning were as tedious as go o'er."[2]

The massacre of Ahimelech and his fellow priests—Abiathar his son alone escapes—is carried out by Doeg the Edomite.

vii

The story then becomes more episodic; events succeed each other in rapid and momentous succession. The Philistines (who by this time must have mastered most of the northern territories of Israel) carry out a raid against Keilah. David, after making oracular inquiry of God, attacks and defeats them. But Keilah, which David has entered, is a fortified city, and Saul thinks that he has David in a trap. Again an inquiry of the oracle: the men of Keilah will, it says, in spite of David's rescue, deliver him up to Saul. So he leaves Keilah, and again becomes a hunted man, in the wilderness of Ziph. The whole scene is intensely vivid. Jonathan and David meet secretly in the wood, and renew their covenant of friendship. But the Ziphites seek to betray David:

> Then came up the Ziphites to Saul to Gibeah, saying, Doth not David hide himself with us in strong holds in the wood, in the hill of Hachilah, which is on the south of Jeshimon?[3]

---

[1] *1 Sam.* 22:14 ff. [2] III. 4. 136. [3] *1 Sam.* 23:19 ff.

Now therefore, O king, come down according to all the desire of thy soul to come down; and our part shall be to deliver him into the king's hand.

And Saul said, Blessed be ye of the Lord; for ye have compassion on me.[1]

I have lingered on this incredible story for several reasons. It forms a compact and exciting miniature epic. It has many of the elements of the traditional romances; the election of the humble, the duel with the giant, the consultation of oracles, the enchanted sword, the raising of a ghost. In the whole cycle, loaded with ironies of *hubris* and of human arrogance, there are perpetual reminders of the classic sequences of Shakespeare's history plays. At every turn of the story there is profound psychological interest; not only in the kings and captains and warriors, but in the temper of the small cities and their peoples. Saul's progress to ruin through something like manic depression is retarded, dramatically, by David's own certainty that Saul is the Lord's anointed. The qualities that are to emerge in David when he reaches his height as the great king, lawyer, poet, economic minister, begin to emerge in his toughness as an outlaw, his magnanimity as an opponent, his ability to inspire the greatest of all proverbial friendships; and, perhaps, his ability to win the love of women.

Across this great tapestry, the pressure from the Philistines always in the background, the women move in their variety; Saul's daughter, Merab, is at first promised to David, then given to another: the other daughter, Michal, who falls in love with David, is to be given for a dowry believed to be certain death. Michal saves her husband's life, but is then given by her father to Phalti, while her former husband is an outlaw. Abigail, soon to be widowed, appears as a model of gracious tactfulness, set off against her churlish and drunken husband; we have the impression that she welcomes the young hero with a modest and becoming delight, after her first marriage of exasperation.

The epic is filled with dramatic happenings. There is David's cutting off of the skirts of Saul's robe in the cave at En-gedi, and the equally daring surprise raid in which he steals Saul's spear and bolster while he sleeps. There is the episode of Nabal and Abigail,

[1] It is not, I think, unduly imaginative to discern the tones of self-pity, of snatching, for reassurance, at some kindness, in this last sentence; one symptom among many of Saul's increasing mania.

202

and David's attempt at something like a protection racket; he has refrained from raiding Nabal's shearers. David makes a temporary alliance with the Philistines, which ceases when the latter mounts a large-scale attack on Israel. Meanwhile there is the classic instance of the Witch of En-dor. Samuel is dead; Saul is desperate for advice which, whether by prophets, dreams or divination by the Urim,[1] have all failed him. It is a mark of the final stage of Saul's mania—there are notorious examples in history—that he should seek this supernatural aid. The witchcraft is illegal, by Saul's own edict,[2] and the witch, justifiably, fears a trap. (We may profitably remind ourselves of the witch-scenes in *Macbeth*, and of their effect on the Shakespearian audience, in view of James I's well-known interests.) Again, we may remember that scene in the *Odyssey*[3] where Odysseus summons the ghost of Tiresias for much-needed advice, and beats aside with the flat of his sword the unwanted ghosts who throng to drink the blood that Odysseus has prepared for them in the trench. The classical ghost rises from the underworld.

> And the woman said unto Saul, I saw gods ascending out of the earth. And he said unto her, What form is he of? And she said, An old man cometh up; and he is covered with a mantle. And Saul perceived that it was Samuel. . . .[4]

viii

'The beauty of Israel is slain upon thy high places: how are the mighty fallen!' David's elegy[5] is the greatest of the Old Testament; like a Greek chorus, it closes the first acts of the tragedy. Yet David has his *moira*, his portion of fate, like Saul and Jonathan. A leaf has been turned in the book that reads in these

> "undetermin'd differences of kings"[6]

but the new reign, that brings David to the height of his power and makes Israel an empire, already has the seeds of doom. The tragedy continues in its quick exciting texture of narrative; the characteristics are a taut economy of language, and the sense of actuality given by the stories. The unit that was Israel is split, coagulates, splits again as

---

[1] The nature of the divinatory *Urim* is uncertain. It is possible that they may have been discs drawn from a pouch: one colour for 'Yes', another for 'No'.
[2] *I Sam.* 28:9.   [3] Bk XI.
[4] *I Sam.* 28:13, 14. 'Gods' are merely supernatural beings.
[5] *2 Sam.* 1:19 ff.   [6] *King John*, II. I. 355.

the dynastic choice develops its inevitable destiny of rebellion, the Elizabethan breach of 'nature'. Around, and every side, are the pressures of the Philistines and of the raiding Bedouin tribes; complicating still further the swiftly moving and dramatic sub-plots. We can discern many of the aspects of the romantic story that are later to become traditional: the outlaw, the magic sword, the sudden raid, the informant; the magnanimity and treachery and ruthlessness of the seeker of power.

It is great literature, but it is not a moral story. The abridged versions that have been so often used in 'religious instruction' fail, I believe, to convey the tremendous momentum, the perennial excitement, of the epic. It is possible that its true character is not to be realized without some physical experience of conditions that are in some way comparable; of the importance of terrain to the man 'hunted like a partridge upon the mountains'; of the good faith or treachery of apparent allies; of the power of the informer; of the suspicious and sudden violences engendered in any occupied territory that lies, always, under the domination of fear and revenge. David's kingdom endures, but immediately we are caught in the cycle of murder, suspicion, intrigue, the revolted son. Is it the doom of the archetypal king from that first fatal anointing, by the voice of the people? or (as it seems to me) an utterly convincing microcosm of the trajectory, and the vanity, of the Hero?

CHAPTER TWELVE

The Bible and Evil

The imagination of man's heart is evil from his youth.
(*Gen.* 8:21)

i

FROM TIME TO TIME indignant letters appear in the newspapers, to the effect that the writers have refused to sing certain verses of the *Psalms*. Common selections for this purpose are:

The Lord said, I will bring again from Bashan, I will bring my people again from the depths of the sea:

That thy foot may be dipped in the blood of thine enemies, and the tongue of thy dogs in the same.[1]

O daughter of Babylon, who art to be destroyed; happy shall he be, that rewardeth thee as thou hast served us.

Happy shall he be, that taketh and dasheth thy little ones against the stones.[2]

It will be seen that I have quoted in each instance the verse that precedes the 'offending' one. The first recalls the hazardous long campaigns to capture the Promised Land: the second is also a cry of agony over the miseries and tortures of the Captivity, a human cry for some ultimate vengeance, divine retribution for the familiar massacres. It is difficult to recapture, imaginatively, the pressures of hatred generated in such a context, unless one has seen, shall we say, the reaction of the resistance party to those who have collaborated with the occupiers of their country, or that of the multitudes of 'displaced persons' who have been driven out of their own countries by political revisions of boundaries. These last offer, perhaps, the nearest analogy in our time to 'the Children of the Captivities'.

[1] 68:22, 23.
[2] 137:8, 9. It is worth noting that St. Augustine interpreted the dashing of the children against the stones as 'the destruction of evil desires'.

In such a context we should also consider the state of mind engendered by this sudden transition of the Host of Israel from the rigours of the desert, the raids by the Bedouin tribes, the prospect (repeatedly emphasized by the divine promise) of the land flowing with milk and honey. Extermination was an essential condition of security and settlement; but there was in addition the problem of the women and children of the host, who would be an easy prey to raiders while the warriors probed the cities of the promise:

> But your wives, and your little ones, and your cattle, (for I know that ye have much cattle,) shall abide in your cities which I have given you;
>
> Until the Lord have given rest unto your brethren, as well as unto you, and until they also possess the land which the Lord your God hath given them beyond Jordan: and then shall ye return every man unto his possession, which I have given you.[1]

So the conquered were to be under the ban, the *cherem*, dedicated to Jehovah, and as such utterly subject to His will. It was, in part, a ritual. The inhabitants of Jericho would have recognized its deadly imminence when they saw their city being circled with measured religious ceremony by the armed host. Therefore—

> ... we took all his cities at that time, and utterly destroyed the men, and the women, and the little ones, of every city, we left none to remain.[2]

Yet however terrible the fate of a whole population put to the sword, we may ponder whether that fate is not more humane than the mutilations and burnings of an innocent population that is the price of all modern war. We may think ironically of one projected sense of that text from *Ecclesiastes*[3]

> Also when they shall be afraid of that which is high, and fears shall be in the way ...

There is indeed something that we may call a 'ferocity of right-eousness' in the Old Testament. The price of intermittent prosperity was an armed watchfulness; and the outcries of the prophets against the invading and enslaving powers are constant and terrible. *Revelation* echoes *Jeremiah* and *Ezekiel* and *Daniel* in its symbolic representations of the attacking Beasts, and their eventual overthrow in some last battle. If deliverance came, the prophets believed, there

---

[1] *Deut.* 3:19, 20. cf. *Josh.* 1:14.   [2] *Deut.* 2:34.   [3] 12:5.

was to be no question of those opportunist alliances, the calling in of foreign allies, that was eventually to split the Kingdom:

> And when the Lord thy God shall deliver them before thee; thou shalt smite them, and utterly destroy them; thou shalt make no covenant with them, nor shew mercy unto them . . .[1]

We may quote a passage from Doughty:

> "Edom and Jeshurun are rivals, and great was the cruelty of the Hebrew arms in these countries. When David was king, his sister's son Joab went and killed of Edomites in the Ghror[2] twelve thousand men, and Joab's brother Abishai killed of them his eighteen thousand, if the Semitic numbers were aught. Edom, be it remembered, and Moab and Ammon, were states to be compared with our smaller counties. Joab's sword went through Edom in six months, until he had made an end of killing every male of Esau, and belike he then made sure of Doeg the king's adversary, and the righteous laughed to the ears, at his calamity; but all was contrary to Moses' word, 'Thou shall not abhor the Edomite for he is thy brother.' "[3]

It is a truism that the Bible records almost any imaginable variety of human evil. There is murder in many forms, and rebellions against 'the Lord's anointed' on a scale and of a variety that suggests comparisons with those of the Wars of the Roses. We have the common revolt of the son against the father, and we recall *Richard II*:

> "O heinous, strong and bold conspiracy!
> O loyal father of a treacherous son!"[4]

Even the Chosen People are split into two warring kingdoms, Israel and Judah, while each sought military alliances with the heathen against their brethren. There is drunkenness, though the episode of Noah is mitigated somewhat by filial piety. A king covets his officer's vineyard, and secures it by an abominable piece of official trickery. A brother steals a birthright by deceiving his blind father, and is himself tricked of the bride of his choice, Rachel, by his prospective father-in-law, so that the latter can retain his services as a bond-labourer. There is almost every known form of 'harlotrye'—to use the

---

[1] *Deut.* 7:2.

[2] Usually spelt *Ghor.* Doughty has a note on the difficulty of transliterating the Arabic gutturals.

[3] *Arabia Deserta*, p. 43. We may notice, but hardly approve, this pastiche of the Biblical style. (*v.* Chapter 4, *supra.*)   [4] V. 3:58.

Chaucerian term—from fornication to sexual perversion. Strange statements find their way into noble visions:

> I know thy works, and charity, and service, and thy patience, and thy works; and the last to be more than the first.

> Notwithstanding I have a few things against thee, because thou sufferest that woman Jezebel, which calleth herself a prophetess, to teach and to seduce my servants to commit fornication, and to eat things sacrificed unto idols.[1]

And the phrase 'The Whore of Babylon'[2] has long been a derogatory epithet in inter-denominational controversy.

The retaliatory provisions of the Law, in mutilation, burning with fire, stoning to death, have offended many; so that the New Testament makes the saving of an adulteress a kind of landmark of the new morality:

> They say unto him, Master, this woman was taken in adultery, in the very act.

> Now Moses in the law commanded us that such should be stoned: but what sayest thou?

> This they said, tempting him, that they might have to accuse him. But Jesus stooped down, and with his finger wrote on the ground, as though he heard them not.

> So when they continued asking him, he lifted up himself, and said unto them, He that is without sin among you, let him first cast a stone at her.[3]

Even an ox that has gored a man or woman to death is to be stoned, and if the beast has not been kept under proper restraint (his temper being known) his owner dies with him.[4]

Some have found offence in the descriptions of the burnt offerings, the disposal of blood and entrails,[5] the complicated rituals of the altar. It has been pointed out that civilized Western man would be less revolted by these descriptions if he had to carry out his own arrangements for butchering his animal food. The majority of the

---

[1] *Rev.* 2:19. See Edmund Gosse's *Father and Son*, and his account of how he, as a small child, stole down to the servants' hall and was given some Christmas pudding. Being afflicted with stomach-ache, he confessed to his father in these words: 'Father, Father, I have eaten of meat sacrificed to idols!'

[2] e.g. *Rev.* 18:2 ff. Babylon is of course a cover-name for the occupational forces of Rome.

[3] *Jn.* 8:4–7. The punishment by stoning is to avoid the actual shedding of blood.

[4] *Ex.* 21:28.   [5] e.g. *Lev.* 8:15 ff.

provisions of the Mosaic Law are admirable sanitary provisions in
the Middle and Far East to-day; as is the cutting of the throat of
beast or bird while it is yet alive—familiar to many in the Mohammedan *halāl*—a wise precaution against eating what may have died
from disease.

ii

One aspect of the evil that may be transmitted and propagated in
missionary work arises through a failure to understand the mind of
those among whom the Bible is being spread; a failure to perceive the
relationship of its teaching to the outlook and traditions of native
peoples and a rigorous and unimaginative projection of Western
ideology. We may quote some illustrative passages:

> "The conflict between missionary and *juju* priest became a struggle
> for power, for minds and souls. African converts, not completely
> understanding the missionary's sermons, confuse the old and new
> religions, interpreting the new in terms of traditional belief."[1]

Again

> "Much of the Old Testament seemed to be about people who were
> a great deal more like the Sousou (a West African tribe) than like
> missionaries. They made sacrifice, they considered circumcision a
> sacred ritual, they fancied gold bangles,[2] they feared leprosy, their
> several wives came into palaver, one with the other. There was pride in
> children, there were tribal wars, curses were feared, diviners consulted,
> and just as in our Sousou stories an animal like Balaam's donkey could
> reproach a man with human speech."[3]

But what we may call the imagery of blood has also strange effects:

> "In the hymns and lessons of the Wesleyan or Evangelical mission-
> aries, they learn of Christ's sacrifice, his death, and the sanctified state
> of those who are 'washed in the Blood of the Lamb'. It becomes easy
> for them to translate this sort of teaching or a hymn such as 'There is a
> Fountain filled with Blood' into terms of their old belief which demands
> human sacrifice to gods of fertility, and the blood of atonement to
> placate ancestral gods. Blood is a key-word. Blood has mystic signifi-
> cance to an African. Blood is life-stuff; life drips away with blood. In

[1] P. R. Moody: from an unpublished thesis on Joyce Cary (p. 128).

[2] 'And they came, both men and women, as many as were willing-hearted, and
brought bracelets, and earrings, and rings, and tablets, all jewels of gold: and every
man that offered an offering of gold unto the Lord.' (*Ex.* 35:22.)

[3] Prince Modupe, *I was a Savage*, London, 1958, p. 928.

the African writings, blood and sacrifice symbolize the amalgamation of missionary Christianity with *juju* worship."[1]

We may quote an interesting use of this emotive 'blood' imagery by D. H. Lawrence; in which Blake's *Tyger* is amalgamated with fragments of liturgical and pseudo-pantheist language:

> "This is one way of transfiguration into the eternal flame, the transfiguration through ecstasy in the flesh. Like the tiger in the night, I devour all flesh, I drink all blood, until the fuel blazes up in me to the consummate fire of the Infinite. In the ecstasy I am Infinite, I become the great Whole, I am a flame of the One White Flame which is the Infinite, the Eternal, the Originator, the Creator, the Everlasting God. In the sensual ecstasy, having drunk all blood and devoured all flesh, I am become the Eternal Fire, I am Infinite.
>
> This is the way of the tiger; the tiger is supreme . . ."[2]

It seems probable that many of the difficulties, and even catastrophes, of early missionary endeavour, as well as of present Western policy in other matters, would have been avoided if such wisdom as this had been kept in mind.

> "Our first task in approaching another people, another culture, another religion, is to take off our shoes, for the place we are approaching is holy. Else we may find ourselves treading on men's dreams. More serious still, we may forget that God was here before our arrival. We have, then, to ask what is the authentic religious content in the experience of the Muslim, the Hindu, the Buddhist, or whoever he may be. We may, if we have asked humbly and respectfully, still reach the conclusion that our brothers have started from a false premise and reached a faulty conclusion. But we must not arrive at our judgement from outside their religious situation. We have to try to sit where they sit, to enter sympathetically into the pains and griefs and joys of their history and see how those pains and griefs and joys have determined the premises of their argument. We have, in a word, to be 'present' with them."[3]

iii

We may turn back to the 'objectionable' passages that concern war and cruelty, the 'cult of blood'. The shortest and most valid answer is that the conduct of war has always and in all countries been marked by ruthlessness, cruelty, massacre of the innocent. We read

---

[1] Moody, *op. cit.*, p. 126.   [2] *The Pluméd Serpent.*
[3] John V. Taylor, *The Primal Vision*, 1963, p. 10. Preface by M. A. C. Warren, p. 10.

in the Bible of the extermination of whole towns and villages; the history of the past half-century records many incidents not less horrible, and often described in less picturesque and restrained language. The hosts of the Israelites were committed, with Jehovah's blessing, to campaigns of conquest; and for a comparatively tiny force there was neither the desire nor the military capacity to take the conquered into slavery, as the great empires around them— Egypt, Assyria, Babylon, Rome—did as a matter of normal practice. The Israelites had no established cities, no consistent apparatus for the partial absorption of a slave population; we may contrast their own highly-organized 'captivity' in Egypt. So village after village is put to the sword. A fortress holds out, and the exasperated besiegers finally reduce it by battering-ram, fire, or stratagem; a massacre ensues. And if a war-chariot is washed by a stream, the blood may well flow from it; as from a battered tank, or a stricken warship.

Probably the Israelites were less cruel than their neighbours. We have no mention of the terrible Assyrian practice of impaling prisoners alive on stakes, of placing rings through their upper lips to lead them on cords, of blinding the sons of princes who have rebelled. There is no cruelty for its own sake, no sadism. Punishments are swift, ruthless, matter-of-fact. The history of Middle and Far-Eastern warfare suggests the comparatively low value placed on human life. There is sadism in plenty in interpretations or commentaries from the Middle Ages onward: we may remember how the Four Torturers of the Wakefield Crucifixion Miracle Play boast of the pain given to their Victim by their brutality in setting up the Cross, or recall the bestial faces of the flagellants as Dürer or Holbein saw them. We remember, too, Swinburne's

"O lips that the live blood faints in, the leavings of racks and rods,
    O ghastly glories of saints, dead limbs of gibbeted gods!"

The Bible narratives are wholly objective, save where some cry of savage triumph lingers to celebrate a 'heroic' action.[1] To a people accustomed to incessant war and raids, the sight of blood seems a less horrifying matter than it does to us. In the perspectives of history, of the holy wars of Christianity and other religions, of forcible conversions and their appropriate mutilations, the bloodshed of the Bible need not offend us.

[1] See p. 85, *supra*.

There is another and more serious aspect of this 'evil'. Until the Reformation the Church had carefully isolated the Bible as a 'dangerous' book. In the hands of the unlearned it opened the way to countless abuses. So did the Miracle and Mystery plays based on it.[1] Without clerical control, without some mediation by learned authority, the Book could be actively dangerous. And if we reflect upon the imperfections—often misleading—of the Greek and Hebrew texts available to Wycliffe and Tyndale, and add them to the obscurities which even now exist, we can see some justification. If, further, we superimpose upon these difficulties the lack of those historical perspectives now afforded by history and archaeology, the 'dangers' may be thought to have been many.

For there were always the dubious circumstances that attach to any book of peculiar sanctity. Its very texts may become amulets, to be worn or even eaten. Its obscurities can become invested with a certain *mana*. They can be distorted, twisted, taken out of context, to form the bases of prophecies, fantasies, numerology. Their rhetorical orotundities can invest the most nonsensical or blasphemous propositions with an aura of credibility and an energy that incites to ill-considered action.[2] The licence of analogical and anagogical speculation still appeals to minds both fanatical and eccentric. It is significant that it has been the Old Testament rather than the New that has provided the pretexts for the wildest excesses of persecution and extermination. The relatively harmless process of using Biblical history as a framework for literary and political satire (as in the work of Dryden) may easily be projected into less innocent antagonisms. The denunciations of the prophets can be readily lifted from their contexts to provide interpretations for crises and Messianic visions, in terms of *Ezekiel*, *Daniel*, or *Revelation* that become impulses to action. Even a New Model Army may draw on the exhortations to righteous annihilation, to justify the constant attraction of a Holy War.

On a different level the Old Testament has provided texts for the belief that material prosperity is the direct reward of righteousness: that poverty, misery, disease are in some way the consequences of hidden or overt sin. This was the view of Job's Comforters, and of the

---

[1] cf. the Anglo-Norman *Manuel des Péchesz*.

[2] Consider for example the account of the preaching renegade in John Buchan's *Salute to Adventurers*; and Hogg's *Memoirs of a Justified Sinner*.

exponents of the *laissez-faire* system of economics. It has been taken to provide precedents for sharp practice of several kinds: Jacob's method of dealing with his uncle Laban's sheep, though it makes no biological sense, is sometimes cited as a precedent.[1] The Parable of the Talents raises in an acute form the age-old controversy over usury; that of the Unjust Steward has been taken to condone a good deal of commercial and political corruption. There are still many dark places in the Parables that require detailed explanation if they are not to be misunderstood. Of such are the Labourers in the Vineyard, and the wedding guests.[2]

Every provision of the Decalogue is broken many times. There are curious, as it were 'local', sins; notably that of removing one's neighbour's landmark, and it is not difficult to imagine the immense significance of that action to a land-hungry people. There are constant diversions into the seductive practices of idolatry; whether out of a desire for novelty, the common-sense practice of inviting one god to a contest of strength with another, (as in the dramatic episode of the priests of Baal and the altar-fire)[3] or because of the perennial attractions of the power of the 'outland' woman to convert such as Samson to her own religion. No doubt there is also the psychological satisfaction of experimenting with a plurality of gods and goddesses, whose individual qualities and modes of behaviour—particularly when they involved a reversion to fertility cults—might be more acceptable to their worshippers than the inflexible and abstracted monotheism of Jehovah. It is a tendency that we may observe in many religions, whether in the search for a kind of multiple responsibility, to obtain mediation at a less exalted level, or merely to obtain the satisfaction of a more 'natural' deity who, like the Baals, had a female consort or counterpart.[4] With the oracular functions of the gods we may group the activities of witchcraft, sorcery and divination, this last shading into legitimate interpretation with the impressive dreams of Pharaoh and Nebuchadnezzar. The sins of witchcraft and spiritualism have their dramatic epiphany in the Cave at En-dor.

[1] See *The Merchant of Venice*, I. 3. 74.

[2] There are many explanations of the Parables: one of the most recent, and most helpful, is that by E. A. Armstrong, *The Gospel Parables*, 1967.

[3] cf. the Indian proverb: 'Your gods or my gods—how do I know which are the stronger?'

[4] We remember the heresy which perceived the Trinity as that of the family—Father, Mother, Child.

iv

To all of this we may make three answers. The Bible, whatever its character as a sacred book, must include, in virtue of its multifarious qualities, the study, and the *exempla* of human evil. If it did not do so, its stature, and its integrity as literature, would be infinitely the less. That is why all attempts to censor, excise, regroup or bowdlerize are, however good the intentions, unsatisfactory, or worse. It is the study of evil because it records the struggle between man's 'erected wit' and his 'infected will';[1] within a human and historical framework that enables us to see this record as a reasonably coherent whole.

The vision of evil must be studied in the perspectives of history. When documentation is scanty, we must train ourselves by 'calling imagination to the aid of reason'. We must, for example, consider the highly-complex meanings of the words so frequently used of the attributes of God—*jealousy, wrath, vengeance*. We must not be afraid to admit, in the earliest perceptions of Jehovah recorded by His people, the relics of a tribal deity; in whom the qualities of the numen of terror seem to be dominant. It is well to remind ourselves of the words of Charles Williams:

> "The God of Genesis is not a kind of supernatural man; he is something quite different which occasionally deigns to appear like a supernatural man."[2]

In literature the necessity for this vision of evil has been expressed in many ways: from Webster's

> "My soul, like to a ship in a black storm
> Is driven, I know not whither."

to Thomas Hardy's

> "For I hold if a way to the better there be, it exacts a full look at the worse."

The vision oscillates and wavers. There is the terrible sentence that seems, in its determinism, to anticipate the Latin tag

> "Quem deus vult perdere, prius dementat."
> I also will choose their delusions.[3]

---

[1] I use the terms of Sidney in his *Apologie for Poetry*.
[2] *He Came Down From Heaven*, p. 143.   [3] *Isa.* 66:4.

Sometimes nature is perceived as cruel, sometimes as kindly and beneficent in contrast to humanity:

> Even the sea-monsters draw out the breast, they give suck to the young ones: the daughter of my people is become cruel, like the ostriches in the wilderness.[1]

so that we think of *King Lear*:

> "If that the heavens do not their visible spirits
> Send quickly down to tame these vile offences,
> It will come,
> Humanity must perforce prey on itself
> Like monsters of the deep."[2]

Yet we are well advised to consider, carefully, and critically, the highly-charged language, the product of physical and mental suffering, in which evil is described; by the greatest of saints, and by the most vigorous of reformers. There appears to be an element in human nature which, under cover of various well-known psychological rationalizations, takes an active pleasure in descriptions of pain, evil, sin. The 'gloomy prophets' have become proverbial, but it is well to study the situations, personal and national, from which their prophetic writings emerge. The opening of the great hymn

> Hora novissima, tempora pessima sunt . . .

appears throughout all Western literature; we should allow for the theme in the total balance of the Bible. Without this we may be blinded to the progressive revelation between the two Testaments; seeing only the imperatives of Jehovah, and not their resolution into the moral ideal that proceeds, through revelation, from the character of God.

[1] *Lam.* 4:3.   [2] IV. 2. 46.

CHAPTER THIRTEEN

The Holy War

But there came a messenger unto Saul, saying, Haste thee, and come; for the Philistines have invaded the land.

(*1 Sam.* 23:27)

'The Philistines be upon thee, Samson!'

(*Jg.* 16:12)

i

THE WARFARE of the Old Testament occupies an appreciable part of its narratives; which are the records of territorial conquest, the struggle and mobilizations for survival, the agonies of the Captivities, the building of Jerusalem, and its final destruction. The setting of the events in time and space are not always clear, and we may attempt at the outset to recall some general conditions under which the wars were fought.

At Sinai, the Israelites have been told of the Promised Land. The exodus from Egypt, the wanderings in the desert, the entry into the Land, become the great epic of their origins; constantly recalled in prophecy, song and praise. The Promised Land is, in fact, divided geographically into four strips. There is the coastal plain, from Gaza to Mount Carmel, the great highway for the invasions from Egypt and the South, and from Assyria and Babylon to the North-East; later for the Crusaders and for Napoleon. In it that mysterious people, the Philistines, had settled, probably arriving at about the same time as the Israelites crossed the Jordan. They existed in a loose confederacy of five main cities:[1] Gaza, Ashkelon, Gath, Lachish and Ekron. These lie astride the Western Road, to Damascus and the North, 'The Highway of the Philistines'. Inland and to the east are the highlands, from the Valley of Jezreel to Beer-sheba, with the Jordan Valley and the Dead Sea as the Eastern boundary. North of the

[1] I am indebted, here as elsewhere, to George Adam Smith, *The Historical Geography of the Holy Land.*

Valley of Jezreel there is the northern sytem of highlands, from Mount Gilboa up to the boundaries of the Tribe of Dan on the slopes of Mount Hermon, and the twin ranges of Lebanon and Hermon. Eastwards there is the Ghor, the great rift of the Jordan Valley, much of it below sea-level. East of that is Trans-Jordania, bounded in its turn to the east by the desert, and, at the time of the entry of the Israelites, occupied by four main kingdoms: Moab, Edom, the Amorites and the Ammonites. After the wanderings in the wilderness, and a sight of the land flowing with milk and honey, the host was compelled to turn back. They were refused rights of passage by Moab and Edom (both kingdoms were to regret this bitterly later on) and, by-passing them, arrived at the northern end of the Dead Sea. Then they have their first serious campaigns: they defeated the Amorites, and Bashan (with its giant king, and famous feral horned cattle); with those successes behind them, they turn to subjugate Moab. There follows the crossing of Jordan, the siege of Jericho, the successive reduction of the Canaanite key-cities to the edge of Philistine territory, and the apportionment of the land among the Twelve Tribes. Under David and Solomon the kingdom was to attain, for a time, its greatest area of influence, stretching to touch the Euphrates in the North, and southwards, to the head of the Gulf of Akaba, including what is now the Negeb. We may note that the second great highway runs from the Gulf northwards through Moab and Edom, the highway which carried the enormously important trade from the copper-mines of Elath and 'all the spices of Arabia'.

ii

Warfare, which is inexorably related to geography, occupies an appreciable part of the Bible. We have already seen the possible effects of war-chronicles in inciting to violence.[1] Of the occupation of the Promised Land we may quote from Gibbon:

"The conquest of the land of Canaan was accompanied with so many wonderful and with so many bloody circumstances, that the victorious Jews were left in a state of irreconcilable hostility with all their neighbours. They had been commanded to extirpate some of the most idolatrous tribes, and the execution of the Divine will has seldom been retarded by the weakness of humanity. With the other nations they were forbidden to contract any marriages or alliances. . . . The descendants of

[1] v. p. 23, supra.

Abraham were flattered by the opinion, that they alone were the heirs of the covenant, and they were apprehensive of diminishing the value of their inheritance, by sharing it too easily with the strangers of the earth."[1]

Gibbon's majestic and biased prose contains something less than the truth. The Israelites emerged from their desert wanderings a fit and hardy race, purged from the results of the flesh-pots of Egypt, if not of those occasionally nostalgic memories. Reports of the Promised Land, and the specimens brought back by the spies, had excited their envy at Kadesh. After the long circuits to avoid territorial violation of Edom and Moab, they had defeated the Amorites and Og of Bashan, and had pressed (if the records speak the whole truth) far to the north. They had achieved by those campaigns confidence and, we may suppose, some coherence as a fighting force. They had crossed the Jordan and invested Jericho at the threshold of their country. We must stand back a little from the picture.

A 'host' with women and children, flocks and herds, moves slowly and cumbrously.[2] So long as it has no fixed bases it dare not leave unreduced fortresses or enemy strongpoints in its rear. The great empires could afford to take captives, to displace whole populations into forms of slavery that might vary between the cruel and the co-operative; but the Israelites had no great city, and no adequate organization to deal with prisoners. Therefore, as a purely practical measure, the enemy had to be put to the sword, their weaponry destroyed, and their horses, the 'mighty ones' of the much-dreaded chariots, killed or maimed against future use against them.

There was, in addition to this practical aspect, the over-riding religious one. Monotheism, stern and uncompromising, is the religion of the desert, as many historians and travellers have noted.[3] We may explain it in part by the arid immensities, the proximity of the stars, the hardness of the living[4] and the promises of ultimate safety and ease by which that hardness is to be alleviated. The entry into Canaan, to a race bred up in the desert, must have been a mental and spiritual shock. Here was a country of hills and forests, green pastures and waters of comfort, full of mystery and of the promise of

[1] *Decline and Fall*, ch. xv.

[2] A fair estimate is, at most, fifteen miles a day between camp and camp.

[3] But the pro-Muslim era produced a plurality of gods: witness Mohammed's long struggle against idolatry.

[4] There is perhaps some analogy with Scottish sectarianism.

a relatively easy, perhaps sensuous life. To the desert dweller a forest, even a tree, can be as numinous as the mysterious ocean itself; so that the Isles become to Isaiah a kind of Atlantis, the magical country on the edge of the known world. But this fertile country, unlike the desert, lends itself to, and even invites, the discovery of a multitude of gods: the genii of high places, of groves, of rivers and fountains. The desire to discover, placate, and worship local deities, under whatever name, is strong. Every high place and grove had its Baal, the indweller of each particular district, and, when placated with sacrifices, a source of prosperity to the inhabitants.

So we have the prohibition:

And ye shall make no league with the inhabitants of the land; ye shall throw down their altars: but ye have not obeyed my voice: why have ye done this?

Wherefore I also said, I will not drive them out from before you; but they shall be as thorns in your sides, and their gods shall be a snare unto you.[1]

Thorns in their sides they were, and remained so. From a military point of view the occupation of the 'Land of Canaan' was anything but a scientific operation. After reducing a number of strongpoints west and north-west of Jericho, the Twelve Tribes were allotted their areas. Dan was the most northerly, up to the slopes of Mt. Hermon. Manasseh, Reuben, and Gilead held Transjordan, the latter as far south as the boundary with the Moabites, the River Arnon. Simeon's territory extended south of Beer-sheba, to the Kenite wilderness, the Gaza Strip, and an indecisive boundary with Edom. But the Israelites were not great builders of cities; perhaps there was a racial memory of Egypt and its bricks. The fortification of Jerusalem under David was their most ambitious work. We must rather imagine the ex-nomads settling into the fertile country, becoming yeoman farmers, and members of an ancestral and religious confederacy of which the weakness was constantly being exposed. Politics and warfare were complicated by their custom, on occasion, of peaceful co-existence, whether from necessity or from some more generous motive. We may give some examples

And the Lord was with Judah; and he drave out the inhabitants of the mountain; but could not drive out the inhabitants of the valley, because they had chariots of iron.

[1] *Jg.* 2:2–3.

And they gave Hebron unto Caleb, as Moses said: and he expelled thence the three sons of Anak.

And the children of Benjamin did not drive out the Jebusites that inhabited Jerusalem; but the Jebusites dwell with the children of Benjamin in Jerusalem unto this day.[1]

The indigenous peoples often became vassals:

Neither did Zebulun drive out the inhabitants of Kitron, nor the inhabitants of Nahalol: but the Canaanites dwelt among them, and became tributaries.[2]

Our picture of the Holy War, after the initial penetration, is therefore of intermittent peace, with a sporadic series of attacks from almost every side: a campaign: defeat or victory: and periods of peace.

iii

The tribal wars develop into almost a standard pattern. The land has 'rest', for ten or forty or fourscore years, under a strong judge capable, we may suppose, of producing some sort of military coherence in the tribal gatherings:

Nevertheless the Lord raised up judges, which delivered them out of the hand that spoiled them . . .

And it came to pass, when the judge was dead, that they returned, and corrupted themselves more than their fathers, in following other gods to serve them . . . they ceased not from their own doings, nor from their stubborn way.[3]

We have therefore the rhythm of prosperity, seduction by the Baals and Ashtaroth, a raid by an enemy, vassalage or slavery, repentance and an outburst of mercy from Jehovah, the emergence of a leader, a battle: and 'the land had rest forty years'. Perhaps the period is more than a poetic cliché; in forty years a new generation of fighting men, their imaginations fed on the past epics of raids and deliverances, would emerge and cohere: often to fall apart again with internal and personal jealousies. (We recall the quarrels among the Greek allies in the *Iliad*.) There are permanent features of the human

---

[1] *Jg.* 1:19–21.   [2] *Jg.* 1:30.
[3] *Jg.* 2:16, 19. Consider the many references to the 'stiff-necked' qualities of the Chosen People: an important aspect of their capacity to survive.

situation. We may quote one instance in which the tones of the dialogue are peculiarly vivid:

And Gaal the son of Ebed came with his brethren, and went over to Shechem: and the men of Shechem put their confidence in him.

And they went into the fields, and gathered their vineyards, and trode the grapes, and made merry, and went into the house of their god, and did eat and drink, and cursed Abimelech.

And Gaal the son of Ebed said, Who is Abimelech, and who is Shechem, that we should serve him? Is he not the son of Jerubbaal? and Zebul his officer? Serve the men of Hamor the father of Shechem: for why should we serve him?

And would to God the people were under my hand! then would I remove Abimelech. And he said to Abimelech, Increase thine army, and come out.[1]

This is a particularly interesting episode. The words of Gaal anger Zebul the ruler of the city, who secretly sends word to Abimelech of Gaal's plot. He advises an ambush, and Abimelech arranges a triple one. Men appear on the mountains in the early morning; we can imagine the dramatic moment of the clans gathering in the mist. Gaal thinks that he sees armed men far off. Then Zebul: 'Thou seest the shadow of the mountains as if they were men.' Now Gaal sees two other bodies of troops 'by the middle of the land' and another on the plains converging on Shechem. Scornfully, Zebul recalls Gaal's boast, and bids him go out and fight. (Here the narrative seems to be defective, for verses 39–41 are in the wrong place.) After a day or two Abimelech mounts a three-pronged attack. One company attacks the gate of the city, while two others cut off and slaughter the people who have gone out to work at the harvest in the field. After a day's fighting the city is taken, and its inhabitants massacred. The ruins are sowed with salt. What is left of Gaal's troops retire to the town's fortress, the tower of Shechem. Abimelech makes his troops cut down boughs, and pile them against the tower, and burns it, 'so that about a thousand men and women die in it'.[2]

Abimelech, flushed with victory, takes the town of Thebez; but in the course of the assault against its citadel, with the same technique

---

[1] *Jg.* 9:26–29.
[2] *Jg.* 9:30-end. We remember that the same fate overtook the impregnable fortress of Lachish. When the Assyrian siege-engines failed, the troops devastated the country for miles around for wood which they piled against the walls.

of fire, a woman defender throws down a piece of millstone, 'and all to brake his skull'.[1] Abimelech orders his sword-bearer to kill him, so that it should not be said that he had been killed by a woman.

In these miniature actions of war and intrigue, jealousy and revenge, we have a kind of epitome of all warfare, of the whole human situation. Longinus[2] noted the emotional effects of the 'names', whether of heroes, places or battles, ennobling the epic context. We may set out some examples. The first, which is rhythmically clumsy, is from Marlowe's *Tamburlaine*: it has, deliberately, a pseudo-barbaric quality of incantation:

> "I left the confines and the bounds of Afric,
> And made a voyage into Europe,
> Where by the river Tyrus, I subdu'd
> Stoka, Podolia and Codemia,
> Then cross'd the sea, and came to Oblia,
> And Nigra Silva, where the devils dance,
> Which in despite of them I set on fire . . ."[3]

Milton reviews the superb troops of Hell with names that reverberate round the world of classical mythology, the Arthurian legend, the long heroic wars that saved Europe from domination by the Turks:

> . . ."though all the giant brood
> Of Phlegra with th'heroic race were join'd
> That fought at Thebes and Ilium, on each side
> Mix't with auxiliar gods; and what resounds
> In fable or romance of Uther's son
> Begirt with British and Armoric knights
> And all who since, baptiz'd or infidel
> Jousted in Ashramont or Montalban,
> Damasco, Marocco, or Trebizond,
> Or whom Biserta sent from Afric's shore
> When Charlemain with all his peerage fell
> By Fontarabbia."[4]

With these examples in mind we may now consider part of the great epic psalm of triumph:[5]

---

[1] Note the Middle English of *A.V.*—'all to brake'.
[2] *A Treatise Concerning Sublimity*, XXIII.   [3] I, 2.
[4] *P.L.* 1. 576 ff. *Phlegra* is the home of the giants in Thessaly: *Uther*, King Arthur; *the baptiz'd* are Charlemagne's troops, the *infidel* the Mohammedan Saracens.
[5] *Ps.* 83; of peculiar interest at the time of writing (1967).

... For, lo, thine enemies make a tumult: and they that hate thee have lifted up the head.

They have taken crafty counsel against thy people, and consulted against thy hidden ones.[1]

They have said, Come, and let us cut them off from being a nation; that the name of Israel may be no more in remembrance.

For they have consulted together with one consent: they are confederate against thee:[2]

The tabernacles of Edom, and the Ishmaelites; of Moab, and the Hagarenes;

Gebal, and Ammon, and Amalek: the Philistines with the inhabitants of Tyre;

Assur also is joined with them: they have holpen the children of Lot: Selah.

Do unto them as unto the Midianites; as to Sisera, as to Jabin, at the brook of Kison:

Which perished at En-dor: they became as the dung for the earth.

Make their nobles like Oreb, and like Zeeb: yea, all their princes as Zebah, and as Zalmunna:

Who said, Let us take to ourselves the houses of God in possession.

O my God, make them like a wheel;[3] as the stubble before the wind ...

It is a kind of epitome, foreshortened as in a Scottish ballad, of the remembered wars. The 'tabernacles' are the tent-dwellers of the nomads. Edom and Moab were victims of early campaigns, though the Edomites were remote kinsfolk. For eighteen years Israel had served Moab;[4] but then the tables were reversed. Their King Eglon, 'a very fat man', was assassinated by Ehud the left-handed Benjamite,[5] who escaped before the crime was discovered. This was the signal for a popular rising; the Israelites came down from the mountain,

[1] The refugees, perhaps in caves (the 'pavilions' of *Ps.* 31 : 20) or in the woods or among the mountains.

[2] The poet exaggerates the amount of co-operation to be expected in the Middle East. There is no historical record of such a confederacy.

[3] The whirling dust-storms.

[4] *Jg.* 3:14. The vividness of the descriptions, the manner in which the poet ranges over the land and its history, is much enhanced by a study of the geography of the land.

[5] The tribe was right-handed; a left-handed assassin has certain advantages in speed and surprise.

and, presumably by forced marches, got to the fords of the Jordan and held them against the routed Moabites:

> And they slew of Moab at that time about ten thousand men, all lusty, and all men of valour; and there escaped not a man. So Moab was subdued that day under the hand of Israel. And the land had rest fourscore years.[1]

The Philistines, the dreaded charioteers of the plains, allied themselves with the Sidonians, later the Phoenicians. Lot was a notorious figure, both for his rescue from Sodom, the turning of his wife into a pillar of salt, and his subsequent drunken incest instigated by his husbandless daughters; from which union came Moab and Ammon, the patriarchs of the enemy tribes.[2]

The Midianites, who according to a rather bad hymn were accustomed to 'prowl and prowl around', were the object of what was perhaps Moses' most striking victory, both for the troops engaged and the results, though we are told nothing of the strategy of the battle or even its locations. There had been an earlier clash with them, under Moses, during the Wanderings: this appears to have been indecisive, but gives some hint as to the size of the 'host of Israel'—about 6,000. Israel's later levies were composed of a thousand men from each of the twelve tribes:[3] a formidable number to control in that terrain. The result is a massacre of the Midianite males, the burning of their cities and the acquisition of a vast amount of booty, mainly in flocks and herds though there are interesting directions for cleansing the metallic portion of the spoil—gold, silver, brass, iron, tin and lead—by 'making it go through the fire'.[4] The spoils themselves are to be divided meticulously; as between those who actually fought, and the rest of the congregation and the Levites. At first the women and children are spared: then, by Moses' command, the male children are slaughtered, with the wives, on the somewhat tenuous ground that

> . . . these caused the children of Israel, through the counsel of Balaam, to commit trespass against the Lord in the matter of Peor, and there was a plague among the congregation of the Lord.[5]

We are told that 32,000 virgins escaped the massacre. The incident of Peor occurs in Balaam's attempted cursing of Israel.[6] The

[1] *Jg.* 3:29–30.
[2] *Gen.* 19. Perhaps this is a fiction to explain the relationship between tribes.
[3] *Num.* 31:5.　　[4] *Ibid.*, 31:22–23.　　[5] *Ibid.*, 31:16.　　[6] *Ibid.*, 23:27–30.

Amalekites, like the Midianites, were a desert tribe from the south: they were one of the most painful thorns in Israel's side. In alliance with the Canaanites they had routed Israel, who had, against Moses' advice, fought them. A graphic picture of a full-scale raid is given in *Judges* 6 and 7.

Israel as usual had done evil in the sight of the Lord, and had even been driven into the 'dens' of the mountains. The oppression lasted seven years. The raiders, Midianites and Amalekites, devastated the cultivated country, and the imagery of the locust-horde was appropriate:

> For they came up with their cattle and their tents, and they came as grasshoppers for multitude; for both they and their camels were without number; and they entered into the land to destroy it.[1]

We should note the factor introduced into these raids by the taming of the camel by the people of the southern deserts. This seems to have been a new dimension of warfare: the speed, range and silence of a camel-corps will be remembered from *The Seven Pillars of Wisdom*, and from the exploits of the Jordanian army. A prophet is raised up who recalls Jehovah's previous care for Israel. Gideon has a vision of an angel, who assures him of Jehovah's support. Gideon's question is, on the face of it, wholly reasonable:

> Oh my Lord, if the Lord be with us, why then is all this befallen us? and where be all his miracles which our father told us of, saying, Did not the Lord bring us up from Egypt? but now the Lord hath forsaken us, and delivered us into the hands of the Midianites.[2]

The orthodox reply is that Israel is being punished for their sins, but this is not made now: Gideon is merely assured that he is to be the saviour of the people. There follows the episode of the unleavened bread, flesh and broth that Gideon brings as an offering to the angel under the oak. The offerings are consumed with fire, and the angel vanishes. Gideon is next enjoined to throw down the altar of Baal, cut down the sacred grove, and sacrifice a bullock on an altar built on the spot. He does this secretly by night for fear of the people. There is a violent controversy when they find that the sacred grove has been desecrated: Joash, Gideon's father, saves his son with the famous phrase

Let Baal plead against him, because he has thrown down his altar.[3]

---

[1] *Jg.* 6:5.   [2] *Ibid.*, 6:13.   [3] *Ibid.*, 6, 32.

iv

Of this warfare as literature it is not easy to write; nor, indeed, is it easy to read as a coherent whole. For the narrative is never continuous. It doubles back on its track in an exasperating way. Accounts of the same events are often conflated. Details often differ: such as those of the names of Moses' wives. There are obvious instances of wrong sequences of events in the battles themselves. There has been some heavily-biased editing, and there are many suspected interpolations. Everything seems to combine to make the record desultory and episodic. We must constantly remind ourselves of the period that this history covers (say from 1250 to 450 B.C.) and keep in mind standards of comparison from other literatures.

It is a record of war, and the morality behind war, which is conditioned as always by the geography and topography of Israel and the great empires that surround it. It is outstanding for its demonstration of the national will to survive in the face of technically impossible odds; both in war and in the captivities. That will is wholly dependent on its belief, however intermittent, partial, subject to human perversions, that the people are under the protection of Jehovah, and that it is His purpose that they should survive. The epic[1] qualities, courage, the great deeds of heroes, are celebrated in poetry, and sustain this Hegelian will. Jerusalem rebuilt and fortified gives a momentary hope of permanence under Solomon. Its power as a symbol may be partly discerned in the report of an Israeli general in the 1967 campaign: 'Our men could never have fought as they did if Jerusalem, and the Wall, had not meant everything to them.'

We should not underestimate the moral effects on a nation of their own recited histories of adventure and fortitude; it seems likely that, in comparison with the passing of the great empires about them, these memories (incorporated continuously into their daily worship) were the strongest impulses to survival. Nor should we forget, among many examples, the adoption of an Old Testament fixity of spirit by Cromwell's New Model Army: how General Wolfe went to his death

---

[1] I use the word in the sense suggested by W. P. Ker in his *Epic and Romance*: the battle, against odds, as the price of survival: whether of the individual, as tribe or a nation. This is founded in reality, the basic facts of living; and is contrasted with the romance, in which the impulse to action is founded upon the *idea*.

after reciting Gray's *Elegy*; nor the memory of that commander who on the Channel Crossing to France in 1944, read aloud to his men from Shakespeare's *Henry V*.

As to strategy, we recognize in history the effect of the positioning of Israel by land and sea. The lessons[1] of its relationship in the warfare of the air have not yet, I think, been fully assessed. History shows us how the invasions, their routes and strategies, have been conditioned by the ground: the lack of any natural harbours from Mt. Carmel to the Delta determine that the invaders must come from the north or south or east until they have secured the plains of Philistia.[2] Jordan remains a permanent and ever-contentious boundary. The campaigns of the Romans, the crusades, of Napoleon and Allenby, follow the ancient routes and the terrain of the battlefields. The basic lessons of surprise, mobility, stratagem and deception, may still be observed and considered in the Old Testament.

As comment on this literature, perhaps the most memorable words are Milton's, and we may quote them at some length:

"But those frequent songs throughout the Law and Prophets beyond all these, not in their divine argument alone, but in the very critical art of composition, may be easily made appear over all the kinds of lyric poesy to be incomparable. These abilities, wheresoever they be found, are the inspired gift of God, rarely bestowed, but yet to some (though most abuse) in every nation; and are of power, beside the office of a pulpit, to inbreed and cherish in a great people the seeds of virtue and public civility, to allay the perturbations of the mind, and set the affections in right tune; to celebrate in glorious and lofty hymns the throne and equipage of God's almightiness, and what he works, and what he suffers to be wrought with high Providence in his Church; to sing victorious agonies of martyrs and saints, the deeds and triumphs of just and pious nations, doing valiantly through faith against the enemies of Christ; to deplore the general relapses of kingdoms and states from justice and God's true worship. Lastly, whatsoever in religion is holy and sublime, in virtue amiable or grave, whatsoever hath passion or admiration in all the changes of that which is called Fortune from without, or the wily subtleties and refluxes of man's thoughts from within; all these things with a solid and treatable smoothness to paint out and describe. . . ."[3]

[1] As of June 1967.
[2] An exception is the Allenby Campaign of 1917.
[3] *The Reason of Church Government*, Bk II.

V

It is not, I think, an exaggeration to suggest that, in the present state and temper of the West, these aspects of warfare constitute a serious obstacle to potential readers of the Bible. There are many complicated reasons, into which we need not enter. But among them is the present intense emotional revulsion from war, often most violent in those who have not experienced it, or its direct effects. There are signs that the three recent campaigns in Israel, and the Russian invasion of Czechoslovakia, have brought us a little nearer towards understanding.

The effort to reconstruct in imagination the whole situation of the Chosen People is an intense one; the weapons, the conventions of warfare, the scale, have all to be reconstituted in our minds. Only then can we see the epic in its rise and fall, as an intermittent and heroic struggle first for living room, and then for the merest freedom to survive. In a previous chapter I have tried to indicate some aspects of the cyclic patterns, under the title of *Character in Action*. Yet the essential elements, the struggle of the human mind against physical and spiritual evil, remain vital in their significance. It is even possible that a future age will return to the historic concept of man's warfare with evil rather than with his irremediable past, and that the imagery linked with the view of morality will, once again, become valid and active. For a last example of the two aspects we may quote a familiar passage:

"The next day they took him and had him into the Armory; where they shewed him all manner of Furniture,[1] which their Lord had provided for Pilgrims, as Sword, Shield, Helmet, Brest plate,[2] *All Prayer*, and Shooes that would not wear out.[3] And there was here enough of them to harness out as many men for the service of their Lord, as there be Stars in the Heaven for multitude.

They also shewed him some of the Engines with which some of his Servants had done wonderful things. They shewed him *Moses* Rod, the Hammer and Nail with which *Jael* slew *Sisera*, the Pitchers, Trumpets and Lamps too, with which *Gideon* put to flight the Armies of *Midian*. They shewed him also the Oxes goad wherewith *Shamger* slew six

[1] i.e. equipment in general, as in Shakespearian usage.

[2] cf. what Browne calls 'the armature of St. Paul'.

[3] magical?-iron shoes are important in folk-lore. For their protective use on the journey to Heaven, see the ballad *The Lyke-Wake Dirge*.

hundred men. They shewed him also the Jaw bone with which *Sampson* did such mighty feats; they shewed him moreover the Sling and Stone with which *David* slew *Goliath* of *Gath*: and the Sword also with which their Lord will kill the Man of Sin, in the day that he shall rise up to the prey."[1]

[1] *The Pilgrim's Progress*, pp. 62–63 (1678 Edn.).

CHAPTER FOURTEEN

'Imitatio'

*(or, Some Aspects of the Use of Biblical Imagery
and Allusion in English Poetry and Prose)*

"The third requisite in our poet or maker is imitation, *imitatio*, to
be able to convert the substance or riches of a poet to his own
use."   (Ben Jonson, *Discoveries.*)

i

THE PURPOSE of this chapter is to invite attention to some of the
many ways in which English writers have made use of the Bible,
directly or obliquely; to suggest some of the overtones, complex and
overlapping images, and shades of meaning of considerable subtlety.
Any teacher of English is aware of the vast amount that is passed
over, and occasionally misunderstood, by the failure of students to
realize such references and overtones; simply because of the desue-
tude in the reading of the Bible. The loss is the more serious when
we realize that in three great centuries of achievement, from the
sixteenth to the nineteenth, such a background was taken for granted.
It is probable that the student of the future will demand footnotes or
glosses to much that his grandfather would have recognized instantly;
in much the same way as portions of literature depending on some
Latin or Greek allusion or quotation, or some well-known myth
which was once familiar to every schoolboy, now requires to be
explained by the teacher.[1] Even more significant is the general
failure to break down and understand Latin and Greek words (of
this the teachers of early literature complain very often), still less to
realize the subtleties with which derivations from those languages
were used in English verse or prose.[2] In this essay I propose to

[1] As, for example, that most important source book, Ovid's *Metamorphoses.*
[2] cf. the overtones in much of Donne, Herbert, Vaughan, Milton.

consider a few examples, which are, necessarily, arbitrary choices. In every instance the whole poem is of course far more rewarding than any analysis of its parts.

We may first take a simple instance, a single verse from Swinburne's *Rococo*:

> "We have heard from hidden places
> What love scarce lives and hears.
> We have seen on fervent faces
> The pallor of strange tears.
> We have trod the wine-vat's treasure
> Whence, ripe to steam and stain,
> Foams round the feet of pleasure
> The blood-red must of pain."

It is not a good poem; it is a strange manifestation, like his own *Dolores*, of the laboured and over-laden pleasure-pain antithesis. The common reader may well be unfamiliar with the word *must*, but he will at least realize that it is a noun. This is confirmed beyond all doubt if he remembers the passages from *Isaiah* that Swinburne is using:

> Who is that cometh from Edom, with dyed garments from Bozrah? this that is glorious in his apparel, travelling in the greatness of his strength? I that speak in righteousness, mighty to save.

> Wherefore art thou red in thine apparel, and thy garments like him that treadeth in the winefat? . . .[1]

Swinburne's poetic energy derives mainly from his rhythms and from turbulent alliterations which do not, as a rule, sustain detailed analysis. But the *raw* grape juice, unfermented and which cannot be preserved, is seen as the outcome of the pleasure of love; with perhaps another echo of the praises of the feet as in themselves beautiful:

> How beautiful upon the mountains are the feet of him that bringeth good tidings, that publisheth peace . . .[2]

Or perhaps the description of the Bride's feet:

> How beautiful are thy feet with shoes, O prince's daughter[3] . . .

[1] 63:1, 2.   [2] *Isa.* 52:7.
[3] *Cant.* 7:1. The description moves from the feet upwards, because she is dancing.

The same image of the wine-press is combined with other Biblical references (though used with no great subtlety or distinction) by Kipling:

> "At the eleventh hour he came,
> But his wages were the same
> As ours who all day long had trod
> The wine-press of the Wrath of God.
>
> When he shouldered through the lines
> Of our cropped and mangled vines,
> His unjaded eye could scan
> How each hour had marked its man. . . .
>
> Since his back had felt no load,
> Virtue still in him abode;
> So he swiftly made his own
> Those last spoils we had not won . . ."[1]

The 'eleventh hour', 'wages', pick up the Parable of the Labourers in the Vineyard. The next stanza depends on the metaphor of the stripped vines of grapes at the end of the harvest; but also perhaps, of 'the little foxes, that spoil the vines'.[2] 'Marked its man' carries no special allusion, and the common idiom impinges, not very happily, on the poem's tone. In the next stanza the references thicken to

> Woe unto you also, ye lawyers! for ye lade men with burdens grievous to be borne . . .[3]

and, rather less fittingly, its allusion of 'virtue still in him abode' to the woman who touched the hem of His garment.[4]

Kipling, as we should expect from his background, upbringing, and the titles to many of the stories, uses Biblical allusion continuously. As an illustration of what is perhaps the most closely-compacted poem we may take two stanzas of 'The Rabbi's Song':[5]

> "If thought can reach to Heaven,
> On Heaven let it dwell,
> For fear thy Thought be given
> Like power to reach to Hell.

---

[1] *The Vineyard.* [2] *Cant.* 2:15.

[3] *Lk.* 11:46, *Mt.* 23:4. Perhaps another dimension of irony is added by the fact that the words are also addressed to the Pharisees.

[4] e.g. *Lk.* 8:44.

[5] From the story 'The House Surgeon': *Actions and Reactions.*

For fear the desolation
  And darkness of thy mind
Perplex an habitation
  Which thou hast left behind.

.   .   .   .   .

Our lives, our tears, as water,
  Are spilled upon the ground;
God giveth no man quarter,
  Yet God a means hath found,
Though Faith and Hope have vanished,
  And even love grows dim—
A means whereby His banished
  Be not expelled from Him.''

Here the basic allusion is to the plea of the Wise Woman of Tekoa to bring back the banished Absalom.[1] The first stanza seems to be almost a *collage* of phrases; we may choose among them. For example—

If I ascend up into heaven, thou art there: if I make my bed in hell, behold, thou art there.[2]

and the famous passage from *Philippians* 4:8

Finally, brethren, whatsoever things are true . . . think on these things.

The fifth and seventh lines suggest

. . . Surely the least of the flock shall draw them out: surely he shall make their habitations desolate with them.[3]

—as well as the perennial image (for which a quotation from Plotinus will serve) 'The body is the garment of the soul'; or

  "The soul's dark cottage, batter'd and decay'd,
    Lets in new Light through chinks that time has made."[4]

The second stanza is even more compacted:

We . . . are as water spilt on the ground, which cannot be gathered up again.[5]

with—

. . . yet doth he devise means, that his banished be not expelled from him.[6]

---

[1] *2 Sam.* 14:4. The story is a favourite of Kipling's: *v.* the use made of it in 'On the Wall'.   [2] *Ps.* 139:8.   [3] *Jer.* 49:20.
[4] E. Waller, 'Of the last Verses in the Book.'   [5] *2 Sam.* 14:14.   [6] *Ibid.*

The fourth line uses *quarter* in the Elizabethan/Jacobean sense (it is not used thus in the Bible) that may recall to us Nathaniel Wanley's poem:

> "Are beds of death so throng'd, or growne so deare
> That a poor skull can get no quarter there?"[1]

ii

But (as we should expect) the richest and most unselfconscious usages are found in Shakespeare[2] and the poetry of the seventeenth century. We may take first of all part of a poem by Herrick:

> "Not as a thief, shalt Thou ascend the mount,
> But like a Person of some high account:
> The *Crosse* shall be Thy *Stage*; and Thou shalt there
> The spacious field have for Thy *Theater*.
> Thou art that *Roscius*, and that markt-out men,
> That must this day act the Tragedian,
> To wonder and affrightment: Thou art He
> Whom all the flux of Nations comes to see;
> Not those poor Theeves that act their part with Thee . . ."

The poem is called 'Rex Tragicus'; clearly, there are overtones of the Aristotelian definition of the tragic here ('person of some high account'). There is also the allusion to 'wonder and affrightment'—is this the 'pity and terror' of the *Poetics*?—as well as the allusion to the famous Roman actor Roscius, of the first century B.C., who was defended by Cicero. He is 'markt out', perhaps, because of the prophecies:[3] 'I, if I be lifted up, will draw all men unto me.'

But we may see other references. The 'poor theeves' are clear: but the first line presumably alludes to the Saviour who will come, at the final judgment, 'like a thief in the night'. 'The Mount' is primarily Calvary, perhaps also The Mount of Olives, Sinai; and the high place on which the new King traditionally meets his death.[4] The 'flux of nations' is a curious term: is it an allusion to the enlargement of the chosen race 'as the sands of the sea-shore for multitude'?

After the initial shock we recognize one of the typical features of seventeenth-century religious poetry; the acceptance of all images,

---

[1] *The Skull.*

[2] For a study of such image-clusters in Shakespeare, see E. A. Armstrong, *Shakespeare's Imagination.*

[3] There may even be a punning reference to the Evangelist.

[4] cf. Lord Raglan, *The Hero.*

pagan and Christian, to exemplify the final glory. Nothing is outside the poetic synthesis that the poet may bring about, since all are part of one accepted unity of being and of praise.

Another and contrasting example may be taken from a famous passage of Donne's 'Second Anniversarie' (1612), an Elegy for the Countess of Bedford. The Countess is the 'immortal Maid', who is perceived as the 'Father' to Donne's own muse.

> "These Hymnes, thy issue, may increase so long
> As till God's great *Venite* change the song.
> Thirst for that time, O my insatiate soul,
> And serve thy thirst, with God's safe-sealing Bowle.
> Be thirstie still, and drinke still till thou goe
> To th' only Health; to be Hydroptique so
> Forget this rotten world; And unto thee
> Let thine owne times as an old storie bee.
> Be not concern'd: studie not why, or when;
> Doe not so much as not beleeve a man.
> For though to erre, be worst, to try truths forth,
> Is far more businesse, than the world is worth.
> The world is but a carkase; thou art fed
> By it, but as a worme, that carkase bred."

Here the 'hymns' are her issue, children (I do not think a further pun is intended) in the sense that she has inspired them. They now form part of the angelic song—perhaps that of *Revelation* 19:6—until the day of judgment, God's great *Venite*, ends or transforms that music.[1] But *Venite* suggests not only the familiar Canticle, but also the promise

> Come unto me, all ye that travail and are heavy laden . . .

Through that phrase we move into the orbit, as it were, of the Communion Service, so that the Chalice fits in logically; besides a multitude of confirming and supporting texts:

> Blessed are they which do hunger and thirst after righteousness . . .[2]
> Ho, every one that thirsteth, come ye to the waters . . .[3]

The 'safe-sealing Bowle' is of course the Chalice—

> Whoso eateth my flesh, and drinketh my blood, hath eternal life.[4]

---

[1] Consider also Donne's *Hymne to God my God in my Sickness.*
[2] *Mt.* 5:6.   [3] *Isa.* 55:1. (*v. infra.*)   [4] *Jn.* 6:54.

and

> This cup is the new testament in my blood . . .[1]

and the sentence, by its massive references, links up with the whole 'contracts' of the Old Testament. In typical manner, the image is then spun out, embodying Donne's 'Paradoxes'. Dropsy is a terrible (and in his age, a common) disease. Yet the desire to drink incessantly leads to the health of the soul, through this Communion; the arrogant pun on the disease again recalls Matthew's text (and many hints from the Psalms), and leads on to 'rotten', a physical feature of the corpse that has died of dropsy, leprosy or venereal disease. We remember Hamlet's dialogue in the graveyard:

> *Hamlet*: How long will a man lie i' the earth before he rot?
>
> *First Clown*: Faith, if he be not rotten before he die—as we have many pocky corpses now-a-days, that will scarce hold the laying-in,—he will last you some eight or nine year.[2]

and the many Shakespearian allusions to the 'rottenness' of the world and the times.

iii

We may pass to another device, not often used (for obvious reasons): a sort of ironic parody or inversion. Here are parts of a poem by A. E. Housman:

> "Ho, everyone that thirsteth
>   And hath the price to give,
> Come to the stolen waters,
>   Drink and your soul shall live.
>
> Come to the stolen waters,
>   And leap the guarded pale,
> And pull the flower in season
>   Before desire shall fail.
>
> It shall not last for ever
>   No more than earth and skies;
> But he that drinks in season
>   Shall live before he dies . . .[3]

To examine the full implications we must set out the first few verses from *Isaiah*:[4]

---

[1] *I Cor.* 11:25.
[3] *More Poems*, No. XXII.

[2] *Hamlet*, V. 1. 168.
[4] 55:1–3.

Ho, every one that thirsteth, come ye to the waters, and he that hath no money; come ye, buy and eat; yea, come, buy wine and milk without money and without price.

Wherefore do ye spend money for that which is not bread? and your labour for that which satisfieth not? hearken diligently unto me, and eat ye that which is good, and let your soul delight itself in fatness.

Incline your ear, and come unto me: hear and your soul shall live; and I will make an everlasting covenant with you, even the sure mercies of David.

The 'righteousness' of Isaiah is in fact inverted by Housman to serve a sexual theme. Illicit intercourse demands its eternal price; the waters are to be 'stolen'—the word is emphasized by repetition. We may, if we wish, remember the common sexual imagery of the well and spring,[1] as well as that of the waters of immortality. The 'guarded pale' is the Garden of Eden, with its overtones of the *hortus clausus* of many literatures; guarded because of the angel with the flaming sword.[2] But it is also the 'pale' of the Elizabethan park, as well as of virginity; and this links up, perhaps, with the many and often wearisome Elizabethan puns on deer and horns.[3]

The pulling of the flower seems a very general aspect of the perennial woman-flower imagery: we may think of Herrick's

"Gather ye rosebuds while ye may . . ."

and of a lesser-known passage from *Wisdom*:[4]

Let us fill ourselves with costly wine and ointments: and let no flower of the spring pass by us . . .

But Housman is also using the famous last chapter of *Ecclesiastes*:

Also when they shall be afraid of that which is high, and fears shall be in the way, and the almond tree shall flourish, . . . *and desire shall fail*: because man goeth to his long home, and the mourners go about the streets.[5]

The line 'It shall not last for ever' inverts Isaiah's

And I will make an everlasting covenant with you . . .

---

[1] e.g. in Yeats' play *At the Hawk's Well*.   [2] *Gen.* 3:24.
[3] *v.* (e.g.) *Love's Labour's Lost*, IV. I. 110; *Venus and Adonis*, l. 229–240. For a similar image from fish-poaching, see *A Winter's Tale*.   [4] 2:7.   [5] 12:5.

and justifies it by the *Ecclesiastes* allusion. But a further irony is perhaps drawn from the unspoken but remembered text:

Heaven and earth shall pass away: but my words shall not pass away.[1]

the 'shall live' being turned with rather clumsy irony to 'before he dies'. The same naïveté is apparent in the last stanza, which I have not quoted.

iv

A striking use of the 'reversed' passage is in the second act of Sean O'Casey's *The Silver Tassie*. The scene is set in France during the 1914–18 war. In the left background there is a ruined monastery, from which, at intervals, can be heard the plainsong of the monks. In front of it is a soldier undergoing field punishment, hands and wrists tied to a gun-wheel in the posture of crucifixion. In the middle foreground there is a huge howitzer, to which a character—the Croucher—intones a hymn. Then comes a reversed form of the famous Valley of Dry Bones passage from *Ezekiel*:[2]

. . . "And I prophesied; and the breath came out of them, and the sinews came away from them, and their bones fell asunder, and they died, and the exceeding great army became a valley of dry bones."

Against this is counterpointed the distant chant from the monastery:

"Accendat in nobis Dominus ignem sui amoris, et flammam aeternae caritatis."

But perhaps the most complex and intricate example is from the second movement of T. S. Eliot's *Ash Wednesday*:

"Lady, three white leopards sat under a juniper-tree
In the cool of the day, having fed to satiety
On my legs my heart my liver and that which had been confined
Shall these bones live? Shall these
Bones live? And that which had been contained
In the bones (which were already dry) said chirping . . ."

The whole poem is concerned with Mount Purgatory, man's progress through purgation to illumination. It is clear that Eliot is using a peculiar layered structure of reference, a frequent device which he uses to gesture, without explicitness, towards the mysteries he is contemplating.

[1] *Mk.* 13:31; *Lk.* 21:33.   [2] 37:1 ff.

238

We may try to follow these gestures by examining the basic material; in which the previous passage from *Ezekiel* is fused with the less familiar narrative of *1 Kings* 19:4. Elijah has fled for his life from Jezebel:

> But he himself went a day's journey into the wilderness, and came and sat down under a juniper tree: and he requested for himself that he might die; and said, It is enough; now, O Lord, take away my life; for I am not better than my fathers.
>
> And as he lay and slept under a juniper tree, behold, then an angel touched him, and said unto him, Arise and eat.
>
> And he looked, and behold, there was a cake baken on the coals, and a cruse of water at his head. And he did eat and drink, and laid him down again.
>
> And the angel of the Lord came again the second time, and touched him, and said, Arise and eat; *because the journey is too great for thee.*

The basic concern of the passage is the need for faith, for renewal of strength on the journey. It is possible that the last sentence suggests that the intended journey was to Mt. Horeb (Sinai) where God had revealed himself to Moses; the cycle completed, as it were, on the Mount of Calvary.[1] Elijah is a devastatingly uncompromising figure, concerned to preserve the tradition against foreign corruptions.

There are many speculative interpretations of the 'three leopards': the three Spirits of the Trinity is one of them. The allusions in the Bible are not helpful; though the leopard is mentioned with the lion by *Hosea*,[2] and though the beast that comes out of the sea in *Revelation*[3] is shaped like a leopard. Perhaps we can, for the moment, rest with the meaning of the beast of great strength, swiftness and cunning, which allures other beasts to it by its smell.

It was, I think, Jones who first drew attention to the 'overlay' of the Biblical passage with Grimm's macabre fairy-tale *The Juniper Tree*, in which a mother cooks her step-children, the familiar Thyestes-type myth.[4]

v

The Bible has furnished ample material for oblique political satire. The most famous example is Dryden's *Absalom and Achitophel*; in

---

[1] cf. Donne's 'identification' of the Tree of Knowledge and the cross: a familiar feature of iconography.   [2] 13:7.   [3] 13:2.

[4] Genesimus Jones, *Approach to the Purpose*, London, 1964.

which David is Charles II, his wife Michal, Catherine of Portugal (who, like Michal, was childless), Absalom is James, Duke of Monmouth; and Achitophel, Ashley Cooper, the Earl of Shaftesbury. The *correspondances* lend themselves readily to the Biblical story. In the passage that follows Solyma is Jerusalem and London. The Ethnic plot is the Popish Plot; the Jebusites are the Roman Catholics, and the Levites are the Presbyterian ministers, displaced from their cures by the Act of Uniformity. The following passage gives some idea of Dryden's method:[1]

> "The Solymaean rout, well versed of old
> In godly faction and in treason bold,
> Cowering and quaking at a conqueror's sword.
> But lofty to a lawful prince restored,
> Saw with disdain an Ethnic plot begun
> And scorned by Jebusites to be outdone.
> Hot Levites headed these; who pulled before
> From the ark, which in the Judges' days they bore,
> Resumed their cant, and with a jealous cry
> Pursued their old beloved theocracy,
> Where Sanhedrin and priest enslaved the nation,
> And justified their spoils by inspiration;
> For who so fit for reign as Aaron's race,
> If once dominion they could find in grace?

. . . . .

> But far more numerous was the hand of such
> Who think too little and who talk too much.
> These out of mere instinct, they knew not why,
> Adored their fathers' God and property,
> And by the same blind benefit of Fate
> The Devil and the Jebusite did hate:
> Born to be saved, even in their own despight
> Because they could not help believing right.
> Such were the tools; but a whole Hydra more
> Remains of sprouting heads too long to score."

Dryden moves with the utmost ease and skill in his energetic and graceful couplet, and refrains from making the scriptural allusions wearisome by over-loading. Within this framework, and the pattern of *Judges*, we may see the steel-pointed allusions; the City mob that had quailed before Cromwell, but whose puritan elements viewed

[1] *Absalom and Achitophel*, i. 513 ff.

Charles II—like David, 'le père de son peuple'—with distrust; the Presbyterian ministers, who had refused—notoriously—the rule of the Bishops. 'Pursued their own beloved theocracy' is the double-barbed sting since in their 'protestation' the ministers were in fact ruled by their own assemblies or 'Sanhedrins', claiming direct guidance from heaven. He glances, too, at the controversy over redemption by grace: 'Because they could not *help* believing right.'

The rabblement—the 'herd' suggests cattle or perhaps swine—are those who 'think too little and who talk too much'. Their religious allegiance is one of self-interest: 'God' and 'property' are given an ironical co-planar value by their position in the line. So will the Jebusites (the Roman Catholics) and the devil. It is typical of baroque imagery that the classical Hydra's head is used quite naturally in the texture.[1]

vi

Over the matter of prose, the main difficulty is to choose from an infinitude of possible examples; selection must again be arbitrary. We may begin with one of Donne's sermons, and consider how he imposes his highly personal style of rhetoric upon the frame of biblical references. We may note afterwards some of the less clear allusions:

"God made the first Marriage, and man made the first Divorce. God married the Body and Soul in the Creation, and man divorced the Body and Soul by death through sin, in his fall. God doth not admit, not justify, not authorize such super-inductions upon such Divorces, as some have imagined: that the soul departing from one body, should become the soul of another body, in a perpetual revolution and trans-migration of souls through bodies, which hath been the giddiness oi some Philosophers to think; Or that the body of the dead should become the body of an evil spirit, that that spirit might at his will, and to his purposes inform, and inanimate that dead body; God allows no such super-inductions, no such second Marriages upon such Divorces by death, no such disposition of soul or body, after their dissolution by death. But because God hath made the band of Marriage indissoluble but by death, farther than man can die, this Divorce cannot fall upon man. As far as man is immortal, man is a married man still, still in possession of a soul, and a body too. And man is forever immortal in

[1] Compare, perhaps, the blend of Christianity and classical imagery in Shake-speare's *Richard II*.

both: immortal in his soul by preservation, and immortal in his body by reparation, in the Resurrection. For, though they be separated *a Thoro et Mensa*, from Bed and Board, they are not divorced; though the soul be at the Table of the Lamb, in Glory, and the body but at the table of the Serpent, in dust; though the soul be *in lecto florido*, in that bed which is always green, in an everlasting spring, in Abraham's Bosom; and the body but in that green-bed, whose covering is but a yard and a half of Turf, and a Rug of Grass, and the sheet but a winding sheet, yet they are not divorced; they shall return to one another again, in an inseparable reunion in the Resurrection. . . ."[1]

The first reference is of course to Eden. The attack is then turned on the believers in metempsychosis, and Donne uses his favourite device, a triple hammer-blow (the word-rhythms lengthening with the force of each beat):

doth not ădmĭt, not jŭstĭf̆y̆, not aŭthŏrĭze

the whole leading to the heavy latinized key-word 'superinductions'.[2] Because of this sermon-rhetoric, he returns again and again to the central idea, attacking it from different angles. The second paragraph follows logically: it is an insistence on individuality after death. But it is possible that we miss, if we read rapidly, some of the allusions

. . . immortal in his soul by preservation . . .
(. . . 'preserve thy body and soul unto everlasting life')

and

immortal in his body by reparation
(. . . 'in remembrance that Christ died for thee')

The legal language of divorce—*a thoro et mensa*—leads on to the idea of *board*, and so to 'the Table of the Lamb' ('Thou spread'st a table before me') but the complex idea of 'the table of the Serpent' plays on the serpent-worm identification, as well as the return of the body to dust, and the passage from *Genesis* 3:

. . . Dust shalt thou eat . . .

In florido lecto—note how the Latin is always translated, as for a mixed audience—picks up once again Psalm 23:

He maketh me to *lie down* in *green pastures*

---

[1] *Sermons*, No. LXXX.

[2] Perhaps paraphrasable as 'further illegitimate consequences deduced in imagination from the known facts'.

progressing to the homely 'Rug of grass', a superb imaginative stroke.[1]
We remember an image of a similar kind.

When the churchyards swell with the waves and billows of the dead.[2]

vii

Finally we may take an extract from a classic 'imaginative' life of
Jesus, George Moore's *The Brook Kerith*:

> "Upon this he took them to a mountainside where the rock was
> crumbling, and he said: you see this crumbling rock? Once it held
> together, now it is falling into sand, but it shall be built up into rock
> again, and again it shall crumble into sand. At which they drew
> together silent with wonder, each fearing to ask the other if the Master
> were mad, for though they could see that the rock might drift into sand,
> they could not see how sand might be built up again into rock.
>
> Master, how shall we know thee when thou returnest to us? Wilt thou
> be changed as the rock changes? Wilt thou be sand or rock? It was
> Andrew that had spoken; and Philip answered him that the Master will
> return in a chariot of fire, for he was angry that a fellow of Andrew's
> stupidity should put questions to Jesus whether they were wise or
> foolish; but could they be aught else than foolish coming from him?
> Andrew, persisting, replied: but we may not be within sight of the Master
> when he steps out of his chariot of fire, and we are only asking for a
> token whereby we may know him from his Father. My Father and thy
> Father, Andrew, Jesus answered, the Father of all that has lived, that
> lives, and that shall live in the world; and the law over the rock that
> crumbles into sand and the sand that is built up into rock again, was in
> that rock before Abraham was, and will abide in it and in the flower
> that grows under the rock till time everlasting."

Here we have a kind of refraction of the language of the New
Testament, which is self-consistent and far removed from pastiche.
The allusions are clear; the projection of the various rock imagery of
the Bible, Ezekiel's (and Blake's) chariot of fire, and the text 'before
Abraham was, I am'. The 'household language' is combined with
occasional archaisms, but these go almost unnoticed: 'Upon this',
'aught else', 'whereby' and indeed serve to emphasize the credibility
of the dialogue which retains the second person singular. It will be

---

[1] cf. Yeats, *To a Shade* (Glasnevin is a cemetery in North Dublin)
"Go, unquiet wanderer,
And gather the Glasnevin *coverlet*
About your head till the dust stops your ear". . .

[2] *Sermons.*

noted that there is no 'poetic' prose structure, only a pellucid rippling rhythm which carries the narrative foreword. Moore frequently uses this blend of New Testament and modern diction—as in the use of 'crumbling', 'stupidity', 'persisting'; resolving it in the last sentence by a more directly allusive rhythm.[1]

Doughty's *Arabia Deserta* is perhaps a special case of Biblical stylistic influence: justified by travel in Bible lands and by a kind of infection of the desert. We may take a single instance:[2]

> "The Semitic East is a land of sepulchres; Syria, a limestone country, is full of tombs, hewn, it may be said, under every hill side. Now they are stables for herdsmen, and open dens of wild creatures.[3] Kings and counsellors of the earth built them desolate places; but Isaiah mocked in his time those 'habitations of the dead'. These are lands of the faith of the resurrection. Palmyra, Petra, Hejra, in the ways of the desert countries, were all less oases of husbandmen than great caravan stations. In all is seen much sumptuousness of sepulchres; clay buildings served for their short lives and squared stones and columns were for the life of the State. The care of sepulture, the ambitious mind of man's mortality, to lead eternity captive, was beyond measure in the religions of antiquity, which were without humility.[4] The Médain funeral chambers all together are not, I think, an hundred. An hundred monuments of well-faring families in several generations betoken no great city. Of such we might conjecture an old Arabian population of eight thousand souls; a town such as *Aneyza* at this day, the metropolis of Nejd."

We may glance briefly at Doughty's technique. He seems to have in mind *Isaiah* 22:16:

> What hast thou here? and whom hast thou here, that thou hast hewed thee out a sepulchre here, as he that heweth him out a sepulchre on high, and that graveth an habitation for himself in a rock?

The preceding 'desolate places' is also a quotation, but might be from one of many sources—*Job*, *Psalms*, *Isaiah*, *Ezekiel*. 'To lead eternity captive' is an adaptation from the familiar 'Thou hast led

---

[1] cf. (of many possible references) *Ps.* 41:13: 'blessed be God from everlasting to everlasting'.

[2] *Travels in Arabia Deserta*, one volume edition, 1926, p. 169.

[3] e.g. *Jer.* 9:11: 'I will make Jerusalem a den of dragons'.

[4] cf. Sir Thomas Browne, *Urn Burial*, V. 16.
"Pyramids, arches, obelisks, were but the irregularities of vainglory, and wild examples of ancient magnanimity."

captivity captive.'[1] But the style is vitiated by archaisms which are not of the Bible, but which come rather from the Wardour Street diction of the original edition (1888).

viii

We have, perhaps, four main divisions of the 'imitatio':

The partial but deliberate imitation of Biblical language and syntax, as in Bunyan, Carlyle, Doughty; which is individual, idiosyncratic, and seems unlikely to be of any importance in the future.

The wider but indefinable effect of what we may call the 'infection' of the best aspects of the Biblical style; its energy, dignity, restraint, and a certain directness which arises, at least in part, from the Hebrew which has few subordinate clauses, and works by short rapid thought-units. Its comparatively simple vocabulary is at once its strength and its weakness; as is also the reliance, for the terms of its imagery, upon unfamiliar modes of living and (sometimes) of thought. But I have used the word 'infection' deliberately, with some thought of Tolstoy's aesthetic; but more in the sense that 'Longinus', and many after him, advocated the reading of the classics:

> ... even so from the great genius of the men of old do streams pass off to the souls of those who emulate them, as though from holy caves ...[2]

Or if we care to transpose it into modern terms,

> Nor is there singing school but studying
> Monuments of its own magnificence.[3]

On a lower level, perhaps, this is sound advice:

> "When you are in doubt which of two words to choose, choose the one which you would think is more likely to be found in the Bible."[4]

A notable example of this 'infection', taken unconsciously and with complete control, is in a book I have mentioned already: George Adam Smith's *The Geography of the Holy Land*.

Secondly, there is a mass of history, parable, proverbs, mythologem and imagery which over five centuries has been absorbed into every literary and artistic form. Until this century this constituted a reservoir of direct and indirect allusion, as of images in depth, to

---

[1] cf. *Ps.* 68:18.   [2] *A Treatise on the Sublime*, XIII. *op. cit.*
[3] W. B. Yeats, 'Sailing to Byzantium.'
[4] G. Townsend Warner, *On the Writing of English*.

Western literature. In combination with learning in the classics (always less widespread, and never so embedded in the consciousness of a large range of readers) it formed a treasure-house of linguistic richness whose importance cannot be overstressed. In combination with the 'household language' of many ages it offers a peculiarly rich and economical mode of statement. That the recovery of its meaning is a process that grows more difficult as these aspects of our culture diminish is a truism. The same is true of many areas of literary scholarship; that of Shakespeare provides the simplest example. The recent attacks on Milton would have puzzled our more educated grandfathers; with the triple tools of Biblical learning, classical scholarship, and some European and Renaissance history, there is little in, say, *Paradise Lost* that would not, for at least two hundred years after its date, have been relatively clear.

To glance at even a fraction of the imagery drawn from Biblical sources would be an impossible task. Shakespeare's vast debt in the way of 'imitatio' conscious and unconscious, has been noted by many writers.[1] Some of it is obscure to the present-day reader. Few respond immediately to such references as Hamlet's

> "O Jephthah, judge of Israel, what a treasure hadst thou!"[2]

or to Othello's

> "Like the base Indian, threw a pearl away
> Richer than all his tribe . . ."[3]

or even to Shylock's composite reminiscence of the prophet:

> "I had it of Leah when I was a bachelor: I would not have
> given it for a wilderness of monkeys."[4]

More complex is Milton's amalgam of *Genesis*, Plato, *Job* and, perhaps, *Psalms* and *Revelation* in the 'Ode on the Morning of Christ's Nativity':

> "Such musick (as 'tis said)
> Before was never made,

---

[1] See, e.g., R. Noble, *Shakespeare and the Bible*; E. Armstrong, *Shakespeare's Imagination*.   [2] II. 2. 408.   [3] V. 2. 346.

[4] *Merchant of Venice*, III. 1. 119. Is the superb richness of the phrase compounded of 'the waste howling wilderness' of *Deut.* 32:10, and the grotesque birds of *Ps.* 102:6?

But when of old the sons of morning sung,
While the Creator Great
His constellations set,
  And the well-balanc'd world on hinges hung,
  And cast the dark foundations deep,
  And bid the weltring waves their oozy channel keep.

Ring out ye Crystall sphears,
Once bless our human ears,
  (If ye have power to touch our senses so)
And let your silver chime
Move in melodious time;
  And let the Base of Heav'ns deep Organ blow,
  And with your ninefold harmony
  Make up full consort to th' Angelike symphony."

ix

We may conclude by some quotations from Northrop Frye:

"Once our view of the Bible comes into proper focus, a great mass of literary symbols from *The Dream of The Rood* to *Little Gidding* begins to take on meaning."[1] . . . "The Bible may thus be examined from an aesthetic or Aristotelian point of view as a single form, as a story in which pity and terror, which in this context are the knowledge of good and evil, are raised and cast out. Or it may be examined from a Longinian point of view as a series of ecstatic moments or points of expanding apprehension. This approach is in fact the assumption on which every selection of a text of a sermon is based. Here we have a critical principle which we can take back to literature and apply to anything we like, a principle in which the "holism", as it has been called, of Coleridge and the discontinuous theories of Poe, Hulme, and Pound are reconciled."[2]

[1] *Anatomy of Criticism*, p. 316.   [2] *Ibid.*, p. 326.

CHAPTER FIFTEEN

'Towards the Values'

i

THIS LAST CHAPTER is an inevitable yet terrifying development of what we have been considering. We are committed to a strange indeterminate country in which Beliefs, Dogmas, Ethics and Morals, History and Aesthetics, seem to shift, coalesce, converge and diverge perpetually. Yet for our purpose it is necessary to attempt some simplification, within the terms we have postulated: even at the price of distortion, and the certainty of giving offence to some. Let us keep tenaciously to two governing propositions; that all 'literary' values are in the last resort subordinate to what is communicated, the thing *said*; and that there is no 'modern' critical vocabulary for dealing with literature which concerns the numinous or the supernatural.[1]

I begin by assuming four kinds of value which I propose to call religious, ethical, historical, and personal.

The religious values will, of course, override all others; subject to our assent to C. S. Lewis' proposition that the Bible is 'remorselessly and continuously sacred'.[2] Within this broad condition we should include those who believe, in various degrees, in its verbal inspiration; the fundamentalists who are not prepared to allow anything less than the literal veracity of its total contents; 'liberal' theologians who feel profound doubts on the historicity of portions of the narrative, and who have found it essential to compromise (to whatever

---

[1] I am aware of the implications of this statement. I have in mind such terms as 'sublime', 'awful', 'majestic', 'noble', 'exalting', which can be traced back to 'Longinus' and in particular, to his re-interpretation at the hands of the eighteenth-century critics. Much Victorian criticism of the Bible employs these terms: which assume our ability to respond to 'great thoughts' expressed in 'an eminence and excellence of language'.

[2] *v.* p. 12, *supra*. But many of us would take exception to all three words, unless they were defined in more depth.

extent, and whatever the critical apparatus that they employ) with the humanist-agnostic positions; the 'demythologizers' who have produced, whatever their reservations, interpretations of the Biblical stories (in both Testaments) without any necessary belief in any historical veracity of the acts and sayings described, but who appear to allow analogical, allegorical, or typological truths to be inferred from the myth or mythologem, in a religious situation which they sometimes call existential.

Behind these categories there appear to be certain overriding aspects of belief which we can perhaps attempt to summarize. God exists; He is all-wise and all-powerful. He has manifested Himself uniquely through His Chosen People. His care is for the individual and for the individual soul, which is immortal. The Bible is the unified, but not progressively constant, revelation of His attributes, which include justice, mercy, forgiveness. In return, He demands constant and exclusive worship and love. To the philosopher He is by definition unknowable except through the mystery of the Incarnation, and we can approach Him only through faith and certain intermittent apprehensions of His nature. The main channels of these apprehensions are symbol and imagery.

There is in man an innate tendency to sinfulness, symbolized by the story of the Fall. This expresses itself in the Bible as history, both of nations and of individuals, and incurs God's punishment, which may be assuaged by repentance.

The New Testament proclaims both an ethical development, fundamental in character, of the Law of the Old Testament, already shown in an evolutionary state; as well as a fulfilment of the millennial events that are adumbrated or prophesied in it.

The new Law is made possible by the Incarnation, in the personality of Christ; in whom godhead and manhood co-exist simultaneously, and for the first and last time. Through Him is made the final and complete sacrifice for sin. The fact of the Incarnation is the vital belief on which Christianity depends, and which, unaccepted, involves the collapse of all further speculation. Out of the life and teaching of Christ comes the certainty of eternal life for the individual, whatever the form, and at whatever the time, of His coming in judgment.[1]

Through Him, man has access to the divine Grace.

[1] 'Then cometh the end . . .'

These beliefs presuppose the *fact* of the supranatural as a force at work in the world, beyond and above any apprehended aspect of 'natural' law.[1] Man's intellectual powers to apprehend these aspects of the godhead are intermittent and partial. Where these fail, faith may enter.

With the acceptance of these propositions all other values contained in the Bible become, not irrelevant, but subordinate or auxiliary; that is, the literary statement may, by its power to induce specific responses, conduce to the acceptance of those values, but can in no possible way become a substitute for the dogmatic elements which grow out of, or are elicited from, the whole book.

ii

If the supranatural elements in these beliefs are excluded, we are driven to a consideration of the Bible as affirming a series of ethical propositions which can be assessed as 'values'. Many of them would command full assent, even though the conditions of Original Sin, Incarnation, Atonement, Personal Immortality and Grace were excluded. Others are only valid in a specific context. We may attempt a brief list of these values as they appear to-day in Western civilization.

It is probable that monotheism (in whatever form) would be approved, rather than any conception of a plurality of gods, though the prevalence of Bacon's 'idols of the market-place' is notorious. An acceptance of monotheism implies no commitment to Christianity, but it is probable that insufficient attention is paid to the varieties of monotheism in other important religions.

Both fornication and adultery have been modified, in the common view (but not in that of the Churches), as unqualified sins; for a variety of social and physical reasons. So, too, with the Biblical strictures against sexual perversions, with which recent legislation has dealt lightly.

The prohibitions against perjury,[2] land-grabbing,[3] cheating of all

[1] See, e.g., C. S. Lewis' exposition of the concepts of 'natural' and 'divine' law in *Miracles*.

[2] 'False Witness.' It is not easy to imagine the vital importance of this unless one has had some experience of an Eastern law-court.

[3] Removing one's neighbour's land-mark. And *v. Isa.* 5:8. We may note this does not apply to international affairs.

kinds (but particularly over false weights and measures) would receive, in theory, universal assent.

Injunctions as to justice and charity to the poor and oppressed, the 'fatherless and widows', are also unexceptionable; and it is not difficult to see a steady though intermittent development, as civilization progresses, in the application of these principles.

There are strong *exempla*, in both Testaments, for racial tolerance and intolerance, and for the eventual brotherhood of man;[1] as well as warnings against violence and lies:

> Thou shalt not raise a false report: put not thine hand with the wicked to be an unrighteous witness.
>
> Thou shalt not follow a multitude to do evil; neither shalt thou speak in a cause to decline after many to wrest judgement.[2]

The prophet Amos attacked the extortion and luxury of the rich, the misery of the poor. Elijah championed Naboth against the wealth and power of King David. Christ's emphasis on the virtues of the poor and humble, and that ultimate reward which has been used to condone so many social injustices, needs no stress.

iii

Or we can consider the values as they emerge from the Bible as history: history fragmented, subject to editings and interpolations, often written out of oral tradition long after the events had occurred: but which forms, in spite of all adverse conditions and destructive criticism, a linear structure that has, in its scope and unity, no rival in literature. We have here, and here alone, the evolution of a small tribal community into a considerable empire under Solomon; and its subsequent disintegration. It contains in itself the most ample material for the study of an underlying philosophy of history. We see law evolving from case-law to code, becoming ossified by its own complexity, purging and renewing itself again. In warfare we may deduce, and transpose into other settings in times and weaponry, principles of that art that still stand. Above all, we can see in the history of Israel the centrifugal forces that appear to act on all states and empires; internal dissensions, the emergence and fall of leaders;

---

[1] Against the massacres of the Old Testament (*v.* Ch. XIII) we must set the compassion of the story of Ruth, and of the woman of Samaria; besides Isaiah's prophecy. Above all, there is the extension of the promise from the Law to the Gentiles.   [2] *Ex.* 23:1, 2.

diplomatic transactions of great complexity and often of great folly. Isaiah attacks those who would form a futile alliance with Egypt in order to resist Assyria, Jeremiah has a vision of the hopelessness of continuing the conflict with the all-powerful Babylon.[1] We may admire Christ's resistance to all hints that He might become the popular leader against the implacable Roman power.[2] He foresaw (as did Jeremiah) that military resistance in such a context was not only hopeless but would involve the final destruction of Jerusalem. Perhaps the most important lesson from the history of war is that of the need to estimate, without emotion, the chances and the consequences of the success of any enterprise; and, if it appears likely to succeed, of the long-term implications of success which have become of increasing and disastrous importance. The text 'Who goeth a warfare any time at his own charges?' (*1 Cor.* 9:7) reads ironically now.

It is a history of which the substantial accuracy is certified by archaeology and what contemporary documentation remains: setting aside always the fragments of folk-lore and magic, embedded in its deeper fossil layers. It is small enough and compact enough to be studied as a unity, for the acid of time has eaten away most of the irrelevancies. Among the lessons to be drawn from it (and which are, I think, still incomplete) are explanations of the persistence of the Jewish spirit of blood and race, its preservation of its characteristics in the 'remnant', over five thousand years.[3] And those explanations would take into account not only the passing of the great empires, Egypt, Assyria, Persia, Philistia, Babylon, Turkey, that surrounded them, but the fate of the hostile tribes whose names survive only in the laconic accounts of *Exodus*, *Chronicles* and *Kings*, and in the epic songs and psalms.

It is a commonplace that the survival, the projection of the Old Testament into the New, determines the whole character of Christianity. The account of its development and varying courses has been written many times, from many points of view, and it would be both impertinent and otiose to attempt to summarize them.[4] In all such histories we can trace a progress that is often devious, self-destructive,

[1] 37:17.

[2] As, for example, in the 'trap' question over the tribute money. (*Mt.* 22:17.)

[3] See, e.g., Arland Ussher, *The Magic People.*

[4] Perhaps one would instance Gibbon's *Decline and Fall*, and Butterfield's *Christianity and History*, as polar contrasts.

productive at times of the most intense cruelty and suffering, yet which moves steadily forward with an enduring bond. These considerations should not blind us to the often appalling consequences; yet we may quote Butterfield:

> "It is impossible to measure the vast difference that ordinary Christian piety has made to the last two thousand years of European history: but we shall have some inkling of that difference if the world continues its present drift towards paganism. Here is a fact which blots out and supersedes everything that can be said against the churches in European history."[1]

The last division is what I have called the personal aspect, for lack of a better word. I have in mind the purely 'poetic' values, considered just as they might be approached in poets whose work is written out of assumptions and propositions that do not command the full assent of the reader.[2] Let us imagine the situation of the agnostic who, with some training in the disciplines of our own and other literatures, is persuaded to return to the Bible with the assurance that it has no palpable design upon him, but that some measure of concentrated study is needful, in addition to 'the willing suspension of disbelief'.

We should make the point before he begins that the Bible is an immensely difficult and complicated collection of books. To approach to some understanding of it in its general setting involves the study of its framework and background in history, geography, ethnology, politics, and sociology. And this study, for any serious student, extends over three and a half thousand years. No other work of literature even approaches it in demanding such a wide, diffused and heterogeneous frame of reference. It is possible, by contrast, to master in outline the philosophy, social and political history, and natural sciences of the seventeeth century in a year's intensive study, after which the reader may feel that he has begun to penetrate the second layer of the meanings of its poetry, drama and prose.[3] Three years' study will provide a reasonable background for a working knowledge of the age of Chaucer; five would be needed for Dante. Yet we expect students to approach a highly complex work with attitudes

[1] Butterfield, *Christianity and History*, pp. 131–132.

[2] A very large number of the great writers would, if we are honest, come into this category. It is also clear that the assent of the common reader to their assumptions has varied, notoriously, in the past.

[3] See, e.g., L. C. Martin, *An Experiment in Depth*; E. Auerbach, *Mimesis*; C. Coffin, *John Donne and the New Philosophy*; R. Tuve, *A Reading of George Heebert*.

which are blocked from further development because of early training; or its lack.

For it seems probable that the indifference or contempt with which many regard the Bible as a 'book' is conditioned by the teaching of what was once called 'Divinity', afterwards 'Religious Knowledge', and now 'Religious Instruction'. Confusions of different kinds are implicit in the whole situation. Some of them arise out of political and sociological considerations. Others have their origins in what can be described as an intelligent groping towards a solution, which has only engaged the full attention of educationalists in the last few decades. If 'Instruction' confines itself to purely historical considerations—at worst, the sequences of the Kings of Judah, the political implications of the rise and fall of the Northern and Southern kingdoms, or the Journeys of St. Paul—the teaching may easily become arid and even pointless. If it is confined to some of the great dramatic episodes, such as, say, the accounts of the creation and of the flood, the sacrifice of Isaac, the episodes of Samson, Jonah, or Esther (the list is endless), the teacher is faced with the probability that what was accepted in childhood as fact has to be reinterpreted allegorically, and that out of this allegory, symbolism, and imagery certain highly complicated and abstract ideas must evolve. But what was thought in childhood is not readily transposed afterwards into a wholly different key. Even more difficult is the task of emptying the words of their familiar meanings, and attempting to discuss just what they may mean in the context of the Bible. The destruction of a scaffolding, accepted unquestioningly from a very early age, is often accompanied by a growth of cynicism when attempts are made at some kind of apologetics by teachers of less than genius,[1] and this cynicism may extend destructively to the whole attitude towards religion.

It is an ironical fact that, at the very age when the religious choice is often made, the relevance of the Bible may be relegated to the category of the fairy-tales, the fairy-tales in an unfamiliar, repetitious and sometimes boring idiom. The problem is being tackled, on many fronts, with intelligence and sympathy.[2] One suspects that, here as

---

[1] We may note that the situation is often made very much worse if the subject is taught both peripherally in the curriculum and by teachers who may be themselves unskilled, reluctant, or even cynical. All these masks are quickly penetrated by an adolescent audience.

[2] See, e.g., T. R. Young, *A Basis for Religious Education*, 1967.

elsewhere, the teacher of intelligence and experience is not too common.

For any adult approach to the Bible will demand a study of its language, metrics, imagery, and philosophical backgrounds, with an attention at least as profound as that involved in the understanding of Shakespeare. In addition it will demand a supreme effort of imagination to grasp the patterns involved; for it cannot be too often emphasized that the Bible is an Eastern book, and that any reading of it should demand at least some reading of comparable non-sacred books. One of its greatest dangers lies in the uncritical application of it to the ethos of the West.[1] It is equally dangerous to read it solely in the light of Western morals. Without a specifically religious approach it will be necessary to impose a high degree of critical selection to an extent to which no other work offers any comparison.[2] For purposes of instruction we could discard perhaps a fifth of the total as without value as literature, uninteresting as history, and as having little bearing on the central concerns of all great literature, the relationship of man to man, of man's soul to God.

iv

There is a further aspect which must be considered. The 'new reader', at school or elsewhere, may have heard many portions of the Bible read aloud, and with varying degrees of understanding in that powerful instrument of communication, the reader's voice. The lessons will be taken from various lectionaries, themselves organized on plans more or less admirable, but which presuppose some continuity of attention. But even so they are often meaningless; the brief introductory phrases which are now fashionable do not get us very far. A study of the faces of the average congregation at the average lesson-reading is highly revealing. It is arguable that many sermons would be better if they could be wholly devoted to an explanation of one of the Lessons, which in that event would have to follow or form part of it. We should thus be able to emphasize what is often left obscure: the continuity of the Old and New Testaments.

This 'new reader' will require at least the rudiments of textual knowledge, and he will be sympathetic with the problems of all such

[1] See Chapter 12, 'The Bible and Evil'.
[2] There are deserts in Homer and Dante: but we are seldom tempted to ruthless excisions.

books and the conditions under which they come into print.[1] It is desirable to have this knowledge in order to confront the manifest inconsistencies, interpolations, lacunae, and those portions of the texts which are corrupted in varying degrees; and in particular the re-telling of a similar body of stories by different authors or editors.[2]

He would then, in his consideration of this literature, marshal all his previous knowledge and experience of poetic, of imagery, rhythm and diction, comparing always the West with the East, and remembering how deep and complex are the root-systems in the past. He should be prepared to consider the emergence and functions of the perennial archetypes. And when he has made these preparations he must then confront the thing said. He may come to the conclusion that the interpretation of the Bible, as a whole, turns on the acceptance, in the widest terms, that there is ultimately a supernatural Power with which man must be concerned. He may be driven to reflect on the eternal problem of whether such a power does exist: and on the language in which that power might be approached in the attempt, which is always doomed to failure, to describe or apprehend it. He will reflect, perhaps, on the attempts that have been made to approach this knowledge of Zeus;[3] he will read his Plato, and perhaps the *Summa Theologica*. He will reflect that in the Bible he has encountered studies of human nature more complex and varied than those of Homer and Aeschylus, less complex and less varied than those he has found in Shakespeare. He will be aware of the embodiment, 'veiled in allegory and illustrated in symbol', of the most profound aspects of the human situation. Among them will be the variety and persistence of human evil, and the persistence and nobility of a divine hope.

He will be aware of lyric, elegiac, and nature poetry as strong and moving as anything in English literature: and of a love-poetry which is the fountain-head of much, perhaps all, the less ambivalent Western writing in that kind.[4] He will—after some initial difficulty—become aware of a panoramic view of history, the more perspicuous because of its tiny scale; in which the seminal principles of politics,

---

[1] See, e.g., H. J. Chaytor, *op. cit.*

[2] Such as the similarities and discrepancies between portions of the books of *Samuel* and *Chronicles*.   [3] I have in mind A. B. Cook's *Zeus*.

[4] There is, for example, nothing of the divided mind, the *odi et amo* theme.

law, war, and diplomacy can be studied in their aspects of perennial wisdom, and perennial folly.

But overriding all else he will be aware of the problem, re-stated constantly and from many angles of experience, of evil and suffering: the theodicy which lies at the heart of all tragedy. From Job through the great prophets, from Isaiah's Suffering Servant to the Crucifixion, the crooked questions are everywhere. And while the reader may reject the ideas related to the Christian atonement, he will be confronted throughout secular tragedy with the fact, or the appearance of fact, that this form involves, in some measure, the suffering or death of the innocent. It is true that 'the wages of sin is death'. It is as true to say that it is not necessarily, and almost never only, the death of the sinner.

V

I suggest that the initial approach to the Bible as Literature is of value in clearing up a number of historical and critical difficulties under which so many labour to-day. We can make use of the normal methods of literary study that are applicable to texts; texts that may be corrupted in many ways, or subjected to tendentious editing and interpolation. We know that contradictions and inconsistencies are inherent in any writing assembled and transmitted under these conditions; and that these inconsistencies have no relevance to the *total* nature of the assertions made. We know that every literature absorbs from its surrounding cultures, as every writer draws upon his predecessors and contemporaries; it is again irrelevant that the Bible should owe so much to neighbouring cults, folklore, traditions, rituals. This is what we should expect in any evolving work of this scope and intention, assembled in such a manner. Literary criticism of the 'mythical' elements tells the same story. The basic patterns may often be found elsewhere; it is sufficient to estimate their value in their context. So far from attempting to demythologize, we may be grateful for the massive and continuous enrichment by the mythologems of the human imagination. The many coincidences with pagan religions and myths constitute no argument for or against Christianity. The fact that Christ's teaching can be shown to have sources in contemporary or traditional teaching is again no more relevant than to deprecate Shakespeare or Coleridge for embodying, and making into new things, the sources that they used.

And we should bear in mind the sentence from *The Golden Bough*:

"So many apparently divergent lines converge
towards the cross on Calvary."

So, too, with image and symbol. We are dealing with language in all its attempts to gesture towards what cannot be expressed. That the heavenly city should be described in terms of human royalty—thrones, crowns, music—is not an example of childish naïveté, but an attempt to make certain imaginative statements under the immense limitations of language. So the discussions as to whether God is or is not to be perceived 'out there' or 'up there' are no more relevant than our tolerant acceptance of the Greek deities as based on Mount Olympus. The attempts to apprehend the divine by the channels of physical sensation—as in *The Song of Songs* or the poems of St. John of the Cross, or Donne, or Hopkins—become instantly comprehensible when we reflect that these different levels of apprehension are integral in all consideration of great literature.

If we read and re-read the Bible with these common aspects in mind, it seems to achieve a new focus, that of a great and diverse epic, 'a nexus of states of being'.[1] It invites the response of all great literature: wonder, delight, exaltation. We achieve a kind of liberation from the need to consider it as fact, or history, or as inerrant authority. We shall examine carefully, but with an open mind, the history of those human institutions which seek to proclaim any kind of inerrancy. We are free to jettison parts of it, as we do of Milton or of Wordsworth. But in this new focus a strange thing happens. It achieves as we read a strange authority and power as a work of literature. It becomes one with the Western tradition, because it is its single greatest source. It reveals to us its own microcosmic yet universal world, a pattern in which the two Testaments, with all their contrasts, merge and coalesce.

vi

At some point the ways divide. We may read and criticize the Bible as history, tragedy, sociology, law. We may gesture towards its qualities as epic or lyric poems, on larger or smaller scales; we may attempt to analyse that poetic finality of statement which, struggling miraculously out of the darkness of three alien languages into what

[1] Charles Williams, *He Came Down From Heaven*, p. 13.

some have called the twilight of our own, is discernible everywhere in the sources of our own thoughts, 'embodied in the mystery of words'. The extension of awareness, the nourishment and strengthening of the creative imagination is, as Shelley and Coleridge know, in its nature divine.

Yet this response, if we achieve it, is in no sense a substitute for the Christian view. At best it may serve to bring the Bible into a new and luminous perspective. It may prepare us for the consideration of the numinous. It cannot, I think, lead us to the Christian apprehension. For this we need a different and higher type of insight.

It was the philosopher Whitehead who pointed out that man's central problem was to reconcile the finite and the infinite. It seems that the task becomes more urgent as we grow older. As the literary approach exhausts itself we begin to perceive this infinite. There is no language in which it can be expressed; but the greatest poets and mystics have known it, beyond what the voice can carry. So Wordsworth:

> "Imagination—here the Power so called
> Through sad incompetence of human speech,
> That awful Power rose from the mind's abyss
> Like an unfathered vapour that enwraps,
> At once, some lonely traveller. I was lost;
> Halted without an effort to break through;
> But to my conscious soul I now can say—
> 'I recognize thy glory': in such strength
> Of usurpation, when the light of sense
> Goes out, but with a flash that has revealed
> The invisible world, doth greatness make abode,
> There harbours; whether we be young or old,
> Our destiny, our being's heart and home,
> Is with infinitide, and only there;
> With hope it is, hope that can never die,
> Effort, and expectation, and desire,
> And something evermore about to be.
> Under such banners militant, the soul
> Seeks for no trophies, struggles for no spoils
> That may attest her prowess, blest in thoughts
> That are their own perfection and reward,
> Strong in herself and in beatitude
> That hides her . . ."[1]

[1] *Prelude*, VI 1850, 592 ff.

It would not be difficult to point out the roots of this passage; the recognition of glory, the dominance of hope, are among them.

But this essay began with some consideration of the Bible as offering a simplification as well as high complexity. One aspect of simplification is a return to innocence and its essentials. A passage from Reinhold Niebuhr is relevant:

"Spiritual health in both individuals and societies is an achievement of maturity in which some excellency of childhood is consciously reclaimed, after being lost in the complexities of life. It is an inner integrity not on this but on the other side of inner conflict; it is sincerity not on this side but the other side of a contrite recognition of the sinfulness of the human heart; it is trust in the goodness of life not on this but the other side of disillusionment and despair; it is naïveté and serenity not on this but the other side of sophistication. In no case is the exact outlook of the child reclaimed. What is at the end is never really like the beginning. Yet something of the beginning must be in the end, if the end is not to be pure dissolution. In both morals and culture, life and history are therefore constant battles 'to become as little children', to arrest that in growth which is delay, to prevent multiplicity from destroying unity, to prevent increased knowledge from enervating the zest for life and to prevent the atrophy of the imagination in the growth of the mind."[1]

[1] *Beyond Tragedy*, London, 1938, pp. 151–152.

Bibliography

The Cambridge History of the Bible, ed. S. L. Greenslade.
The Bible in a New Age, ed. L. Klein.
The Study of the Bible Today and Tomorrow, ed. H. R. Willoughby, Chicago, 1947.
On the Authority of the Bible: some recent studies by C. F. Evans, J. Burnaby, etc., London, 1966.
Peake's Commentary on the Bible, ed. M. Black and H. H. Rowley, London, 1962.
Vocabulary of the Bible, ed. J.-J. von Allmen. With an Introduction by H. H. Rowley, London, 1958.

ARMSTRONG, E. A., Shakespeare's Imagination (Revised edn.) Nebraska, 1963.
— The Folklore of Birds, New York, 1969.
— The Gospel Parables, London, 1967.
AUERBACH, E., Mimesis, Princeton, 1953.

BALY, DENIS, The Geography of the Bible, London, 1957.
BARFIELD, OWEN, Poetic Diction, A Study in Meaning, London, 1952.
BEVAN, E. R., Symbolism and Belief, London, 1938.
BODKIN, MAUD, Archetypal Patterns in Pottery, Oxford, 1934.
— Studies of Type Images in Poetry, Religion and Philosophy, Oxford, 1951.
BRUCE, F. F., The English Bible: a history of translation, London, 1961.
BUTTERFIELD, SIR HERBERT, Christianity and History, London, 1949.
BUTTERWORTH, C. C., The Literary Lineage of the King James Version 1340–1611.

CARPENTER, S. C., The Bible View of Life, London (2nd Edn.), 1955.
CEADEL, E. B. (ed.), Literatures of the East, London, 1935.
CHAYTOR, H. J., From Script to Print, Cambridge, 1945.
COPE, GILBERT, Symbolism in The Bible and The Church, London, 1959.
COULTON, G. G., Medieval Panorama, Cambridge, 1947.

261

DAICHES, DAVID, *Literary Essays*, Edinburgh, 1956.
— *The King James Version of The English Bible*, Chicago, 1941.
DAMON, S. FOSTER, *William Blake, His Philosophy and Symbols*, London, 1924.
DEANESLEY, M., *The Lollard Bible*, Cambridge, 1920.
DILLISTONE, F. W., *Christianity and Symbolism*, London, 1955.
— (ed.), *Myth and Symbol*, London, 1966.
DODD, C. H., *New Testament Studies*, Manchester, 1967.
— *The Authors of The Bible.*
DRIJVERS, P., *The Psalms, their Structure and Meaning*, London, 1967.

FARRER, A., *A Rebirth of Images*, London, 1949.
FRANKFORT, H. H. A., *et al.*, *Before Philosophy*, Chicago, 1946; Pelican Books, 1959.
FROMM, ERICH, *The Forgotten Language*, London, 1952.
FRYE, NORTHROP, *Anatomy of Criticism*, Princeton, 1957.
FUNK, R. W., *Language, Hermeneutic, and Word of God*, New York, 1966.

GARDINER, J. H., *The Bible as English Literature*, London, 1906.
GOOD, E. M., *Irony in the Old Testament*, London, 1965.
GRIERSON, H. J. C., *The English Bible*, London, 1943.

HATTO, A. T., *EOS*, The Hague, 1965.
HART, H. ST J., *A Foreword to the Old Testament*, London, 1951.
HIRST, DÉSIRÉE, *Hidden Riches*, London, 1964.
HOSKYNS, SIR EDWYN AND DAVEY, NOEL, *The Riddle of the New Testament*, London, 1958.

JAMES, E. O., *The Ancient Gods*, London, 1960.
JONES, GENESIMUS, *Approach to the Purpose: a study of the poetry of T. S. Eliot*, London, 1964.
JUNG, G. C., *Memories, Dreams and Reflections*, London, 1963.
— *Modern Man in Search of a Soul*, London, 1933.
JUNG, G. C., AND KERÉNYI, C., *Introduction to a Science of Mythology*, London, 1951.

KELLER, WERNER, *The Bible as History*, London, 1957.
KER, W. P., *Epic and Romance*, London, 1908.
KITAMORI, KAZOH, *Theology of the Pain of God*, London, 1966.

LANGER, SUSANNE K., *Philosophy in a New Key*, Oxford, 1942.
LAWRENCE, D. H., *The Symbolic Meaning*, London, 1962.
LEWIS, C. S., *They Asked for a Paper*, London, 1962.
— *Miracles*, London, 1947.
— *The Allegory of Love*, Oxford, 1936.
'LONGINUS', *A Treatise Concerning Sublimity*, Tr. A. O. Prichard, Oxford, 1926.
LOWES, J. LIVINGSTON, *Essays in Appreciation*, Boston, 1936.
— *Of Reading Books*, London, 1930.

MÂLE, ÉMILE, *The Gothic Image*, 1910, Fontana Press, 1961.
MARTZ, L. L., *The Poetry of Meditation*, Yale, 1954.
MOULTON, R. G., *The Literary Study of the Bible*, London, 1906.
MOULTON, R. G., et al., *The Bible as Literature*, London, 1899.

NEUMANN, ERICH, *The Origins and History of Consciousness*, London, 1954.
NIEBUHR, REINHOLD, *Beyond Tragedy*, London, 1938.
NOBLE, R., *Shakespeare's Biblical Knowledge . . .*, London, 1935.

OESTERLEY, W. O. E., *A Fresh Approach to the Psalms*, London, 1937.
OTTO, RUDOLPH, *The Idea of the Holy*, Oxford, 1923.

PANOVSKY, IRWIN, *Studies in Iconology*, New York, 1939 (Edn. of 1962).
PFEIFFER, R. H., *Introduction to the Old Testament*, London, 1952.
POPE, H., *English Versions of the Bible* (revd. S. Bullough, 1952).

RAHNER, FR. HUGO, *Greek Myths and Christian Mysteries*, London, 1963.
RAINE, KATHLEEN, *Defending Ancient Springs*, Oxford, 1967.
RICHARDSON, A., AND SCHWEITZER, W., *Biblical Authority for Today*, London, 1951.
RICHARDSON, KATHLEEN (ed.), *A Theological Word-Book of the Bible*, London.
ROWLEY, H. H., *The Unity of the Bible*, London, 1953.
— *The Relevance of the Bible*, London, 1941.
— *The Authority of the Bible*, London, 1950.

SCHOLEM, G. G., *On to Kabbalah and its Symbolism*, London, 1965.
SHELLY, J., *Rhythmical Prose in English and Latin*, Church Quarterly Review, April 1912.

SMITH, GEORGE ADAM, *The Historical Geography of the Holy Land*, London, 1899, 25th Edn., 1931, Fontana Library, 1966.
SPENCER, THEODORE, *Death and Elizabethan Man*, New York, 1960.
STEVENSON, W. B., *The Poem of Job*, London, 1947.
SUTCLIFFE, E. F., *Providence and Suffering in the Old and New Testaments*, London, 1953.

TAYLOR, JOHN V., *The Primal Vision*, London, 1963.
TEMPEST, N. R., *The Rhythm of English Prose*, Cambridge, 1930.
TEMPLE, W., *Mens Creatrix*, London, 1917.
THOMAS, D. WINTON (ed.), *Documents from Old Testament Times*, London, 1958.
— *Understanding the Old Testament*, London, 1967.
TUVE, R., *A Reading of George Herbert*, London, 1952.
— *Elizabethan and Metaphysical Images*, Chicago, 1947.

USSHER, ARLAND, *The Magic People*, London, 1950.

VICO, GIAMBATTISTA, *The New Science* (ed. Bergin and Fisch), Cornell, 1948.

WATTS, ALAN A., *Myth and Ritual in Christianity*, London, 1954.
WEIGHT, L. A., *The English New Testament from Tyndale to R.S.V.*, 1949.
WHEELWRIGHT, PHILIP, *The Burning Fountain* (New Edn.), Indiana, 1968.
WHITE, FR. VICTOR, *God and the Unconscious*, London, 1952.
WHITEHEAD, A. N., *Dialogues* (Recorded by L. Price), Boston, 1954.
— *Religion in the Making*, Cambridge, 1926.
WILLEY, BASIL, *Christianity Past and Present*, Cambridge, 1952.
WILLIAMS, CHARLES, *He Came Down from Heaven*, London, 1950.
— *Selected Writings* (chosen by A. Ridler), Oxford, 1961.
WIND, E., *Pagan Mysteries in the Renaissance*, London, 1958.
WOOD, J., *Job and the Human Situation*, London, 1966.

The Main Bibles

Wycliffite Bible (Jon Wycliffe, *c.* 1330–1384).
Gutenberg Bible, 1450–1455.
The 1462 Bible (Mainz), 1462.
Biblia Pauperum (with woodcuts), *c.* 1465.
Tyndale's New Testament, 1525–1526.
Coverdale's, 1535.
The Matthew Bible, 1537. (The first to be licensed by the King.)
The Great Bible, 1539–1540.
Geneva Bible, 1560. (This was Shakespeare's Bible.)
Bishop's Bible, 1568.
Clementine Bible, 1592 (Vulgate Text).
Douai Old Testament, 1609. (N.T. 1582.)
King James Bible, 1611. (A.V.)
Revised Version, 1881–1885. (R.V.)
Revised Standard Version, 1946–1952. (R.S.V.)
Confraternity Version, 1952.
The New English Bible, N.T. 1961, *O.T.* 1970.

OTHER VERSIONS

The Twentieth Century New Testament, 1902.
James Moffat, *N.T.* 1913. *O.T.* 1924; one-vol. edition, 1928.
Edgar J. Goodspeed, *The Complete Bible*, 1927, revd. 1935.
'Basic English', *N.T.* 1940, Complete Bible, 1949.
The Berkeley Version, *O.T.* 1945, complete, 1959.
Ronald A. Knox, *O.T.* 1949. *N.T.* 1945; one-vol. edition, 1949.
J. B. Phillips, *Letters to Young Churches*, 1947; *New Testament in Modern English*, 1958.
E. V. Rieu, *Penguin Translations*: 1952 and 1957.
The Jerusalem Bible, 1968.

Index